SPELLING WORKOUT

Phillip K. Trocki

Modern Curriculum Press
Parsippany

EXECUTIVE EDITOR Wendy Whitnah

PROJECT EDITOR Diane Dzamtovski

EDITORIAL DEVELOPMENT
DESIGN AND PRODUCTION The Hampton-Brown Company

ILLUSTRATORS Anthony Accardo, Joe Boddy, Harry Briggs, Roberta Collier-Morales,
Mark Farina, Meryl Henderson, Masami Miyamoto, Rik Olson, Doug Roy,
John Sandford, Rosalind Solomon.

PHOTO CREDITS 5, Ralph Nelson, Jr./Culver Pictures; 9, Uniphoto/Pictor;
13, Lawrence Migdale/Photo Researchers; 17, Long Beach Public Library
and Information Center; 20, Archive Photos;
29, Stuart Dee/Image Bank; 33, Jeff Spielman/Image Bank;
37, Karl H. Maslowski/Photo Researchers; 41, J. Cochin/Image Bank;
45, Bob Daemmrich/Uniphoto; 53, Michael Newman/Photo Edit;
57, John Spragens, Jr./Photo Researchers; 61, G. Colliva/Image Bank;
65, George Lepp/Comstock; 69, Images Unlimited/Image Bank;
77, Michael S. Thompson/Comstock; 85, Virginia P. Weinland/Photo Researchers;
89, The Bostonian Society/Old State House; 93, Gil C. Kenny/Image Bank;
101, D.O.E./Science Source/Photo Researchers; 105, Grant Huntington;
109, Courtesy of David Barry; 113, Steve Dunwell/Image Bank;
117, Peter Beck/Uniphoto; 125, Jim Mendenhall/Courtesy of the SimonWiesenthal
Center; 128, Courtesy of International Peace Garden; 129, Bruce Hands/Comstock;
133, Karl Hentz/Image Bank; 137, James L. Schaffer/Photo Edit.

COVER DESIGN The Hampton-Brown Company
COVER PHOTO Steve Satushek/Image Bank

Typefaces for the cursive type in this book were provided
by Zaner-Bloser, Inc., Columbus, Ohio, copyright, 1993.

Copyright © 1994 by Modern Curriculum Press, Inc.
An imprint of Pearson Learning
299 Jefferson Road, PO Box 480
Parsippany, New Jersey 07054-0480
http://www.pearsonlearning.com

ISBN 0-8136-2845-8

18 V0SV 09/2013

Name _____

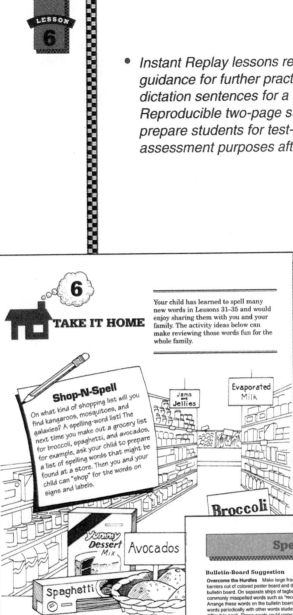

Instant Replay Test

Side A

Read each set of words. Fill in the circle next to the word that is spelled correctly.

1. (a) fraigrant   (c) fragrent
   (b) fragrant   (d) fraigrent

2. (a) perfer   (c) prefer
   (b) perferr   (d) preffer

3. (a) hemisphere   (c) hemispheer
   (b) hemisfere   (d) hemisfeer

4. (a) icicels   (c) icicles
   (b) icycles   (d) icycels

5. (a) doub   (c) doute
   (b) dowt   (d) doubt

6. (a) nowlege   (c) knowlege
   (b) knowledge   (d) nowledge

7. (a) schedual   (c) scedule
   (b) schedule   (d) skedual

8. (a) sketching   (c) schetching
   (b) scetching   (d) skeching

9. (a) hymms   (c) hymns
   (b) himms   (d) hims

10. (a) younique   (c) unieque
    (b) yuneek   (d) unique

11. (a) resgned   (c) risgned
    (b) resigned   (d) rezined

12. (a) cartredge   (c) cartrege
    (b) cartridge   (d) cartrage

13. (a) gnarled   (c) gnrled
    (b) narld   (d) narled

30

- *Instant Replay lessons review spelling objectives, give guidance for further practice of List Words, and provide dictation sentences for a **Final Replay Test.** Reproducible two-page standardized tests to help prepare students for test-taking are supplied for assessment purposes after each Instant Replay lesson.*

*Reproducible **Take It Home Masters** that also follow each Instant Replay lesson strengthen the school-home connection by providing ideas for parents and students for additional practice at home.*

Suggested games and group activities make spelling more fun.

13

Meeting the Needs of Your ESL Students

Spelling is the relationship between sounds and letters. Learning to spell words in English is an interesting challenge for English First Language speakers as well as English as a Second Language speakers. You may want to adapt some of the following activities to accommodate the needs of your students—both native and non-English speakers.

Rhymes and Songs

Use rhymes, songs, poems, or chants to introduce new letter sounds and spelling words. Repeat the rhyme or song several times during the day or week, having students listen to you first, then repeat back to you line by line. To enhance learning for visual learners in your classroom and provide opportunities for pointing out letter combinations and their sounds, you may want to write the rhyme, song, poem, or chant on the board. As you examine the words, students can easily see similarities and differences among them. Encourage volunteers to select and recite a rhyme or sing a song for the class. Students may enjoy some of the selections in *Miss Mary Mack and Other Children's Street Rhymes* by Joanna Cole and Stephanie Calmenson or *And the Green Grass Grew All Around* by Alvin Schwartz.

Student Dictation

To take advantage of individual students' known vocabulary, suggest that students build their own sentences incorporating the List Words. For example:

Mary ran.
Mary ran away.
Mary ran away quickly.

Sentence building can expand students' knowledge of how to spell words and of how to notice language patterns, learn descriptive words, and so on.

Words in Context

Using words in context sentences will aid students' mastery of new vocabulary.

- Say several sentences using the List Words in context and have students repeat after you. Encourage more proficient students to make up sentences using List Words that you suggest.
- Write cloze sentences on the board and have students help you complete them with the List Words.

Point out the spelling patterns in the words, using colored chalk to underline or circle the elements.

Oral Drills

Use oral drills to help students make associations among sounds and the letters that represent them. You might use oral drills at listening stations to reinforce the language, allowing ESL students to listen to the drills at their own pace.

Spelling Aloud   Say each List Word and have students repeat the word. Next, write it on the board as you name each letter, then say the word again as you track the letters and sound by sweeping your hand under the word. Call attention to spelling changes for words to which endings or suffixes were added. For words with more than one syllable, emphasize each syllable as you write, encouraging students to clap out the syllables. Ask volunteers to repeat the procedure.

Variant Spellings   For a group of words that contain the same vowel sound, but variant spellings, write an example on the board, say the word, and then present other words in that word family *(cake: rake, bake, lake).* Point out the sound and the letter(s) that stand for the sound. Then add words to the list that have the same vowel sound *(play, say, day).* Say pairs of words *(cake, play)* as you point to them, and identify the vowel sound and the different letters that represent the sound *(long a: a_e, ay).* Ask volunteers to select a different pair of words and repeat the procedure.

Vary this activity by drawing a chart on the board that shows the variant spellings for a sound. Invite students to add words under the correct spelling pattern. Provide a list of words for students to choose from to help those ESL students with limited vocabularies.

Synonyms

Write a List Word that means the same or almost the same as the word or phrase given.

1. needed   _required_   7. timetable   _schedule_
2. feast   _banquet_   8. old   _antique_
3. amount   _quantity_   9. wisdom   _knowledge_
4. one of a kind   _unique_   10. method   _technique_
5. admit   _acknowledge_   11. choir   _chorus_
6. meet standards   _qualify_   12. repairs locks   _locksmith_

Missing Words

Circle the List Word that belongs in each sentence. Write the correct word on the line.

1. The cat tiptoed along the _____, making a little song.
chorus   (keyboard)   chemistry   _keyboard_

2. Fred's beautiful paintings are proof of his _____ talent.
qualify   (remarkable)   acknowledge   _remarkable_

3. The _____ of our voices bounced back from across the lake.
quantity   technique   (echoes)   _echoes_

4. Dad polished the _____ on his car with a soft cloth.
(chrome)   technical   schedule   _chrome_

5. Karen _____ down to play with the little puppy.
required   (knelt)   echoes   _knelt_

6. The loud music gave me a _____
keyboard   schedule   (headache)   _headache_

7. By studying computer science, he gained _____ knowledge.
(technical)   chemistry   qualify   _technical_

8. Before she became a scientist, she received her degree in _____.
(chemistry)   knowledge   technique   _chemistry_

Lesson 1 ▪ /k/, /kw/, and /n/   7

Flex Your Spelling Muscles

Writing

Put yourself into a movie about a space adventure with a _remarkable_ robot. Write the dialogue that takes place when you first meet this _unique_ character. If you like, add descriptions that go with the actions.

Proofreading

This dialogue from the movie "My Friend Is a Robot" has ten mistakes. Use the proofreading marks to correct them. Then write the misspelled List Words correctly on the lines.

Proofreading Marks
◯ spelling mistake
≡ capital letter
⊙ add period

ROBOT: (in a panicky voice) I'm having (tecnicle) difficulties. I'm losing all of my (knowlege) Now I know what a (headake) feels like! you must (skeduel) time to make the (requred) repairs⊙

IRMA: (rolling her eyes in amusement) Don't panic! All you need is to have your batteries recharged⊙

ROBOT: (more frantic) Hurry up and recharge them! I'm quickly becoming a useless pile of (krome)

1. _technical_   4. _schedule_
2. _knowledge_   5. _required_
3. _headache_   6. _chrome_

Now proofread your own dialogue. Correct any errors.

Go for the Goal

Take your Final Test. Then fill in your Scoreboard. Send your mistakes to the Word Locker.

SCOREBOARD	
number correct	number wrong

★ ★ ★ ★ ★ ★ ★ All-Star Words ★ ★ ★ ★ ★ ★ ★

knothole   mechanic   plaque   quiz   kindling

Draw a simple sketch that gives a clue to the meaning of each All-Star Word. Then trade picture clues with a partner. Try to write the All-Star Word that fits each of your partner's sketches.

8   Lesson 1 ▪ /k/, /kw/, and /n/

⊙ **Spelling Strategy** Make three columns on the board, labeled /k/, /kw/, and /n/. Say each List Word and ask a volunteer to come to the board and write the word in the appropriate column (or columns, if the word contains more than one of the sounds). Ask a second volunteer to circle the letter or letters that stand for the /k/, /kw/, or /n/ sound.

Flex Your Spelling Muscles   *Page 8*

As students complete the **Writing** activity, encourage them to brainstorm ideas, write a first draft, revise, and proofread their work. The **Proofreading** exercise will help them prepare to proofread their dialogues. To publish their writing, students may want to get together with a partner to perform their scenes for the class.

✍ Writer's Corner

You may want to bring in reviews of movies, TV shows, or plays from your local newspaper. Encourage students to write responses to the reviews, telling whether or not they agree with them. Or invite students to write their own review of a favorite movie or show.

Go for the Goal/Final Test

1. The *chemistry* teacher conducted an experiment.
2. The bat is *unique* because it is a flying mammal.
3. The pianist's fingers flew over the *keyboard.*
4. A swimming pool holds a large *quantity* of water.
5. What a terrific speech she gave at the *banquet!*
6. Pitchers practice to improve their *technique.*
7. My father gave me this *antique* spoon.
8. I want to *acknowledge* your valuable help.
9. The goalie's *remarkable* speed helped us to win.
10. The *echoes* of happy voices rang out clearly.
11. I *knelt* down to pat Tina's pet rabbit.
12. Her *knowledge* of music is amazing.
13. What a relief to finally see the *locksmith!*
14. Did the school *chorus* perform at graduation?
15. A glass of water might soothe your *headache.*
16. Does the school *require* that everyone take gym?
17. Many electricians attend *technical* schools.
18. To *qualify* for this job, I must complete the course.
19. Does that *schedule* tell what time the bus leaves?
20. Becky polished the *chrome* on her car.

Remind students to complete the Scoreboard and write any misspelled words in their Word Locker.

★★ **All-Star Words** You may want to point out that the All-Star Words follow the spelling rule and model drawing a sketch for a List Word.

Lesson 2

Objective
To spell words with hard and soft *c* and *g;* with *dge*

Correlated Phonics Lesson
MCP Phonics, Level F, Lesson 2

Warm Up
Page 9

In "Hard Rock," students learn about the hardest substance on the earth—a diamond. Ask students which information they found the most surprising and invite them to share other facts they may know about diamonds or other jewels.

Call on volunteers to say the boldfaced words and identify the sounds spelled with *c* and *g*.

On Your Mark/Warm Up Test
1. That *crystal* chandelier is really beautiful!
2. The corners of the frame form a right *angle.*
3. Gloria and Jamal are *engaged* to be married.
4. Tall people have an *advantage* in basketball.
5. John *pledges* to do his homework every night.
6. The graphite in the pencil is made from *carbon.*
7. Cheese spread is made from *processed* cheese.
8. Was that *medicine* prescribed by a doctor?
9. Lisa planned a birthday *celebration* for her dad.
10. The heat caused the *icicles* to melt.
11. Our *language* changes as new words are added.
12. To meet the deadline, Ali must *budget* his time.
13. After two wrong *guesses,* I got the answer.
14. Milk must be kept in the *refrigerator.*
15. When you *conjugate* verbs, you list their forms.
16. Clare dreamed about a *magical* journey.
17. The porpoise is an *intelligent* animal.
18. Kathy put a new *cartridge* in the tape recorder.
19. I hope the vase I bought is a *genuine* antique.
20. Do you have a *recipe* for lasagna?

Pep Talk/Game Plan
Pages 10–11

Introduce the spelling rule and have students read the List Words aloud, telling which sound the *c* or *g* stands for in each word. Then encourage students to look back at their Warm Up Tests and apply the spelling rule to any misspelled words.

As students work through the **Spelling Lineup,** **Alphabetical Order,** and **Definitions** exercises, remind them to look back at their List Words or in their dictionaries if they need help. For the **Spelling Lineup,** point out that some words are used as answers more than once.

 See **Rhymes and Songs,** page 14

Warm Up
What is the hardest substance found on the earth?

Hard Rock

Have you ever heard the expression "diamonds are forever"? Diamonds can last as long as they take to make. They are made of **carbon.** That's the same substance as the graphite in your pencil. Nature, however, takes a longer time to create diamonds. Diamonds become **processed** over millions of years, and it all takes place nearly 100 miles below the earth's surface. Miners have to move tons of rock to dislodge a single ounce of diamonds.

A diamond is the hardest substance found on the earth. In fact, nothing can cut a **genuine** diamond except another diamond. Cutting a diamond is a very delicate process. To turn a rough diamond into a gem, flat surfaces called *facets* are carefully carved out of the stone. To increase the sparkle, each facet is ground at a certain **angle.**

Diamonds were first discovered in India more than 2,000 years ago. Ancient people thought this type of **crystal** had **magical** powers. They were thought to bring luck, power, good health, and long life. It has been a custom for a man to give a woman a diamond ring when they are **engaged** to be married. They are still used as symbols of love, but they also have other less romantic uses. Today we use diamonds to make phonograph needles and medical tools. The space program used diamonds in a window of a spacecraft that went to Venus. It was the only windowlike matter that would not be destroyed by the heat and atmospheric pressure of this far-off planet.

Look back at the boldfaced words in the selection. What do you notice about the sounds made with the letters **c** and **g**?

On Your Mark

Take your Warm Up Test. Then check your spelling with the List Words on the next page.

9

Pep Talk

The letter **g** makes a hard sound, as in angle, and a soft sound, as in magical. The letters **dge** often spell the soft **g** sound, as in cartridge. The letter **c** makes a hard sound, as in carbon, and a soft sound, as in recipe. Be careful when spelling words with **c** or **g**, because their sounds can easily be confused with **s** or **j**.

LIST WORDS

1. crystal
2. angle
3. engaged
4. advantage
5. pledges
6. carbon
7. processed
8. medicine
9. celebration
10. icicles
11. language
12. budget
13. guesses
14. refrigerator
15. conjugate
16. magical
17. intelligent
18. cartridge
19. genuine
20. recipe

Game Plan

Spelling Lineup

Write each List Word under the correct heading. Some words are used more than once.

g, as in giant	c, as in card
1. engaged	16. crystal
2. pledges	17. carbon
3. advantage	18. icicles
4. language	19. conjugate
5. budget	20. magical
6. refrigerator	21. cartridge
7. magical	
8. intelligent	**c, as in cinema**
9. cartridge	22. processed
10. genuine	23. medicine
	24. celebration
g, as in gate	25. icicles
11. angle	26. recipe
12. engaged	
13. language	
14. guesses	
15. conjugate	

10 Lesson 2 ■ Hard and Soft c and g; dge

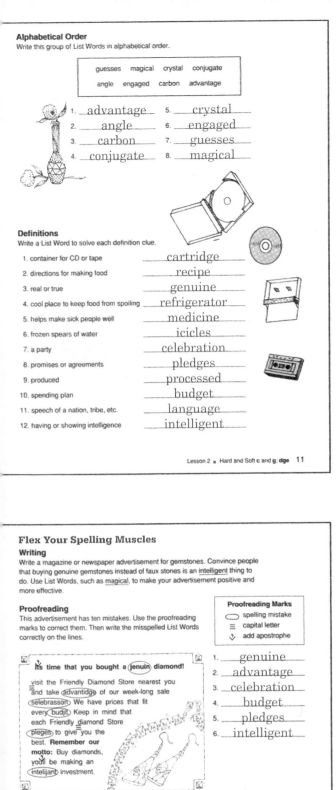

Alphabetical Order
Write this group of List Words in alphabetical order.

| guesses | magical | crystal | conjugate |
| angle | engaged | carbon | advantage |

1. advantage
2. angle
3. carbon
4. conjugate
5. crystal
6. engaged
7. guesses
8. magical

Definitions
Write a List Word to solve each definition clue.

1. container for CD or tape — cartridge
2. directions for making food — recipe
3. real or true — genuine
4. cool place to keep food from spoiling — refrigerator
5. helps make sick people well — medicine
6. frozen spears of water — icicles
7. a party — celebration
8. promises or agreements — pledges
9. produced — processed
10. spending plan — budget
11. speech of a nation, tribe, etc. — language
12. having or showing intelligence — intelligent

Flex Your Spelling Muscles
Writing
Write a magazine or newspaper advertisement for gemstones. Convince people that buying genuine gemstones instead of faux stones is an intelligent thing to do. Use List Words, such as magical, to make your advertisement positive and more effective.

Proofreading
This advertisement has ten mistakes. Use the proofreading marks to correct them. Then write the misspelled List Words correctly on the lines.

Proofreading Marks
- ⟅ spelling mistake
- ≡ capital letter
- ⌄ add apostrophe

Its time that you bought a jenuin diamond!
visit the Friendly Diamond Store nearest you and take advantidge of our week-long sale selebrasson! We have prices that fit every budjit. Keep in mind that each Friendly diamond Store pleges to give you the best. **Remember our motto:** Buy diamonds, youll be making an intelijant investment.

1. genuine
2. advantage
3. celebration
4. budget
5. pledges
6. intelligent

Now proofread your own advertisement. Fix any mistakes.

Go for the Goal
Take your Final Test. Then fill in your Scoreboard. Send your mistakes to the Word Locker.

SCOREBOARD

| number correct | number wrong |

★ ★ ★ ★ ★ ★ ★ ★ All-Star Words ★ ★ ★ ★ ★ ★ ★ ★

foliage   gallery   recently   capacity   midget

Create a crossword puzzle that contains the All-Star Words. Write clues and draw a blank grid. Trade puzzles with a partner and try to solve each other's clues.

Page 12

⊙ **Spelling Strategy**   Write each List Word containing c on the board and invite the class to
• identify the letter that follows the c
• say the word and tell whether the c is hard or soft. Follow the same procedure with List Words that contain g. Point out to students that when they see c or g followed by e or i, they should try the soft sound when pronouncing it. Help them conclude that c and g are usually soft before e or i.

Flex Your Spelling Muscles
As students complete the **Writing** activity, encourage them to brainstorm ideas, write a first draft, revise, and proofread their work. If necessary, discuss the definition and pronunciation of the word *faux*. The **Proofreading** exercise will help students prepare to proofread their advertisements. To publish their writing, they may want to tape-record their ads.

✍ Writer's Corner
Invite the class to formulate questions such as What is the fastest land animal? or What is the world's tallest mountain? Students can search for answers in an almanac or similar reference books.

Go for the Goal/Final Test
1. **Carbon** is a very common chemical.
2. Look how clear that **crystal** is!
3. Are you surprised that pigs are **intelligent?**
4. Here's my **recipe** for cheese bread.
5. The accountant helped me **budget** my money.
6. Make sure you take the **medicine** each day.
7. The two lines meet at a sharp **angle.**
8. The film was about a **magical** land.
9. Can you find a **cartridge** for this tape player?
10. Endurance is an **advantage** in a marathon.
11. The machine **processed** the food in seconds.
12. The silver is **genuine,** but the stone is fake.
13. How many verbs can you **conjugate** in Latin?
14. The **icicles** on my house finally melted!
15. After winning, the team had a **celebration.**
16. Mary **pledges** to clean her room once a week.
17. The ring shows they are **engaged** to be married.
18. Will you learn French as a second **language?**
19. You can make three **guesses** before you give up.
20. Our **refrigerator** is not keeping the food cold.
 ✗ technical
Remind students to complete the Scoreboard and write any misspelled words in their Word Locker.

★★ **All-Star Words**   You may want to point out that the All-Star Words follow the spelling rule. Suggest that students first arrange the All-Star Words, then draw a grid based on that arrangement.

Lesson 3

Objective
To spell words in which *f, ff, ph,* and *gh* spell /f/

Correlated Phonics Lesson
MCP Phonics, Level F, Lesson 4

Warm Up   *Page 13*
In this selection, students learn about a unique parade in which floats are covered with millions of flowers. Ask students if they have ever seen the Tournament of Roses Parade and invite them to talk about their own experiences with parades.

Call on volunteers to say each boldfaced word and name the letter or letters that stand for the /f/ sound.

On Your Mark/Warm Up Test
1. Rosa **photographed** each member of her family.
2. A police **officer** directed traffic on the street.
3. The winning runner flashed a **triumphant** smile.
4. I'll save my money until I can **afford** a bike.
5. Athletes exercise to **toughen** their muscles.
6. At graduation, **fifteen** students received awards.
7. Alice likes plums, but I **prefer** peaches.
8. Aunt Miranda is a **physician** at City Hospital.
9. This bouquet of roses is so **fragrant!**
10. The students wrote a **pamphlet** on bicycle safety.
11. Chato plays the **saxophone** in the school band.
12. The scientists searched for an **effective** cure.
13. What country grows the most **coffee?**
14. A **phrase** is a group of words or musical notes.
15. Should I **hyphenate** this word?
16. What a **magnificent** view this is!
17. Do you have **sufficient** supplies for your hike?
18. Our coaches **emphasize** regular exercise.
19. Canada is in the Northern **Hemisphere.**
20. My first attempt to skateboard was **laughable.**

Pep Talk/Game Plan   *Pages 14–15*
Introduce the spelling rule and have students read the List Words aloud. Discuss the spelling of the /f/ sound in each word and point out that *photographed* contains two instances of /f/. Then encourage students to look back at their Warm Up Tests and apply the spelling rule to any misspelled words.

As students work through the **Spelling Lineup,** **Missing Words,** and **Alphabetical Order** exercises, remind them to look back at their List Words or in their dictionaries if they need help.

 See **Variant Spellings,** page 14

Warm Up
How many flowers does it take to cover a Tournament of Roses Parade float?

Flower Power
Every year in Pasadena, California, there's a parade called the Tournament of Roses. It is considered by many to be the only parade of its kind, as well as the most **photographed** event in the world. The focus of this parade, held every January 1st, is the display of hundreds of floats, all made of flowers. In one float, you might find a giant sun made of thousands of daffodils. In another, a ship made of **fragrant** carnations and roses parades by. Who is responsible for making these **magnificent** floats?

One of the parade's top floral float designers is Raul Rodriguez. He does not have an easy job. Floats are never reused, so he must create different designs every year. As soon as the parade ends, he begins his work for the next year. First, his designs are drawn and perfected. Next, the framework is constructed. This can take months. Finally, one week before the parade, millions of flowers are carefully attached to the frame. Fortunately, Rodriguez has a **sufficient** number of volunteers to help him.

Most artists **prefer** to see their work displayed in galleries and museums. Rodriguez, however, goes one step further. He rides his art as it parades for millions of viewers. Few artists can boast of that many admirers seeing their work!

 Look back at the boldfaced words in the selection. How many different ways is the /f/ sound spelled?

On Your Mark
Take your Warm Up Test. Then check your spelling with the List Words on the next page.

13

Pep Talk
The /f/ sound can be spelled four different ways:
f, as in fifteen; **ff,** as in coffee;
ph, as in photographed; **gh,** as in laughable.

LIST WORDS
1. photographed
2. officer
3. triumphant
4. afford
5. toughen
6. fifteen
7. prefer
8. physician
9. fragrant
10. pamphlet
11. saxophone
12. effective
13. coffee
14. phrase
15. hyphenate
16. magnificent
17. sufficient
18. emphasize
19. hemisphere
20. laughable

Game Plan
Spelling Lineup
Write each List Word in the correct category to show how the /f/ sound is spelled.

/f/, as in final	/f/, as in photo
1. fifteen	10. photographed
2. prefer	11. triumphant
3. fragrant	12. physician
4. magnificent	13. pamphlets

/f/, as in sheriff	14. saxophone
5. officer	15. phrase
6. afford	16. hyphenate
7. effective	17. emphasize
8. coffee	18. hemisphere
9. sufficient	

	/f/, as in enough
	19. toughen
	20. laughable

14   Lesson 3 ■ /f/

Missing Words

Write the List Word that completes each sentence.

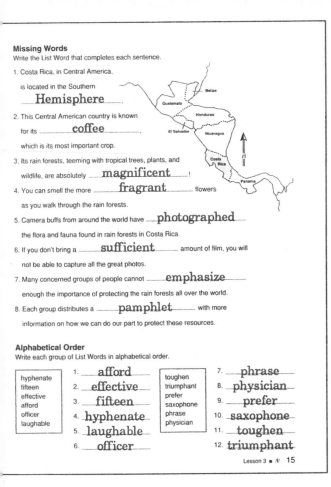

1. Costa Rica, in Central America,

   is located in the Southern

   __Hemisphere__

2. This Central American country is known

   for its _____ __coffee__ _____

   which is its most important crop.

3. Its rain forests, teeming with tropical trees, plants, and

   wildlife, are absolutely __magnificent__ !

4. You can smell the more _____ __fragrant__ _____ flowers

   as you walk through the rain forests.

5. Camera buffs from around the world have _____ __photographed__

   the flora and fauna found in rain forests in Costa Rica.

6. If you don't bring a _____ __sufficient__ _____ amount of film, you will

   not be able to capture all the great photos.

7. Many concerned groups of people cannot _____ __emphasize__ _____

   enough the importance of protecting the rain forests all over the world.

8. Each group distributes a _____ __pamphlet__ _____ with more

   information on how we can do our part to protect these resources.

Alphabetical Order

Write each group of List Words in alphabetical order.

hyphenate fifteen effective afford officer laughable	1. __afford__ 2. __effective__ 3. __fifteen__ 4. __hyphenate__ 5. __laughable__ 6. __officer__	toughen triumphant prefer saxophone phrase physician	7. __phrase__ 8. __physician__ 9. __prefer__ 10. __saxophone__ 11. __toughen__ 12. __triumphant__

Lesson 3 ■ /f/ 15

Flex Your Spelling Muscles

Writing

Write a newspaper article about a parade. Were the floats effective or laughable? Describe the sights, smells, and sounds. Were there any fragrant flowers?

Proofreading

Mayor Green's speech, to be given at a parade, has ten mistakes. Use the proofreading marks to correct them. Write the misspelled List Words correctly on the lines.

Proofreading Marks	
◯	spelling mistake
≡	capital letter
∧	add something

good day to all of my fellow citizens! Have you ever seen such a (magnifisent) parade? I'm told that there are (fifteen) more floats this year than at last year's parade. I can't (enfasize) enough how much this parade means to our town. That's why I'm surprised that my opponent thinks that we can't (aforde) a parade every year. what a (lauphable) idea! I say that we can't afford not to ∧hold a parade. our town needs to celebrate its (triumfant) history. Thank y∧ou.

1. __magnificent__   6. __triumphant__
2. __fifteen__
3. __emphasize__
4. __afford__
5. __laughable__

Now proofread your newspaper article. Fix any mistakes.

Go for the Goal

Take your Final Test. Then fill in your Scoreboard. Send your mistakes to the Word Locker.

SCOREBOARD

number correct	number wrong

★ ★ ★ ★ ★ ★ ★ ★ **All-Star Words** ★ ★ ★ ★ ★ ★ ★ ★

affection   fender   phenomenon   roughen   orphanage

Divide the All-Star Words between you and a partner. Write both a real and a fake definition for your words. Trade papers. Can each of you match the All-Star Words with their correct meanings?

16   Lesson 3 ■ /f/

◉ **Spelling Strategy**   Write each List Word on the board, but use an incorrect spelling for /f/ (*ophicer* for *officer*). Then call on volunteers to point to the incorrect spelling, rewrite the word correctly, and circle the correct spelling.

Flex Your Spelling Muscles   *Page 16*

As students complete the **Writing** activity, encourage them to brainstorm ideas, write a first draft, revise, and proofread their work. The **Proofreading** exercise will help them prepare to proofread their newspaper articles. Before they begin the exercise, remind students that the proofreading mark ∧ is used to add something. It could be a space, a comma, a question mark, or an exclamation mark. To publish their writing, students may want to pretend they are commentators at a parade and read their articles aloud.

✍ **Writer's Corner**

Students might enjoy looking through *Chase's Annual Events* to learn about unusual celebrations, such as Goof-Off Day and Kazoo Day. Suggest that students select an event that occurs on their birthday and write a paragraph telling why they would or would not like to attend the event.

Go for the Goal/Final Test

1. Barbara practices her *saxophone* every day.
2. Bob's paintings are *magnificent!*
3. In Wales, Kathy *photographed* many castles.
4. When Naomi was *fifteen,* she moved to Kansas.
5. Did we have *sufficient* rainfall this season?
6. I would *prefer* to stay home and read my book.
7. My father is an *officer* in the Marine Corps.
8. What *effective* ways for studying did you learn?
9. Mr. Bates hoped that he could *afford* a new car.
10. Don't forget to use the *phrase* "thank you."
11. Brazil is in the Southern *Hemisphere.*
12. A skunk is certainly not a *fragrant* animal.
13. The dentist gave me a *pamphlet* about tooth care.
14. The sun can *toughen* and damage your skin.
15. *Hyphenate* words between their syllables.
16. Our attempt to move the couch was *laughable.*
17. A veterinarian is a *physician* who treats animals.
18. The *coffee* plant has bright red berries.
19. Ian felt *triumphant* when he won the race.
20. Did you *emphasize* the important points?

Remind students to complete the Scoreboard and write any misspelled words in their Word Locker.

★★ **All-Star Words**   You may want to point out that the All-Star Words follow the spelling rule and model writing a fake definition for a List Word.

23

Lesson 4

Objective
To spell words with *gn*, *wr*, and *tch*

Correlated Phonics Lesson
MCP Phonics, Level F, Lesson 9

Warm Up
Page 17

In "The Spruce Goose," students may be surprised to learn about an airplane that is even bigger than today's jumbo jets. Invite students to discuss the Spruce Goose and other interesting airplanes.

Point out that the picture in the box shows Howard Hughes. Then ask volunteers to say each boldfaced word and identify the letters that stand for /n/, /r/, or /ch/.

On Your Mark/ Warm Up Test
1. Do you do warm-up *stretches* before you run?
2. The book *designer* chose a heavy cream paper.
3. That antique *wristwatch* is really beautiful!
4. The dog *fetched* the stick from the stream.
5. The family ate breakfast at the *kitchen* counter.
6. We found *wreckage* from the ship on the beach.
7. Mack wanted to find out how *wrestling* is scored.
8. I returned the *crutches* after my leg healed.
9. The scout used a *hatchet* to split the logs.
10. The villagers feared the *wrath* of their leader.
11. The two runners are *unmatched* in ability.
12. Rita dabbed some *cologne* behind her ears.
13. The puppy *scratched* a hole in the screen door.
14. He *resigned* after twenty years in his profession.
15. Some artists do all their *sketching* outdoors.
16. A police officer helped the *foreigner* find a hotel.
17. Did you meet the governor during the *campaign?*
18. The shutters were blown *awry* by the wind.
19. What a *gnarled* appearance that tree has!
20. Queen Victoria *reigned* for many years.

Pep Talk/Game Plan
Pages 18–19

Introduce the spelling rule and have students read the List Words aloud. Point out the pronunciation of *awry* (ə rī´), and give its meaning and the meanings of other unfamiliar words (*gnarled, wrath*). Then encourage students to look back at their Warm Up Tests and apply the spelling rule to any misspelled words.

As students work through the **Spelling Lineup,** **Word Clues,** and **Dictionary** exercises, remind them to look back at their List Words or in their dictionaries if they need help.

 See **Spelling Aloud,** page 14

Warm Up

Do you know of any planes larger than today's jumbo jets?

The Spruce Goose

Do you think an airplane with a wingspan longer than a football field is far-fetched? An aviator named Howard Hughes imagined one. Because Hughes was also one of the world's richest men, he did more than just imagine it. He was the **designer** and builder of it.

Construction of this marvel began in 1942, during World War II. Hughes planned to use his giant plane to transport troops to foreign battlefields. Plans for his plane went **awry**. Metal was scarce in wartime, so he built the plane out of birch, a kind of wood. By the time his plane was completed, the war was over. The "Spruce Goose," as it was nicknamed, seemed like a dead duck. People said that if it ever got off the ground, little would be left but a **wreckage** of matchsticks. Hughes decided to prove them wrong. On November 2, 1947, he flew the plane on its one and only flight. The goose traveled for one mile. Future flights in this aircraft of **unmatched** size were cancelled.

For years, the Spruce Goose was on display in Long Beach, California. Recently, it has been moved to McMinnville, Oregon, for display at the Evergreen AirVenture Museum. Visitors will see how a modern "jumbo" jet could easily fit beneath the outstretched wooden wings of the goose. Maybe Hughes didn't lay an egg after all!

 Look back at the boldfaced words in the selection. Say the words. Listen for the /n/, /r/, and /ch/ sounds. What do you notice about how these sounds are spelled?

On Your Mark

Take your Warm Up Test. Then check your spelling with the List Words on the next page.

17

Pep Talk

Sometimes you don't hear every letter in a word. The letters **gn** can spell the /n/ sound, as in <u>designer</u>, but the **g** is silent. The letters **wr** can spell the /r/ sound, as in <u>wrath</u>, but the **w** is silent. The letters **tch** can spell the /ch/ sound, as in <u>scratched</u>, but the **t** is silent.

LIST WORDS
1. stretches
2. designer
3. wristwatch
4. fetched
5. kitchen
6. wreckage
7. wrestling
8. crutches
9. hatchet
10. wrath
11. unmatched
12. cologne
13. scratched
14. resigned
15. sketching
16. foreigner
17. campaign
18. awry
19. gnarled
20. reigned

Game Plan

Spelling Lineup
Write each List Word under the correct heading. One word will be written twice.

/n/ spells gn
1. designer
2. cologne
3. resigned
4. foreigner
5. campaign
6. gnarled
7. reigned

/r/ spells wr
8. wristwatch
9. wreckage
10. wrestling
11. wrath
12. awry

/ch/ spells tch
13. stretches
14. wristwatch
15. fetched
16. kitchen
17. crutches
18. hatchet
19. unmatched
20. scratched
21. sketching

18 Lesson 4 ■ gn, wr, and tch

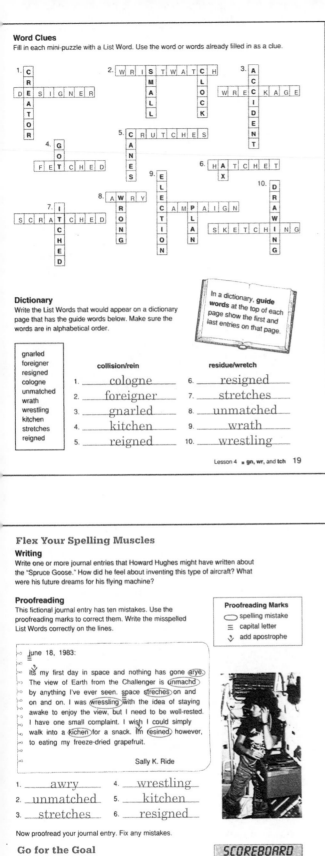

Word Clues

Fill in each mini-puzzle with a List Word. Use the word or words already filled in as a clue.

(crossword puzzle)

1. DESIGNER / CREATOR
2. WRISTWATCH / SMALL / CLOCK
3. ACCIDENT / WRECKAGE
4. GO / FETCHED
5. CRUTCHES / CANES
6. HATCHET / EX
7. SCRATCHED / ITCHED
8. AWRY / WRONG
9. ELECTION / CAMPAIGN / PLAN
10. DRAW / DRAWING
SKETCHING

Dictionary

Write the List Words that would appear on a dictionary page that has the guide words below. Make sure the words are in alphabetical order.

> In a dictionary, **guide words** at the top of each page show the first and last entries on that page.

gnarled
foreigner
resigned
cologne
unmatched
wrath
wrestling
kitchen
stretches
reigned

collision/rein
1. cologne
2. foreigner
3. gnarled
4. kitchen
5. reigned

residue/wretch
6. resigned
7. stretches
8. unmatched
9. wrath
10. wrestling

Lesson 4 ■ gn, wr, and tch   19

Flex Your Spelling Muscles

Writing

Write one or more journal entries that Howard Hughes might have written about the "Spruce Goose." How did he feel about inventing this type of aircraft? What were his future dreams for his flying machine?

Proofreading

This fictional journal entry has ten mistakes. Use the proofreading marks to correct them. Write the misspelled List Words correctly on the lines.

Proofreading Marks
⬯ spelling mistake
≡ capital letter
⋎ add apostrophe

> june 18, 1983:
>
> Its my first day in space and nothing has gone arye. The view of Earth from the Challenger is unmachd by anything I've ever seen. space streches on and on and on. I was wressling with the idea of staying awake to enjoy the view, but I need to be well-rested. I have one small complaint. I wish I could simply walk into a kichen for a snack. Im resined, however, to eating my freeze-dried grapefruit.
>
> Sally K. Ride

1. awry
2. unmatched
3. stretches
4. wrestling
5. kitchen
6. resigned

Now proofread your journal entry. Fix any mistakes.

Go for the Goal

Take your Final Test. Then fill in your Scoreboard. Send your mistakes to the Word Locker.

SCOREBOARD
number correct	number wrong

★ ★ ★ ★ ★ ★ ★ All-Star Words ★ ★ ★ ★ ★ ★ ★ ★

gnomes   wring   wrench   twitch   stitched

Write a riddle for each All-Star Word leaving a space for the answer. Switch riddles with a partner. See if you can write the correct answers.

20   Lesson 4 ■ gn, wr, and tch

◎ **Spelling Strategy**   With a partner, students can write *gn, wr,* and *tch* on separate cards. Then they can take turns saying the List Words aloud and using them in sentences. For each word, the partner who is listening holds up the appropriate card or cards—to show whether *gn, wr,* and/or *tch* is in the word—and spells the word aloud.

Flex Your Spelling Muscles   *Page 20*

As students complete the **Writing** activity, encourage them to brainstorm ideas, write a first draft, revise, and proofread their work. The **Proofreading** exercise will help them prepare to proofread their journal entries. To publish their writing, students may want to create a bulletin-board display with their journal entries and drawings of the Spruce Goose.

✍ **Writer's Corner** _____

> Encourage students to look in an encyclopedia or a library book to learn more about famous aircraft. Students can create "flight" cards based on their favorite planes, then share or trade their cards with one another.

Go for the Goal/Final Test

1. The character's **wrath** is shown in Chapter 1.
2. Was the **wreckage** from the storm removed?
3. Those pine trees have **gnarled** trunks.
4. Do you see the artist who is **sketching** the tree?
5. When he sprained his ankle, Al needed **crutches.**
6. Watch how the cat **stretches** when it first wakes.
7. We'll eat dinner at the **kitchen** table.
8. This French **cologne** smells wonderful!
9. Queen Elizabeth II has **reigned** since 1953.
10. Why can't a **foreigner** visit that temple?
11. The tablecloth was blown **awry** in the wind.
12. That old **hatchet** is too dull to chop wood now.
13. My new **wristwatch** is shockproof and waterproof.
14. Fundy's tides are **unmatched** by any in the world.
15. Yuka **resigned** from her job to take a better one.
16. A political **campaign** takes time and money.
17. The sharp chair legs **scratched** the wood floor.
18. Is sumo **wrestling** a popular sport in Japan?
19. This suit was made by a famous **designer.**
20. A student **fetched** a chair for the guest.

Remind students to complete the Scoreboard and write any misspelled words in their Word Locker.

★★ **All-Star Words**   You may want to point out that the All-Star Words follow the spelling rule and provide an example of a riddle for one of the words.

Lesson 5

Objective

To spell words that contain silent consonants

Correlated Phonics Lessons

MCP Phonics, Level F, Lessons 1, 4

Warm Up
Page 21

In this selection, students find out about a "coat" that isn't a piece of clothing. Ask students what kinds of symbols people wear today (i.e., brand names, T-shirt slogans) and what their coat of arms would look like if they had one.

Encourage students to look back at the boldfaced words. Ask volunteers to say each word and identify the silent consonant or consonants.

On Your Mark/Warm Up Test

1. I **doubt** that I will attend the party.
2. **Knickers** are sometimes worn by golfers.
3. Can you read the date on that old **tombstone?**
4. A streak of **lightning** lit up the evening sky.
5. If you borrow money, you are in **debt** to someone.
6. A water **softener** removes iron from water.
7. The people believed that the king was **almighty.**
8. We made a **solemn** promise to be friends forever.
9. **Fasten** the leash on the dog's collar.
10. We heard the tea kettle **whistling** on the stove.
11. What fabulous **castles** we saw in Europe!
12. Louisa added the numbers in the **column.**
13. Did Mozart write **hymns** as well as symphonies?
14. An owl uses its sharp **eyesight** to find food.
15. Felipe was **listening** to a talk show on the radio.
16. Uncle Bert is a very successful **plumber.**
17. Lorraine Hansberry was a famous **playwright.**
18. When did the city **condemn** that old building?
19. **Moisten** the stamp with your tongue.
20. Lamar coated the fish fillet with bread **crumbs.**

Pep Talk/Game Plan
Pages 22–23

Introduce the spelling rule and have students read the List Words aloud, identifying the silent consonant in each word. Then encourage students to look back at their Warm Up Tests and apply the spelling rule to any misspelled words.

As students work through the **Spelling Lineup, Comparing Words,** and **Missing Words** exercises, remind them to look back at their List Words or in their dictionaries if they need help.

 See **Tape Recording,** page 15

26

Silent Consonants

Warm Up

How many sleeves are there in a coat of arms?

Coat of Arms

Imagine watching a football game where both teams wore the same uniforms and all players had the same number on their shirts. Even if you had excellent **eyesight**, it would be hard to tell who was who.

During the Middle Ages, when noble knights defended their kings' **castles**, there were no such things as uniforms. Each knight was dressed in a suit of armor that made him look like other knights. The knight's face was covered by a metal plate, too. How was one army of knights able to recognize who was on their side and who was the enemy? The knights came to solve the problem by wearing a "coat of arms" over their armor. The coat of arms was a shirt showing a symbol or shield. Often, the shield, too, bore the colors of the king who had hired the knight. Then, when each **column** of knights approached each other in battle, there was no **doubt** as to who was **fighting** for whom.

The days of knighthood are long past. Coats of arms, however, can still be found today. Many schools and organizations have special symbols called "seals." Families, too, may have their own shields called "family crests." Like the knights' shields, these crests contain symbols and colors that represent the family's history.

 Say the boldfaced words in the selection. Do you hear all of the consonants in each word? What do you notice about some of the consonants?

On Your Mark

Take your Warm Up Test. Then check your spelling with the List Words on the next page.

21

Pep Talk

Use the following rules to help you spell words with silent consonants:

- Silent **t** often comes before **en** or **le**, as in fasten and castles.
- Silent **b** often comes before **t**, as in debt, or after **m**, as in crumbs.
- Silent **n** often follows **m**, as in hymns.
- Silent **k** often comes before **n**, as in knickers.
- Silent **gh** often follows **i**, as in eyesight.

LIST WORDS

1. doubt
2. knickers
3. tombstone
4. lightning
5. debt
6. softener
7. almighty
8. solemn
9. fasten
10. whistling
11. castles
12. column
13. hymns
14. eyesight
15. listening
16. plumber
17. playwright
18. condemn
19. moisten
20. crumbs

Game Plan

Spelling Lineup

Write each List Word in the category that tells what silent consonant or consonants it contains.

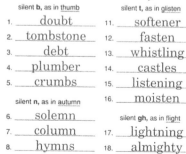

silent **b**, as in thumb

1. doubt
2. tombstone
3. debt
4. plumber
5. crumbs

silent **n**, as in autumn

6. solemn
7. column
8. hymns
9. condemn

silent **k**, as in knife

10. knickers

silent **t**, as in glisten

11. softener
12. fasten
13. whistling
14. castles
15. listening
16. moisten

silent **gh**, as in flight

17. lightning
18. almighty
19. eyesight
20. playwright

22 Lesson 5 ■ Silent Consonants

Comparing Words

Study the relationship between the first two underlined words. Then write a List Word that has the same relationship with the third underlined word.

1. Poet is to poem as ___playwright___ is to play.
2. Birds are to nests as kings are to ___castles___
3. Peas are to vegetables as ___hymns___ are to songs.
4. Tie is to shoes as ___fasten___ is to seatbelts.
5. Huge is to big as ___almighty___ is to powerful.
6. Music is to hearing as colors are to ___eyesight___
7. Drops are to water as ___crumbs___ are to bread.
8. Sandals are to shoes as ___knickers___ are to trousers.
9. Keep is to promise as pay is to ___debt___
10. Television is to watching as radio is to ___listening___

Missing Words

Write a List Word to complete each sentence.

1. Without a ___doubt___, Dan is the best singer in the chorus.
2. Use the cold water to ___moisten___ the towel.
3. Instead of calling a ___plumber___, mother fixed the leak herself.
4. The List Words appear in a long ___column___ on page 22.
5. They were ___whistling___ a tune as they raked the leaves.
6. The granite ___tombstone___ of Paul Revere is in this graveyard.
7. The Health Department had to ___condemn___ the hotel due to unsanitary conditions.
8. Fabric ___softener___ will make the towels soft and fluffy.
9. The thunder and ___lightning___ startled us.
10. I knew the man was worried when I saw his ___solemn___ look.

Flex Your Spelling Muscles

Writing

Write a mystery story titled "The Case of the Missing Coat of Arms." Use List Words to help you create an eerie mood. Perhaps you can add some lightning or whistling winds.

Proofreading

The book review has eight mistakes. Use the proofreading marks to correct them. Write the misspelled List Words correctly on the lines.

Proofreading Marks
◯ spelling mistake
≡ capital letter
⊙ add period

There are so many drawings in The True Book of knights and Cassels that you can spend hours looking at just one page. This book will take you to thirteenth century europe You'll see a solum knighthood ceremony You'll spot an unlucky knight who is in det after losing a joust and a lucky knight who gets to lassen his lady's scarf.

1. ___Castles___
2. ___solemn___
3. ___debt___
4. ___fasten___

Now proofread your mystery story. Fix any mistakes.

Go for the Goal

Take your Final Test. Then fill in your Scoreboard. Send your mistakes to the Word Locker.

SCOREBOARD

number correct	number wrong

★ ★ ★ ★ ★ ★ ★ All-Star Words ★ ★ ★ ★ ★ ★ ★

knuckles   thistle   numb   throughout   corps

Write an exclamatory sentence that includes each of the All-Star Words. Then erase the All-Star Words and switch papers with a partner. Fill in the missing words.

◎ **Spelling Strategy** Invite students to get together with a partner and write the List Words. Then partners can pronounce each word, point to the silent consonant or consonants, and explain the spelling rule that applies to the silent letter or letters. Challenge students to think of other words that contain silent b, n, k, t, and gh.

Flex Your Spelling Muscles   Page 24

As students complete the **Writing** activity, encourage them to brainstorm ideas, write a first draft, revise, and proofread their work. The **Proofreading** exercise will help them prepare to proofread their mystery stories. To publish their writing, students may want to
• present their mystery stories as plays
• create a mystery story magazine.

✍ Writer's Corner

Students might be interested in looking at Steven Caney's *Kids' America* or a similar book to help them design their own coat of arms or personal seal. Encourage students to attach their emblems to their desks, books, or folders.

Go for the Goal/Final Test

1. The *tombstone* was made of pink granite.
2. The chorus recorded several old English *hymns.*
3. A witness takes a *solemn* oath to tell the truth.
4. Teachers must *condemn* disruptive behavior.
5. Hannah is *whistling* a song.
6. I finally paid my *debt* to the bank!
7. Pigeons ate the *crumbs* on the ground.
8. Who's *listening* to the ballgame on the radio?
9. Please *fasten* the latch on the door.
10. Glaucoma is a disease that affects *eyesight.*
11. Dew will *moisten* the grass and make it sparkle.
12. Ben Franklin learned that *lightning* is electricity.
13. If you *doubt* the truth of a fact, look it up.
14. That wave just destroyed two sand *castles!*
15. When did your aunt become a licensed *plumber?*
16. Fabric *softener* makes clothes soft and fluffy.
17. In the 1920s, men's *knickers* were fashionable.
18. The *almighty* ruler promised to bring peace.
19. Arthur Miller is a renowned American *playwright.*
20. The words are listed in a long *column.*

Remind students to complete the Scoreboard and write any misspelled words in their Word Locker.

★★ **All-Star Words** You may want to point out that the All-Star Words follow the spelling rule and review the definition of an exclamatory sentence.

Lesson 6 • Instant Replay

Objective
To review spelling words with /k/, /kw/, and /n/; hard and soft *c* and *g*, *dge*; /f/; *gn*, *wr*, and *tch*; and silent consonants

Time Out
Pages 25–28

Check Your Word Locker Based on your observations, note which words are giving students the most difficulty and offer assistance for spelling them correctly. Here are some frequently misspelled words to watch for: *knowledge, schedule, icicles, genuine, physician, emphasize, cologne, campaign, solemn,* and *column.*

To give students extra help and practice in taking standardized tests, you may want to have them take the Review Test for this lesson on pages 30–31. After scoring the tests, return them to students so that they can record their misspelled words in their Word Locker.

After practicing their troublesome words, students can work through the exercises for **Lessons 1–5.** Before they begin each exercise, you may want to go over the spelling rule.

🏠 **Take It Home** Invite students to collect the List Words in **Lessons 1–5** at home. Suggest that they look for words in books, magazines, and newspapers, and listen for them on the radio and TV. For a complete list of the words, encourage students to take their *Spelling Workout* books home. Students can also use Take It Home Master 1 on pages 32–33 to help them do the activity. Invite them to compare their lists at school and to discuss which words they located most frequently.

Name _____

Instant Replay • Lessons 1–5

LESSON 6

Time Out
Some words are spelled differently than you might expect. Some sounds, like /f/ and /k/, are spelled more than one way. The letters g and c have a hard and a soft sound. Some words contain silent letters.

Check Your Word Locker
Look at the words in your Word Locker. Write your most troublesome words from Lessons 1 through 5.

_____

_____

Practice writing your troublesome words with a partner. Say the words and point out to your partner what part of the word is spelled differently than you expected.

Lesson 1
Sounds can be spelled in different ways. <u>K</u>eyboard, ac<u>k</u>nowledge, e<u>ch</u>oes, and antique all have the /k/ sound. <u>Qu</u>alify has the /kw/ sound. <u>Kn</u>elt has the /n/ sound.

List Words
chorus
schedule
keyboard
quantity
banquet
required
knowledge
antique
knelt
unique

Write a List Word that means the same or almost the same as the word given.

1. piano — keyboard
2. necessary — required
3. timetable — schedule
4. amount — quantity
5. singers — chorus
6. feast — banquet
7. old — antique
8. unequaled — unique
9. bowed — knelt
10. understanding — knowledge

25

Lesson 2
The letter **g** makes a hard sound, as in <u>g</u>uage, and a soft sound, as in bud<u>g</u>et.
The letter **c** makes a hard sound, as in magi<u>c</u>al, and a soft sound, as in <u>c</u>elebration.

List Words
crystal
engaged
medicine
icicles
language
guesses
intelligent
cartridge
genuine
recipe

Write a List Word to complete each sentence.

1. I like the way that **language** sounds when it is spoken.
2. Anna was **engaged** two years before she got married.
3. My doctor told me to take this **medicine**
4. The **recipe** requires two cups of flour.
5. So far, all your **guesses** have been wrong.
6. An **intelligent** dog learns tricks easily.
7. Is that a **genuine** ruby or a fake?
8. Many fine goblets are made from **crystal**
9. This **cartridge** does not fit my tape player.
10. Every winter, long **icicles** form.

Lesson 3
The /f/ sound can be spelled with **f, ff, ph,** and **gh,** as in <u>pref</u>er, a<u>ff</u>ord, <u>ph</u>rase, and tou<u>gh</u>en.

List Words
officer
afford
toughen
fifteen
prefer
physician
fragrant
pamphlet
phrase
hemisphere

Write the List Word that belongs in each group.

1. catalog, booklet, — pamphlet
2. seven, thirteen, — fifteen
3. sergeant, captain, — officer
4. globe, planet, — hemisphere
5. word, sentence, — phrase
6. scented, perfumed, — fragrant
7. save, spend, — afford
8. like, desire, — prefer
9. strengthen, stiffen, — toughen
10. nurse, medic, — physician

26 Lesson 6 ■ Instant Replay

28

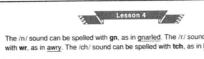

Lesson 4

The /n/ sound can be spelled with **gn**, as in <u>gn</u>arled. The /r/ sound can be spelled with **wr**, as in <u>awry</u>. The /ch/ sound can be spelled with **tch**, as in ki<u>tch</u>en.

List Words

stretches
fetched
wrath
wristwatch
gnarled
resigned
sketching
foreigner
awry
wreckage

Find List Words that mean the same as the underlined words in the sentences. Write the words on the lines.

1. By my <u>clock</u>, it's almost noon. __wristwatch__
2. The apology ended my <u>fury</u>. __wrath__
3. Tim <u>reaches</u> for the box on the top shelf. __stretches__
4. That tree is so <u>twisted</u>! __gnarled__
5. Eileen <u>quit</u> after a week. __resigned__
6. He is a <u>stranger</u> to our land. __foreigner__
7. Kirk <u>brought</u> the book I left behind. __fetched__
8. The storm left <u>damage</u> everywhere. __wreckage__
9. Dad is <u>drawing</u> a boat. __sketching__
10. Our plans for the trip went <u>wrong</u>. __awry__

Lesson 5

Some words contain silent letters, such as the **t** in sof<u>t</u>ener, the **b** in plum<u>b</u>er, the **n** in colum<u>n</u>, the **k** in <u>k</u>nickers, and the **gh** in almi<u>gh</u>ty.

List Words

doubt
knickers
lightning
debt
solemn
fasten
hymns
condemn
moisten
crumbs

Write the List Word to match each clue.

1. short pants __knickers__
2. declare unfit for use __condemn__
3. make damp __moisten__
4. comes with storms __lightning__
5. something owed __debt__
6. be uncertain about __moisten__
7. songs of praise __hymns__
8. not laughing __solemn__
9. bits of bread __crumbs__
10. attach or join __fasten__

Lesson 6 ▪ Instant Replay **27**

Lessons 1–5

List Words

recipe
intelligent
moisten
knowledge
chorus
prefer
fetched
wristwatch
genuine
knickers
medicine
sketching
wrath
hemisphere

Write the List Word next to its dictionary sound-spelling.

1. (res´ə pe) __recipe__
2. (mois´ən) __moisten__
3. (kôr´əs) __chorus__
4. (fech´t) __fetched__
5. (jen´yo͞o in) __genuine__
6. (med´ə sən) __medicine__
7. (rath) __wrath__
8. (in tel´ə jənt) __intelligent__
9. (nä´lij) __knowledge__
10. (prē fur´) __prefer__
11. (rist´wäch) __wristwatch__
12. (nik´ərz) __knickers__
13. (skech´iŋ) __sketching__
14. (hem´i sfir´) __hemisphere__

Go for the Goal

Take your Final Replay Test. Then fill in your Scoreboard. Send any misspelled words to your Word Locker.

SCOREBOARD

number correct	number wrong

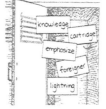

Clean Out Your Word Locker

Look in your Word Locker. Cross out each word you spelled correctly on your Final Replay Test. Circle the words you're still having trouble with. Add the words you circled to your Spelling Notebook. What do you notice about the words? Watch for those words as you write.

1. I have no **doubt** that I will finish on time.
2. In the picture, Grandfather is wearing **knickers.**
3. Fine **crystal** shines more brightly than glass.
4. Not everyone becomes **engaged** before marrying.
5. A police **officer** guarded the payroll.
6. I can finally **afford** the bike I want!
7. This belt **stretches** enough to fit my father.
8. I bought a **wristwatch** with a big face.
9. How many members does the **chorus** have?
10. A standard piano **keyboard** has eighty-eight keys.
11. **Lightning** just lit up the sky!
12. No one should go into **debt** for luxury items.
13. Luckily this **medicine** is paid for by insurance.
14. Those falling **icicles** might hurt someone.
15. Raking without gloves will **toughen** your hands.
16. My aunt lived in that house for **fifteen** years.
17. Pedro **fetched** his mother's purse for her.
18. Investigators studied the **wreckage** for clues.
19. The **quantity** of water is not enough to run a mill.
20. The **banquet** was given in honor of the mayor.
21. His face was serious and **solemn.**
22. Please **fasten** the gate when you leave.
23. German is the **language** spoken in my home.
24. I made several bad **guesses** on the test.
25. Some people **prefer** to take winter vacations.
26. Only a **physician** can prescribe those pills.
27. Although he was full of **wrath,** his voice was calm.
28. No one ever **resigned** from this job.
29. The guard has no **knowledge** of any visitors.
30. Isn't a lifeguard **required** at the lake?
31. Which composer wrote those **hymns?**
32. The judge will **condemn** such behavior.
33. An **intelligent** person thinks before acting.
34. The pen has an ink **cartridge.**
35. Your garden is so **fragrant!**
36. This **pamphlet** names the birds in this area.
37. Mr. Dubois is **sketching** plans for a house.
38. No **foreigner** may vote in our elections.
39. Katy needed a copy of the latest train **schedule.**
40. That **antique** store has a suit of armor for sale.
41. If the mixture seems dry, **moisten** it with water.
42. The hikers left only **crumbs** on their plates.
43. Do you think their affection for us is **genuine?**
44. Does the **recipe** call for noodles or rice?
45. That is a **phrase,** not a complete sentence.
46. Australia is in the Southern **Hemisphere.**
47. The curtains were blown **awry** by the breeze.
48. How **gnarled** those old tree branches are!
49. As the queen entered, everyone **knelt** before her.
50. That artist has a **unique** way of showing motion.

Clean Out Your Word Locker   After writing each word, students can identify the spelling of a consonant sound they learned in **Lessons 1–5** or point to a silent consonant.

Instant Replay Test

Side A

Read each set of words. Fill in the circle next to the word that is spelled correctly.

1. (a) fraigrant   (c) fragrent
   (b) fragrant   (d) fraigrent

2. (a) perfer   (c) prefer
   (b) perferr   (d) preffer

3. (a) hemisphere   (c) hemispheer
   (b) hemisfere   (d) hemisfeer

4. (a) icicels   (c) icicles
   (b) icycles   (d) icycels

5. (a) doub   (c) doute
   (b) dowt   (d) doubt

6. (a) nowlege   (c) knowlege
   (b) knowledge   (d) nowledge

7. (a) schedual   (c) scedule
   (b) schedule   (d) skedual

8. (a) sketching   (c) schetching
   (b) scetching   (d) skeching

9. (a) hymms   (c) hymns
   (b) himms   (d) hims

10. (a) younique   (c) unieque
    (b) yuneek   (d) unique

11. (a) resgned   (c) risgned
    (b) resigned   (d) rezined

12. (a) cartredge   (c) cartrege
    (b) cartridge   (d) cartrage

13. (a) gnarled   (c) gnrled
    (b) narld   (d) narled

Instant Replay Test

Side B

ead each set of words. Fill in the circle next to the word that
spelled correctly.

4.   (a) moysten   (c) moysen
    (b) moisen   (d) moisten

5.   (a) det   (c) deabt
    (b) debt   (d) dett

6.   (a) ristwach   (c) wristwatch
    (b) wristwach   (d) ristwatch

7.   (a) intelligient   (c) intelligent
    (b) intelligant   (d) inteligent

8.   (a) chorus   (c) choris
    (b) choress   (d) coris

9.   (a) foureigner   (c) fourener
    (b) foregner   (d) foreigner

0.   (a) afford   (c) afourd
    (b) aford   (d) afored

1.   (a) knealt   (c) nealt
    (b) kneelt   (d) knelt

2.   (a) phisician   (c) phisitian
    (b) physician   (d) physitian

3.   (a) solemn   (c) solumn
    (b) solum   (d) sollumn

4.   (a) cristal   (c) crystal
    (b) crystle   (d) cristle

5.   (a) recipee   (c) recipe
    (b) resippy   (d) resipe

TAKE IT HOME

Your child has learned to spell many new words and would enjoy sharing them with you and your family. The following activities will provide both a review of the words in Lessons 1–5 and a lot of family fun!

Homey Words

School isn't the only place where spelling words are found—there may be dozens of them floating around your house! Encourage your child to collect these words by looking for them in books, magazines, and newspapers, and by listening for them on the radio or TV. Keep a piece of paper and a pencil handy to jot down each spelling word he or she finds.

Our home-improvement **pamphlet stretches** your household **budget.** Are you **listening** closely? Here's how to **qualify** for a free copy!

chorus
angle
debt

Word Decoding

Can you and your child decode the secret writing? Use the key to help you write the spelling words represented by the numbers and symbols. Then use the letters in the box to complete the message.

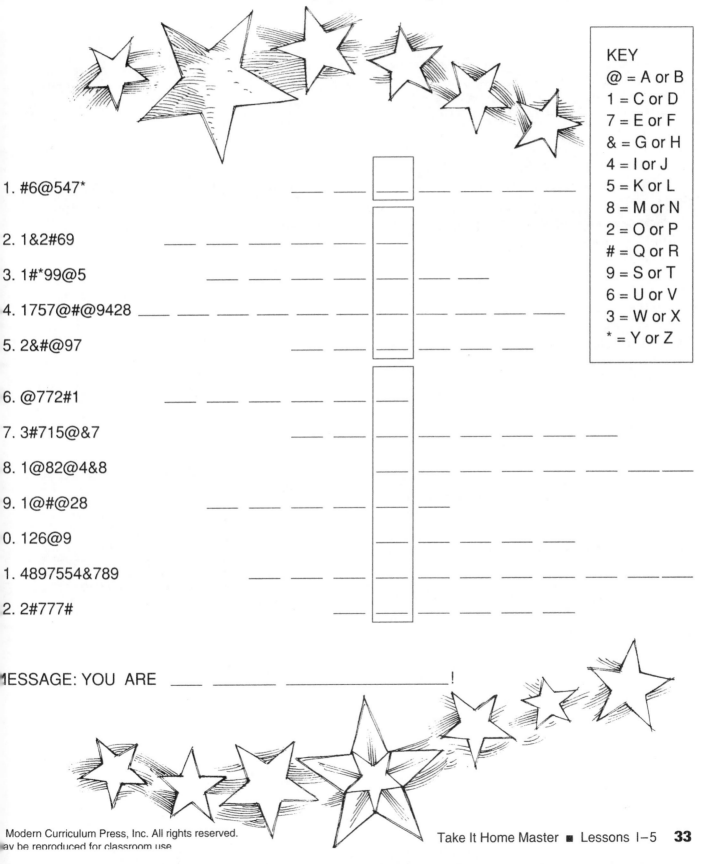

KEY
@ = A or B
1 = C or D
7 = E or F
& = G or H
4 = I or J
5 = K or L
8 = M or N
2 = O or P
# = Q or R
9 = S or T
6 = U or V
3 = W or X
* = Y or Z

1. #6@547* ___ ___ ☐ ___ ___ ___ ___

2. 1&2#69 ___ ___ ___ ☐ ___ ___

3. 1#*99@5 ___ ___ ___ ☐ ___ ___ ___

4. 1757@#@9428 ___ ___ ___ ___ ___ ☐ ___ ___ ___ ___

5. 2&#@97 ___ ___ ___ ☐ ___ ___

6. @772#1 ___ ___ ___ ☐ ___ ___

7. 3#715@&7 ___ ___ ___ ___ ☐ ___ ___ ___

8. 1@82@4&8 ___ ___ ___ ___ ☐ ___ ___ ___

9. 1@#@28 ___ ___ ___ ☐ ___ ___

0. 126@9 ___ ___ ☐ ___ ___

1. 4897554&789 ___ ___ ___ ___ ___ ___ ☐ ___ ___ ___ ___

2. 2#777# ___ ___ ☐ ___ ___ ___

MESSAGE: YOU ARE ___ ___ ___ ___ !

Lesson 7

Objective
To spell words in which *s* sounds like /s/, /z/, and /zh/

Correlated Phonics Lesson
MCP Phonics, Level F, Lesson 5

Warm Up   *Page 29*
In this selection, students read about a special job—firemedic—that requires you to be a daredevil. After reading, invite students to discuss careers they are interested in and what they think about being a firemedic.

Encourage students to look back at the boldfaced words. Ask volunteers to say the words and identify the different sounds that *s* stands for.

On Your Mark/Warm Up Test
1. The **purpose** of the meeting is to elect officers.
2. Tien maintained his **composure** during the match.
3. A healthy lifestyle can prevent many **diseases.**
4. Everyone at the party wore **casual** clothes.
5. Are farm workers hired on a **seasonal** basis?
6. Identical twins **resemble** each other very closely.
7. Use the map scale when **measuring** distance.
8. Marie and her **husband** jog every day.
9. The sled dogs are in **position** to begin the race.
10. Lucy is both a **visual** and an auditory learner.
11. Nick pressed his **trousers** before the dance.
12. How many musical **instruments** can Nancy play?
13. We got the most **desirable** seats in the hall!
14. The swimming **instructor** also teaches diving.
15. Lawanda took a **leisurely** stroll through the park.
16. Bonuses will go to the most **deserving** workers.
17. The aerobics class is held in the **gymnasium.**
18. Carl's **version** of what happened is inaccurate.
19. How much money is in the club's **treasury?**
20. Colorado **usually** has great skiing in February.

Pep Talk/Game Plan   *Pages 30–31*
Introduce the spelling rule and have students read the List Words aloud. Discuss the meanings of unfamiliar words, such as *leisurely* and *composure.* Then encourage students to look back at their Warm Up Tests and apply the spelling rule to any misspelled words.

As students work through the **Spelling Lineup, Synonyms,** and **Puzzle** exercises, remind them to look back at their List Words or in their dictionaries if they need help.

 See **Charades,** page 15

34

/s/, /z/, and /zh/   LESSON 7

Warm Up
What kind of career might require you to be a daredevil?

Double-duty Daredevils
A stunt performer and a race-car driver are **usually** thought of as daredevils. Either one of these could be considered a dangerous position. Some say that such people tempt danger on **purpose.**

There's a career field for those who find it **desirable** to have a bit of risk and danger in their work. It's not **casual** work, though. In fact, it's lifesaving work. A person who is this version of a "daredevil" is called a "firemedic."

A firemedic really does the jobs of two people. He or she is a trained firefighter and a paramedic. This means that he or she can give medical help in an emergency. Both professions require a great deal of training. Becoming a firefighter requires many hours of **instruction** and practice. A paramedic learns information both in school and in a hospital. A person who is qualified in both of these areas is **deserving** of credit.

In many places it would be too expensive to hire firefighters as well as paramedics. A firefighter is often called to a scene where there's an injury. Having been trained in both medicine and firefighting, a firemedic is prepared for almost anything.

It takes a special kind of person to want to be a firemedic. It **usually** means giving up leisure time for the extra training. Months of study and practice are part of the program. However, firemedics claim that the feeling of satisfaction their careers offer is well worth the sacrifices.

 Say the boldfaced words in the selection. Notice the sound that the letter **s** makes in each word. How many different sounds for **s** do you hear?

On Your Mark
Take your Warm Up Test. Then check your spelling with the List Words on the next page.

29

Pep Talk
The letter s can stand for different sounds. For example, in the word purpose, the letter s spells the /s/ sound. In the word resemble, the letter s spells the /z/ sound. In the word usually, the letter s spells the /zh/ sound.

LIST WORDS
1. purpose
2. composure
3. diseases
4. casual
5. seasonal
6. resemble
7. measuring
8. husband
9. position
10. visual
11. trousers
12. instruments
13. desirable
14. instructor
15. leisurely
16. deserving
17. gymnasium
18. version
19. treasury
20. usually

Game Plan
Spelling Lineup
Write each List Word under the sound that s stands for. One word will be written twice.

/s/, as in secure
1. purpose
2. seasonal
3. instruments
4. instructor

/z/, as in music
5. diseases
6. seasonal
7. resemble
8. husband
9. position
10. trousers
11. desirable
12. deserving
13. gymnasium

/zh/, as in pleasure
14. composure
15. casual
16. measuring
17. visual
18. leisurely
19. version
20. treasury
21. usually

30   Lesson 7 ● /s/, /z/, and /zh/

Synonyms

Write a List Word that means the same or almost the same as the word or phrase given.

1. reason — purpose
2. generally — usually
3. worth wanting — desirable
4. teacher — instructor
5. informal — casual
6. unhurried — leisurely
7. self-control — composure
8. look like — resemble
9. weighing — measuring
10. money or funds — treasury
11. ailments — diseases
12. placement — position
13. worthy — deserving
14. tools — instruments
15. variation — version

Puzzle

Fill in the crossword puzzle by writing a List Word to answer each definition clue.

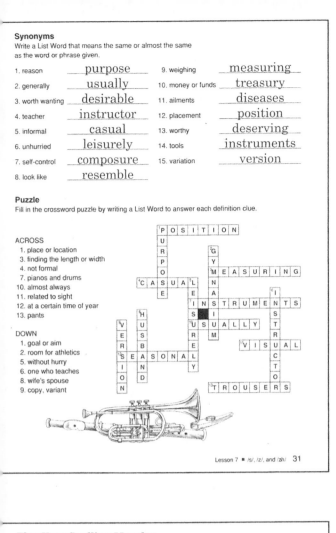

ACROSS
1. place or location
3. finding the length or width
4. not formal
7. pianos and drums
10. almost always
11. related to sight
12. at a certain time of year
13. pants

DOWN
1. goal or aim
2. room for athletics
5. without hurry
6. one who teaches
8. wife's spouse
9. copy, variant

Lesson 7 ■ /s/, /z/, and /zh/ 31

Flex Your Spelling Muscles

Writing

Write a brief speech praising people, such as firemedics, who perform an important job. Explain why those people are deserving of praise. Do they show composure in difficult situations?

Proofreading

This want ad has twelve mistakes. Use the proofreading marks to correct them. Then write the misspelled List Words correctly on the lines.

Proofreading Marks
◯ spelling mistake
≡ capital letter
∧ add something

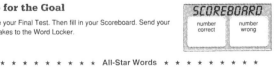

Gerry's Gymnassiem
Hiring Now
We need an instruckter to work in our after-school program. the purpuse of our program is to help children become good sports. Experience teaching team sports, such as baseball, soccer, or basketball, is a must. Knowledge of first aid is dezirabul. Cazuall dress is okay. It you're interested in this possision please contact: Sally O'Connell, pauline Heaney, or Ari Geiger.
Telephone: **1-800-WRK-OUTS.**

1. Gymnasium
2. instructor
3. purpose
4. desirable
5. Casual
6. position

Now proofread your speech. Fix any mistakes.

Go for the Goal

Take your Final Test. Then fill in your Scoreboard. Send your mistakes to the Word Locker.

SCOREBOARD
number correct	number wrong

★ ★ ★ ★ ★ ★ ★ ★ **All-Star Words** ★ ★ ★ ★ ★ ★ ★ ★ ★

releases   resolve   foreclosure   intrusion   diffuse

Write a newspaper headline for each All-Star Word. Then, erase the All-Star Word. Trade headlines with a partner. Complete each other's headlines by writing the missing words.

32 Lesson 7 ■ /s/, /z/, and /zh/

◎ **Spelling Strategy** Write each of these headings at the top of a column on the board:

s sounds like /s/
s sounds like /z/
s sounds like /zh/

Call on volunteers to come to the board, write a List Word in the appropriate column, and circle the s or s's. Then invite the class to pronounce the word, stressing the sound or sounds that s stands for. Ask students which word can be written in more than one column (*seasonal*).

Flex Your Spelling Muscles   *Page 32*

As students complete the **Writing** activity, encourage them to brainstorm ideas, write a first draft, revise, and proofread their work. The **Proofreading** exercise will help them prepare to proofread their speeches. To publish their writing, students may want to have a "Careers Day" and give their speeches to the class.

✍ Writer's Corner

The class might want to write to a local chapter of the Red Cross to invite a guest speaker to tell about the work of emergency medical personnel. Have students compile a list of questions to ask.

Go for the Goal/Final Test

1. Did you play basketball in the new *gymnasium?*
2. Modern medicines can cure many *diseases*.
3. First, the stringed *instruments* could be heard.
4. Let's take a *leisurely* stroll after dinner.
5. The *purpose* of the meeting is to plan the menu.
6. The car that uses less gas is more *desirable.*
7. The money in the *treasury* is counted daily.
8. The tailor hemmed the pleated *trousers.*
9. The workers are *measuring* the size of the roof.
10. Please hold your *position* while I'm drawing!
11. What is your *version* of the accident?
12. We ate a *casual* meal on the balcony.
13. At what time does the school bus *usually* come?
14. The joke was *visual,* so it's hard to explain.
15. That bird is a *seasonal* visitor, not a native.
16. The most *deserving* workers received bonuses.
17. I kept my *composure* even though I was scared.
18. You and Jo *resemble* each other.
19. My dad shook hands with my teacher's *husband.*
20. The diving *instructor* stood near the pool.

Remind students to complete the Scoreboard and write any misspelled words in their Word Locker.

★★ **All-Star Words** You may want to point out that the All-Star Words follow the spelling rule and inspire students by displaying newspaper headlines.

Lesson 8

Objective

To spell words in which *sh, su, ti, ci,* and *ch* spell /sh/

Correlated Phonics Lesson

MCP Phonics, Level F, Lesson 6

Warm Up   *Page 33*

In "Hocus Focus," students read about the history of eyeglasses and discover why frames weren't fashionable in the past. After reading, invite students to share their own experiences with selecting and wearing eyeglasses.

Encourage students to look back at the boldfaced words. Ask volunteers to say the words and identify the different spellings of the /sh/ sound.

On Your Mark/Warm Up Test

1. Shouldn't you *insure* that valuable ring?
2. Janelle sent away for *information* about China.
3. Astronauts are pioneers in space *exploration*.
4. Dan was not *ashamed* to express his opinion.
5. When is the next *partial* eclipse of the sun?
6. We will *nourish* the plants with fertilizer.
7. Ms. Ames joined a *social* club to make friends.
8. The store sent a *brochure* about the product.
9. The *invention* of the computer changed our lives.
10. Arriving early will *assure* you of a good seat.
11. His *facial* expression showed great surprise.
12. The doctors' *convention* was held in Tulsa.
13. The maple leaf is the *official* symbol of Canada.
14. What kinds of *machinery* are made here?
15. The sky diver snapped on his *parachute.*
16. We met to *negotiate* a new contract.
17. You will *accomplish* great deeds in your life.
18. Miriam has the *potential* to be a good actress.
19. I truly *appreciate* all your help!
20. When you divide 100 by 4, the *quotient* is 25.

Pep Talk/Game Plan   *Pages 34–35*

Introduce the spelling rule and have students read the List Words aloud. Encourage students to look back at their Warm Up Tests and apply the spelling rule to any misspelled words.

As students work through the **Spelling Lineup, Classification,** and **Missing Words** exercises, remind them to look back at their List Words or in their dictionaries if they need help.

 See **Letter Cards,** page 15

36

Name _____

/sh/

Warm Up

What can you wear to help you see better or to make a fashion statement?

Hocus Focus

Eyeglasses used to be called "spectacles." Before evolving to their present shape, they really were quite a spectacle.

No one is really sure who is responsible for the **invention** of eyeglasses. Using pieces of glass to enlarge the size of words on a printed page goes back to ancient times. Many scholars say that the first glasses were made in Venice, Italy, in about 1280.

Eyeglasses were first put in frames made of leather. They were held in place by tying the leather strips around the wearer's ears. This proved uncomfortable. Later, the Spanish invented frames made of silk ribbons. These, too, were uncomfortable and held the glasses too close to the eyes. To avoid the problem of tightly tied frames, the Chinese found a **partial** solution to **assure** comfort. They added weights to the ribbons. Wearers draped the ribbons over their ears. This held the glasses comfortably—until the wearer turned his or her head too quickly. Then the weights swung around, hitting their owner in the head. Later came frameless glasses that stayed on with a clip over the wearer's nose. In this case, the wearer could see, but the clip interfered with breathing.

The big breakthrough in frames came in London, England, in 1730. An optician, Edward Scarlett, decided to attach the lenses to stiff side pieces.

Even after glasses became more practical, people were **ashamed** to wear them in **social** situations. Today glasses have become a fashion statement. To **appreciate** how things have changed, just take a long look around.

 Say the boldfaced words in the selection. How many ways do you find to spell the /sh/ sound?

On Your Mark

Take your Warm Up Test. Then check your spelling with the List Words on the next page.

33

Pep Talk

The /sh/ sound can be spelled in several ways.
sh, as in shoe
su, as in insure
ti, as in convention and partial
ci, as in facial
ch, as in machinery

LIST WORDS

1. insure
2. information
3. exploration
4. ashamed
5. partial
6. nourish
7. social
8. brochure
9. invention
10. assure
11. facial
12. convention
13. official
14. machinery
15. parachute
16. negotiate
17. accomplish
18. potential
19. appreciate
20. quotient

Game Plan

Spelling Lineup
Write each List Word in the correct category to show how the /sh/ sound is spelled.

/sh/, as in shoe	/sh/, as in motion
1. ashamed	11. information
2. nourish	12. exploration
3. accomplish	13. partial

/sh/, as in machine	14. invention
4. brochure	15. convention
5. machinery	16. negotiate
6. parachute	17. potential
	18. quotient

/sh/, as in glacial	/sh/, as in sure
7. social	19. insure
8. facial	20. assure
9. official	
10. appreciate	

Balloon Popper

34 Lesson 8 ▪ /sh/

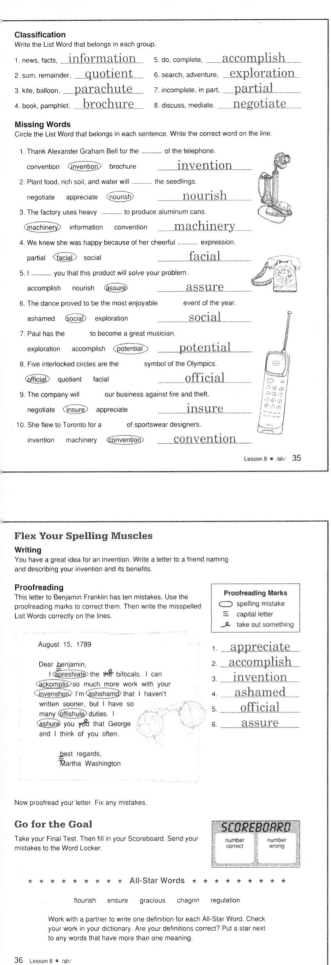

Classification

Write the List Word that belongs in each group.

1. news, facts, __information__
2. sum, remainder, __quotient__
3. kite, balloon, __parachute__
4. book, pamphlet, __brochure__
5. do, complete, __accomplish__
6. search, adventure, __exploration__
7. incomplete, in part, __partial__
8. discuss, mediate, __negotiate__

Missing Words

Circle the List Word that belongs in each sentence. Write the correct word on the line.

1. Thank Alexander Graham Bell for the _____ of the telephone.
   convention (invention) brochure __invention__

2. Plant food, rich soil, and water will _____ the seedlings.
   negotiate appreciate (nourish) __nourish__

3. The factory uses heavy _____ to produce aluminum cans.
   (machinery) information convention __machinery__

4. We knew she was happy because of her cheerful _____ expression.
   partial (facial) social __facial__

5. I _____ you that this product will solve your problem.
   accomplish nourish (assure) __assure__

6. The dance proved to be the most enjoyable _____ event of the year.
   ashamed (social) exploration __social__

7. Paul has the _____ to become a great musician.
   exploration accomplish (potential) __potential__

8. Five interlocked circles are the _____ symbol of the Olympics.
   (official) quotient facial __official__

9. The company will _____ our business against fire and theft.
   negotiate (insure) appreciate __insure__

10. She flew to Toronto for a _____ of sportswear designers.
    invention machinery (convention) __convention__

Lesson 8 ▪ /sh/ 35

Flex Your Spelling Muscles

Writing

You have a great idea for an invention. Write a letter to a friend naming and describing your invention and its benefits.

Proofreading

This letter to Benjamin Franklin has ten mistakes. Use the proofreading marks to correct them. Then write the misspelled List Words correctly on the lines.

Proofreading Marks	
◯	spelling mistake
≡	capital letter
⤴	take out something

August 15, 1789

Dear benjamin,
  I appreshiate the the bifocals. I can ackomplis so much more work with your invenshon. I'm ashshamd that I haven't written sooner, but I have so many offishule duties. I ashure you you that George and I think of you often.

  best regards,
  Martha Washington

1. __appreciate__
2. __accomplish__
3. __invention__
4. __ashamed__
5. __official__
6. __assure__

Now proofread your letter. Fix any mistakes.

Go for the Goal

Take your Final Test. Then fill in your Scoreboard. Send your mistakes to the Word Locker.

SCOREBOARD

number correct	number wrong

★ ★ ★ ★ ★ ★ ★ ★ **All-Star Words** ★ ★ ★ ★ ★ ★ ★ ★

flourish   ensure   gracious   chagrin   regulation

Work with a partner to write one definition for each All-Star Word. Check your work in your dictionary. Are your definitions correct? Put a star next to any words that have more than one meaning.

36 Lesson 8 ▪ /sh/

◉ **Spelling Strategy** To help students recognize the different ways to spell the /sh/ sound, write *sh, su, ti, ci,* and *ch* on the board as separate column headings. Invite the class to tell you which column each List Word belongs in, then write the word in that column. Call on a volunteer to come to the board, point to the letters that spell the /sh/ sound, and say the word aloud.

Flex Your Spelling Muscles   *Page 36*

As students complete the **Writing** activity, encourage them to brainstorm ideas, write a first draft, revise, and proofread their work. The **Proofreading** exercise will help them prepare to proofread their letters. To publish their writing, students may want to make drawings or diagrams to accompany their letters and create a bulletin-board display titled "What's New?"

✍ **Writer's Corner**

You may want to bring in ads for eyeglasses from your local newspaper or from an eyewear catalog. Invite students to create their own fashionable frames and to write an ad for them.

Go for the Goal/Final Test

1. I'm not **ashamed** to admit the truth.
2. The factory installed new production **machinery.**
3. Bjorn and Sue **appreciate** the gifts that you sent.
4. Was the lightbulb Edison's greatest **invention?**
5. I took my first **parachute** jump last April.
6. Ms. Hall is **partial** owner of a large shoe store.
7. The **quotient** is the answer in a division problem.
8. I **assure** all my customers of satisfaction.
9. Carlos has a **brochure** sent by Camp Longacre.
10. The chickadee is the **official** state bird of Maine.
11. The king will sponsor the **exploration.**
12. This hotel has the **potential** for worldwide fame.
13. We'll **negotiate** a contract that is fair.
14. She removed her makeup with **facial** tissues.
15. Robins catch worms to **nourish** their young.
16. Where will the next writers' **convention** be held?
17. An atlas is a good source of **information.**
18. What a hard task that was to **accomplish!**
19. I'll **insure** my new car against damage or loss.
20. Many people play golf for **social** reasons.

Remind students to complete the Scoreboard and write any misspelled words in their Word Locker.

★★ **All-Star Words** You may wish to point out that the All-Star Words follow the spelling rule and review the concept of a multiple-meaning word.

37

Lesson 9

Objective

To spell words with the letters *sc*

Correlated Phonics Lesson

MCP Phonics, Level F, Lesson 8

Warm Up   *Page 37*

In "Something Fishy," students learn about spiders that sometimes eat fish for their dinners. After reading, invite students to read aloud the part of the selection they liked the best and to tell about spiders they have seen.

Encourage students to look back at the boldfaced words. Ask volunteers to say the words and identify the different sounds that *sc* stands for.

On Your Mark/Warm Up Test

1. The smell of roses **scented** the garden.
2. Although still an **adolescent,** Khiam is very tall.
3. Wind **scattered** the leaves in many directions.
4. You can use these **scissors** to cut the cloth.
5. Did you do a **scientific** experiment on gravity?
6. The **screaming** siren woke up the whole family.
7. The weight lifter flexed his powerful **muscles.**
8. The water in that tap is capable of **scalding** you.
9. This **scenery** is so beautiful!
10. How lovely the **crescent** moon is!
11. The **descending** climbers met a happy crowd.
12. Will you use clay or wood for your **sculpture?**
13. In the book, the hero uses a tunnel to **escape.**
14. The mice **scampered** around in their cage.
15. Why didn't the bus take the **scenic** route?
16. Marie collects **miscellaneous** stamps.
17. What a **fascinating** idea that is!
18. We had **luscious** ripe peaches for dessert.
19. In the armed forces, **discipline** is important.
20. Her **conscience** would not let her do wrong.

Pep Talk/Game Plan   *Pages 38–39*

Introduce the spelling rule and have students read the List Words aloud. Encourage students to look back at their Warm Up Tests and apply the spelling rule to any misspelled words.

As students work through the **Spelling Lineup, Alphabetical Order,** and **Missing Words** exercises, remind them to look back at their List Words or in their dictionaries if they need help.

 See **Picture Clues,** page 15

38

Warm Up

What kind of spider can dine on fish?

Something Fishy

Not all spiders are content to eat only bugs. There are some **fascinating** kinds of spiders that are "anglers," or fishers. They actually catch tadpoles and **miscellaneous** types of tiny fish!

In North America, there are more than a dozen types of fisher spiders. Their angling techniques vary. Most of them scamper swiftly across the water and wait patiently for a passing fish. A fisher spider may be seen **descending** upon a fish that is twice its own size. The capture itself is not the real problem for this eight-legged creature. Because the spider's digestive juices have little effect in the water, the spider has to haul its prey to land. Dragging its **luscious** little treat to land requires hard work, **discipline**, and **muscles**.

Two of these anglers are the raft spider and the nursery-web spider. The raft spider builds its own raft from leaves and its own silk threads. This spider sails out on its raft to wait for its prey. The nursery-web spider is named for the web it weaves to hold its egg sac. It gets a taste for fish now and then, too. Most of the time it stays with the eggs until all have hatched and the young spiders have **scattered**. Once in a while it may venture out across the water for a seafood supper. It may seem strange that a creature that is often eaten by fish can turn the tables and have a fish for lunch!

 Say the boldfaced words in the selection. How many different sounds can you find made by the letters **sc**?

On Your Mark

Take your Warm Up Test. Then check your spelling with the List Words on the next page.

37

Pep Talk

The letters **sc** can make three different sounds:
the /sk/ sound, as in <u>escape</u>
the /s/ sound, as in <u>scissors</u>
the /sh/ sound, as in <u>conscience</u>

LIST WORDS

1. scented
2. adolescent
3. scattered
4. scissors
5. scientific
6. screaming
7. muscles
8. scalding
9. scenery
10. crescent
11. descending
12. sculpture
13. escape
14. scampered
15. scenic
16. miscellaneous
17. fascinating
18. luscious
19. discipline
20. conscience

Game Plan

Spelling Lineup

Write each List Word under the sound **sc** makes.

/s/, as in <u>scene</u>	/sk/, as in <u>scoop</u>
1. scented	13. scattered
2. adolescent	14. screaming
3. scissors	15. scalding
4. scientific	16. sculpture
5. muscles	17. escape
6. scenery	18. scampered
7. crescent	
8. descending	/sh/, as in <u>unconscious</u>
9. scenic	19. luscious
10. miscellaneous	20. conscience
11. fascinating	
12. discipline	

38 Lesson 9 ■ sc

Alphabetical Order

Write this group of List Words in alphabetical order.

scented	1. scalding	8. scissors
scattered	2. scampered	9. screaming
scissors	3. scattered	10. sculpture
scientific	4. scenery	
screaming	5. scenic	
scalding	6. scented	
scenery	7. scientific	
sculpture		
scampered		
scenic		

Missing Words

Write the List Word that completes each sentence.

1. An __adolescent__ is a person between childhood and adulthood.

2. Your body moves by the stretching and tightening of your __muscles__.

3. The bride looked lovely as she was __descending__ the stairway in her gown.

4. The moon is a __crescent__ shape in its first or last quarter.

5. Many people have a "junk drawer" where they store __miscellaneous__ household items.

6. She captured the attention of the entire audience with her __fascinating__ speech on an otherwise boring topic.

7. It takes a lot of __discipline__ to practice the piano every day.

8. Reading is a great way to relax and __escape__ daily stress.

9. Otto, a gourmet chef, cooks __luscious__, tasty meals.

10. Rely on your __conscience__ when deciding whether something is right for you.

Flex Your Spelling Muscles

Writing

Write a nature poem. You can write about a fascinating creature such as a spider, your favorite season, or a scenic place. Use as many List Words as you can.

Proofreading

These nature poems have seven mistakes. Use the proofreading marks to correct them. Write the misspelled List Words correctly on the lines.

Proofreading Marks
- ◯ spelling mistake
- ⌄ add apostrophe
- ∧ add something

Work of Art
A spider web is a fassinating thing.
Its a skulptur made of silky string.

Hungry Night
Crecint Moon, Night has
Taken a bite out of you.
What a lussious meal!

1. fascinating
2. sculpture
3. Crescent
4. luscious

Now proofread your nature poem. Fix any mistakes.

Go for the Goal

Take your Final Test. Then fill in your Scoreboard. Send your mistakes to the Word Locker.

SCOREBOARD

number correct	number wrong

★ ★ ★ ★ ★ ★ ★ ★ **All-Star Words** ★ ★ ★ ★ ★ ★ ★ ★

scrimp   ascend   scour   conscious   scheme

Create a crossword puzzle that includes each of the All-Star Words. You'll need to draw a blank grid and write clues. Use your dictionary if you need help. Switch puzzles with a partner. Write the answers to solve each other's puzzle.

◎ **Spelling Strategy** Write several cloze sentences on the board using List Words. Next to each sentence, include the sound that *sc* stands for in the missing List Word. For example: "A squirrel_____along the branch." /sk/ Call on volunteers to read each sentence, write the correct word in the blank, and circle the letters *sc*.

Flex Your Spelling Muscles   *Page 40*

As students complete the **Writing** activity, encourage them to brainstorm ideas, write a first draft, revise, and proofread their work. The **Proofreading** exercise will help them prepare to proofread their poems. To publish their writing, students may want to submit their poetry to *Children's Digest*, P.O. Box 567B, Indianapolis, IN 46206 or *Stone Soup,* Children's Art Foundation, P.O. Box 83, Santa Cruz, CA 95063.

✎ **Writer's Corner** _____

> The Nature Conservancy helps preserve plants and animals and their environments. To find out about projects in your state, students can write to The Nature Conservancy, 1815 N. Lynn Street, Arlington, VA 22209.

Go for the Goal/Final Test

1. Those strawberries look absolutely **luscious!**
2. Don't let the rabbit **escape** when you feed it.
3. Only a **crescent** of the moon remained visible.
4. Please put the **scissors** back when you finish.
5. We looked at the **scenery** from the bus window.
6. The odor of mothballs **scented** the entire attic.
7. A clear **conscience** is a pleasant companion.
8. I need to buy **miscellaneous** school supplies.
9. Be careful **descending** the stairs!
10. Susan lifts weights to strengthen her **muscles.**
11. An **adolescent** boy gave us directions.
12. Why are papers **scattered** around your room?
13. The puppy **scampered** across the lawn.
14. It requires **discipline** to exercise daily.
15. That river is one of our **scenic** attractions.
16. I read a **fascinating** book about firefighting.
17. Did you see the artist's marble **sculpture?**
18. We are studying these plants in a **scientific** way.
19. Don't burn yourself with that **scalding** water!
20. The audience began **screaming** with excitement.

Remind students to complete the Scoreboard and write any misspelled words in their Word Locker.

★★ **All-Star Words** You may want to point out that the All-Star Words follow the spelling rule. Have students first arrange the All-Star Words, then draw their blank grids based on that arrangement.

Lesson 10

Objective

To spell words in which *ear* spells /ir/ or /ʉr/; *are* spells /er/; and *air* spells /er/

Correlated Phonics Lessons

MCP Phonics, Level F, Lessons 10–11

Warm Up   *Page 41*

In this selection, students read about an exciting new Olympic event called *luging*. After reading, invite students to tell about their favorite Olympic events.

Encourage students to look back at the boldfaced words. Ask volunteers to say each word and identify the sound spelled by *ear, are,* or *air.*

On Your Mark/Warm Up Test

1. In 1849 many miners were *searching* for gold.
2. Black clouds suddenly *appeared* in the sky.
3. The *millionaire* donated funds to the hospital.
4. Sulphur in the air can tarnish *silverware.*
5. Have you *compared* a luge and a bobsled?
6. Please help me carry the boxes up the *stairway.*
7. Pottery of baked clay is called *earthenware.*
8. LuAnn followed the directions *carefully.*
9. We *barely* arrived in time!
10. A checkerboard has red and black *squares.*
11. The mechanic replaced the engine's worn *gears.*
12. Jake is *earning* money by delivering newspapers.
13. The pitcher thought the umpire ruled *unfairly.*
14. I was *unaware* that you were away last week.
15. Duong designs and makes *earrings.*
16. I have an *earnest* desire to become a doctor.
17. Are the students doing *research* in the library?
18. A sad event may cause a person to feel *despair.*
19. We filled out a *questionnaire* for the class.
20. Did the *rehearsal* for the school play go well?

Pep Talk/Game Plan   *Pages 42–43*

Introduce the spelling rule and have students read the List Words aloud. You may also want to point out that *earthenware* contains two of the sounds being studied. Then encourage students to look back at their Warm Up Tests and apply the spelling rule to any misspelled words.

As students work through the **Spelling Lineup, Comparing Words,** and **Missing Words** exercises, remind them to look back at their List Words or in their dictionaries if they need help.

 See **Student Dictation,** page 14

40

---

ear, are, air

Warm Up

How does luge racing differ from sledding?

Super Sledding

An exciting sporting event has **appeared** on the Winter Olympic scene. It's a race run on a fast, lightweight sled called a *luge.* This small, one-person sled has been **compared** to a bobsled. While they are both sleds, the comparison ends there.

A luger lies on his or her back on the luge. When going down a run, the rider's head and feet extend past the length of the sled. In this position, an experienced luger can reach speeds of nearly 80 miles per hour! One of the most amazing things about the luge is the way it is steered. The rider **carefully** moves his or her thighs and upper arms to turn the luge. The movements are **barely** noticeable to spectators.

In luge racing, fearless riders wear little equipment. Their rubber suits are form-fitting with gloves and boots to match. The lugers wear a simple helmet with a face shield. The idea is to reduce the air friction that can slow a sled down.

The luge has been popular in Europe for many years. Many Americans were **unaware** of the sport until recently. Training camps give American athletes a chance to develop their racing skills. These Olympic hopefuls practice in **earnest** for the chance to compete with the world's best lugers.

 Look back at the boldfaced words in the selection. Say the words. Compare the sounds made by the letters **ear, are,** and **air.**

On Your Mark

Take your Warm Up Test. Then check your spelling with the List Words on the next page.

41

Pep Talk

Sometimes the letters **ear** make the /ir/ sound, as in <u>years</u> and <u>appeared</u>.
The letters **ear** can also make the /ʉr/ sound, as in <u>earnest</u> and <u>earning</u>.
Sometimes the /er/ sound can be spelled **are**, as in <u>barely</u> or **air**, as in <u>stairway</u>.

LIST WORDS

1. searching
2. appeared
3. millionaire
4. silverware
5. compared
6. stairway
7. earthenware
8. carefully
9. barely
10. squares
11. years
12. earning
13. unfairly
14. unaware
15. earrings
16. earnest
17. research
18. despair
19. questionnaire
20. rehearsal

Game Plan

Spelling Lineup

Write the List Words that contain the sound given. You will write one word twice.

/ʉr/, as in <u>earth</u>
1. searching
2. earthenware
3. earning
4. earnest
5. research
6. rehearsal

/er/, as in <u>chair</u>
7. millionaire
8. stairway
9. unfairly
10. despair
11. questionnaire

/er/, as in <u>care</u>
12. silverware
13. compared
14. earthenware
15. carefully
16. barely
17. squares
18. unaware

/ir/, as in <u>clear</u>
19. appeared
20. gears
21. earrings

Comparing Words

Study the relationship between the first two underlined words. Then write a List Word that has the same relationship with the third underlined word.

1. <u>Up</u> is to <u>down</u> as ___carefully___ is to <u>carelessly</u>.
2. <u>Wheels</u> are to <u>circles</u> as <u>boxes</u> are to ___squares___.
3. <u>Bracelets</u> are to <u>wrists</u> as ___earrings___ are to <u>ears</u>.
4. <u>Turn</u> is to <u>return</u> as <u>search</u> is to ___research___.
5. <u>Peach</u> is to <u>fruit</u> as <u>fork</u> is to ___silverware___.
6. <u>Footbridge</u> is to <u>cross</u> as ___stairway___ is to <u>climb</u>.
7. <u>Happiness</u> is to <u>joy</u> as <u>sadness</u> is to ___despair___.
8. <u>Review</u> is to <u>test</u> as ___rehearsal___ is to <u>performance</u>.

Missing Words

Write the List Word that completes each sentence.

1. A rescue team is ___searching___ for the lost boy.
2. Mountain bikes are equipped with several ___gears___.
3. She is saving part of the money she is ___earning___ every month.
4. Although the ___earthenware___ pot was very old, it had no cracks.
5. The younger brother didn't appreciate being ___compared___ to his older brother.
6. The sun was shining while it was showering, and a rainbow ___appeared___
7. I was so sick I could ___barely___ get out of bed.
8. She had no idea and was completely ___unaware___ that they were planning a surprise party for her.
9. The defendant was angry and felt that he was treated ___unfairly___ by the judge.
10. He gave an ___earnest___ and moving speech about his fight with the disease.
11. Members will fill out a ___questionnaire___ to participate in the survey.
12. In today's economy, it is not easy to become a ___millionaire___.

Flex Your Spelling Muscles

Writing

Research questionnaire formats (i.e., question-and-answer or multiple choice), and write a questionnaire about a new Olympic sport. Choose an event that you feel should be in the Olympics.

OLYMPICS QUESTIONNAIRE

Instructions: Darken the circle that indicates your response.

1. The Olympic Games should be held every year.
   ○ strongly agree ○ agree ○ disagree ○ strongly disagree
2. The Summer Olympics should always be held in the same country.
   ○ strongly agree ○ agree ○ disagree ○ strongly disagree

Proofreading

These how-to directions for a Trivia Olympics have eleven mistakes. Use the proofreading marks to correct them. Write the misspelled List Words correctly on the lines.

1. You will need two teams and a a judge.
2. Each team has to (reserch) five questions for the other team to answer. Start by (surching) through reference books. List the books where the information (appaired) Work (cairfully).
3. Each correctly answered question is worth 50 points.
4. Each incorrectly answered question results in the opposite team team (erning) a 25-point bonus.
5. At the end of the game, the scores are (compard) The team with the most points wins.

Now proofread your questionnaire. Fix any mistakes.

Proofreading Marks
- ⌒ spelling mistake
- ⊙ add period
- ℘ take out something

1. ___research___
2. ___searching___
3. ___appeared___
4. ___carefully___
5. ___earning___
6. ___compared___

Go for the Goal

Take your Final Test. Then fill in your Scoreboard. Send your mistakes to the Word Locker.

SCOREBOARD

number correct	number wrong

★ ★ ★ ★ ★ ★ ★ ★ All-Star Words ★ ★ ★ ★ ★ ★ ★ ★

concessionaire   smeared   yearn   impair   welfare

Write a mystery story title for each All-Star Word. Then erase the All-Star Word from each title. Switch titles with a partner. Can you fill in the missing words correctly?

◉ Spelling Strategy

To help students associate vowel sounds with their spellings, write *ear* /ir/ or /ur/; *are* /er/; and *air* /er/ in large letters on separate sheets of paper. Tape each sheet in a different corner of the classroom. Then call out each List Word and have students point to the appropriate sheet for the word's vowel sound and spelling. Ask a volunteer to write each List Word on the correct sheet.

Flex Your Spelling Muscles   *Page 44*

As students complete the **Writing** activity, encourage them to brainstorm ideas, write a first draft, revise, and proofread their work. The **Proofreading** exercise will help them prepare to proofread their questionnaires. To publish their writing, students may want to submit the results of their questionnaires to the sports section of a local newspaper.

✍ Writer's Corner

Invite groups of students to consult an almanac to find each year's Olympic winning time or distance for a particular competitive event, such as the 100-meter dash or the broad jump. Students can make line graphs to show the results of the event for several successive competitions.

Go for the Goal/Final Test

1. Rinse the **silverware** with hot water.
2. Josie was **unaware** that she dropped her scarf.
3. Tio used a **questionnaire** to gather opinions.
4. I was **barely** able to lift the box by myself.
5. Astronomers do **research** to learn about stars.
6. Lovely **earthenware** is made in Spain.
7. Does your team have a way of **earning** money?
8. After the storm, a beautiful rainbow **appeared.**
9. The tailor **carefully** stitched the trousers.
10. The **millionaire** left all her money to charity.
11. I felt that the author was criticized **unfairly.**
12. What **despair** that terrible storm left behind!
13. Yesterday she lost one of her favorite **earrings.**
14. **Squares** have four equal sides.
15. Have you **compared** the book with the movie?
16. The orchestra will hold a **rehearsal** today.
17. Daryl helped out by vacuuming the **stairway.**
18. I am **searching** for facts to use in my report.
19. Roberto is **earnest** in his desire to be a poet.
20. Karen adjusted the **gears** on her racing bike.

Remind students to complete the Scoreboard and write any misspelled words in their Word Locker.

★★ All-Star Words

You may want to point out that the All-Star Words follow the spelling rule. Display several mystery books to help students think of titles.

Lesson 11

Objective
To spell words with /ē/

Correlated Phonics Lessons
MCP Phonics, Level F, Lessons 15, 18–19

Warm Up   *Page 45*
In "Olympic Gold," students learn about the athletes in a unique kind of competition. After reading, invite students to discuss competitions in which they have participated.

Ask volunteers to say the boldfaced words and identify the different letters that spell the /ē/ sound.

On Your Mark/Warm Up Test
1. An *athlete* must train regularly.
2. The police officer signaled the car to *proceed.*
3. Please *delete* my name from the list of runners.
4. That animal is in *extreme* danger of extinction.
5. Amy *repeated* the good news to her family.
6. This award is a token of our *esteem* for you.
7. Try to find a *reasonable* solution to the problem.
8. Leon *revealed* the secret only to his friend.
9. My collection of models is finally *complete!*
10. Let me wash that *greasy* pan for you.
11. Painting my room was quite an *achievement!*
12. The governor *squeezed* my hand firmly.
13. What is the cost of overnight package *delivery?*
14. The students rode a *trolley* car to school.
15. *Ecology* is the study of the natural environment.
16. How many *nieces* and nephews does he have?
17. Grandpa *concealed* my present under his coat.
18. The jeweler will *guarantee* my watch for a year.
19. The jury found the witness's story *believable.*
20. Jamie finally *succeeded* at doing a handstand.

Pep Talk/Game Plan   *Pages 46–47*
Introduce the spelling rule and have students read the List Words aloud. Encourage students to look back at their Warm Up Tests and apply the spelling rule to any misspelled words.

As students work through the **Spelling Lineup, Respellings,** and **Classification** exercises, remind them to look back at their List Words or in their dictionaries if they need help. For the **Spelling Lineup,** point out that *delete, revealed,* and *delivery* can be pronounced with the long *e* sound or the short *i* sound in the first syllable. *Believable* can be pronounced with the /ē/ sound or the schwa sound.

 See Variant Spellings, page 14

42

Warm Up
Who are the competitors in the Special Olympics?

Olympic Gold
It takes a special kind of athlete to win an Olympic medal. There are some very special athletes who win every time they compete.

"Let me win, but if I cannot win, let me be brave in the attempt."

After reciting this official oath, each **athlete** is ready to **proceed.** This is no ordinary competition. It's called the Special Olympics.

The competitors are special, indeed. All are developmentally challenged. Yet all have developed the skills and the **esteem** it takes to make them winners.

The Special Olympics began over twenty years ago with a handful of athletes competing in a few track and field events. Today, over a million athletes compete annually in more than 75 events. Like the Summer and Winter Olympic Games that are **repeated** every four years, this series of competitions begins with a parade, during which all the hopeful competitors can be seen by their fans and families.

After every event, the top three athletes are presented with gold, silver, or bronze medals. All the competitors are recognized for their **achievement.** Each competitor, even the one who placed last, is awarded a well-deserved medal.

Most athletes only have to compete against one another. The participants in the Special Olympics go one step further. They compete against themselves—and win.

 Say the boldfaced words in the selection. What vowel sound do you hear in each of these words? How many ways can you find to spell that sound?

On Your Mark
Take your Warm Up Test. Then check your spelling with the List Words on the next page.

45

Pep Talk
The /ē/ sound can be spelled different ways:
- **e,** as in ecology
- **ea,** as in repeated
- **e_e,** as in athlete
- **ey,** as in trolley
- **ee,** as in proceed
- **ie,** as in nieces
- **y,** as in delivery

LIST WORDS
1. athlete
2. proceed
3. delete
4. extreme
5. repeated
6. esteem
7. reasonable
8. revealed
9. complete
10. greasy
11. achievement
12. squeezed
13. delivery
14. trolley
15. ecology
16. nieces
17. concealed
18. guarantee
19. believable
20. succeeded

Game Plan
Spelling Lineup
Write each List Word under the spelling of its /ē/ sound. Some List Words are used more than once.

ee, as in succeed
1. proceed
2. esteem
3. squeezed
4. guarantee
5. succeeded

ea, as in speak
6. repeated
7. reasonable
8. revealed
9. greasy
10. concealed

y, as in apology
11. greasy
12. delivery
13. ecology

ey, as in volleyball
14. trolley

e, as in equal
15. ecology
16. delete
17. believable
18. revealed
19. delivery

ie, as in piece
20. achievement
21. nieces
22. believable

e_e, as in scheme
23. athlete
24. delete
25. extreme
26. complete

46   Lesson 11 ● /ē/

Respellings

Use the accent marks and the pronunciation key in the back of the book to say each respelling below. Then write the List Word that goes with each respelling.

In the dictionary, the respelling tells how to pronounce the word.
delete (dē lēt´)

1. (sək sēd´id) __succeeded__
2. (e stēm´) __esteem__
3. (kən sēld´) __concealed__
4. (dē liv´ə rē) __delivery__
5. (rē vēld´) __revealed__
6. (ri pēt´ əd) __repeated__
7. (ath´ lēt) __athlete__
8. (bē lēv´ə bəl) __believable__
9. (nēs´ iz) __nieces__
10. (ē käl´ ə jē) __ecology__
11. (grē´ sē) __greasy__
12. (trä´ lē) __trolley__
13. (skwēzd) __squeezed__
14. (rē´ zən ə bəl) __reasonable__
15. (prō sēd´) __proceed__
16. (ger ən tē´) __guarantee__

Classification

Write the List Word that belongs in each group.

1. omit, erase, __delete__
2. pressed, kneaded, __squeezed__
3. respect, admiration, __esteem__
4. farthest, utmost, __extreme__
5. total, whole, __complete__
6. train, bus, __trolley__
7. uncles, cousins, __nieces__
8. feat, accomplishment, __achievement__
9. uncovered, exhibited, __revealed__
10. biology, chemistry, __ecology__
11. warranty, promise, __guarantee__
12. fair, sensible, __reasonable__
13. true, likely, __believable__
14. oily, slick, __greasy__
15. advance, move, __proceed__
16. hid, obscured, __concealed__

Lesson 11 ■ /ē/ 47

Flex Your Spelling Muscles

Writing

Write a report about your favorite sports hero. Describe the way in which your hero has succeeded. Try to use as many List Words as you can.

Proofreading

This special message for an award has twelve mistakes. Use the proofreading marks to correct them. Then write the misspelled List Words correctly on the lines.

Proofreading Marks
◯ spelling mistake
≡ capital letter
� take out something

Most Improved ⟨Athleet⟩ of the Year

P. S. 321 recognizes Russ ⟨s⟩amuels for his ⟨acheivment⟩ in track. ⟨a⟩lthough Russ did not win any races, he ⟨suceded⟩ in winning our admiration. At ⟨a⟩ first, Russ could not even ⟨compleet⟩ a 100-yard dash. ⟨i⟩nstead of quitting or giving up, Russ ran each day, even under the most ⟨extream⟩ weather conditions. At Field Day, Russ came in third in the ⟨the⟩ 3-mile race. He has truly earned our ⟨our⟩ highest ⟨esteam⟩.

1. __Athlete__   4. __complete__
2. __achievement__   5. __extreme__
3. __succeeded__   6. __esteem__

Now proofread your report. Fix any mistakes.

Go for the Goal

Take your Final Test. Then fill in your Scoreboard. Send your mistakes to the Word Locker.

SCOREBOARD
| number correct | number wrong |

★ ★ ★ ★ ★ ★ ★ ★ All-Star Words ★ ★ ★ ★ ★ ★ ★ ★

precede   eastward   bleak   folly   siege

Write each List Word. Then, work with a partner to list at least one synonym and antonym for each All-Star Word. Use a thesaurus or an unabridged dictionary to check your work. How many additional synonyms and antonyms can you find?

48 Lesson 11 ■ /ē/

◉ **Spelling Strategy** To call attention to the different ways to spell /ē/, write each List Word on the board and circle the letter or letters that stand for the /ē/ sound or sounds. Ask volunteers to suggest other words that illustrate each of the spelling patterns.

Flex Your Spelling Muscles   *Page 48*

As students complete the **Writing** activity, encourage them to brainstorm ideas, write a first draft, revise, and proofread their work. The **Proofreading** exercise will help them prepare to proofread their reports. To publish their writing, students may want to

• use their reports to create a display in the school gymnasium

• read their reports aloud as TV broadcasts.

✍ Writer's Corner

Students may enjoy writing fan letters to sports figures they admire. A reference librarian can help them locate appropriate addresses. Be sure to tell students that not all the celebrities will respond to their letters.

Go for the Goal/Final Test

1. Linda **squeezed** lemons to make lemonade.
2. Your plan sounds like a **reasonable** one.
3. When the rain stops, our game can **proceed.**
4. On Saturdays, our mail **delivery** is very early.
5. A curtain **concealed** the prize from the audience.
6. Have you **succeeded** in starting the mower?
7. Two of my **nieces** were born on the same day.
8. Once, this **trolley** was pulled by a horse.
9. The teacher **repeated** each spelling word twice.
10. Good nutrition is important for an **athlete.**
11. I read the **complete** book in only an hour!
12. The store will **guarantee** the radio for a year.
13. We are learning about **ecology** in science class.
14. My hands are **greasy** from working on the car.
15. Draw a line through words you want to **delete.**
16. A good actor can make any role seem **believable.**
17. The last page of the book **revealed** the solution.
18. Do you have a warm coat for **extreme** cold?
19. What an **achievement** winning that trophy was!
20. The mayor is held in high **esteem** by the voters.

Remind students to complete the Scoreboard and write any misspelled words in their Word Locker.

★★ **All-Star Words**   You may want to point out that the All-Star Words follow the spelling rule and review the meanings of *synonym* and *antonym.*

Lesson 12 • Instant Replay

Objective

To review spelling words with the sounds /s/, /z/, /zh/; /sh/; with *sc; ear, are, air;* and with /ē/

Time Out
Pages 49–52

Check Your Word Locker Based on your observations, note which words are giving students the most difficulty and offer assistance for spelling them correctly. Here are some frequently misspelled words to watch for: *desirable, brochure, official, appreciate, scissors, muscles, despair, athlete,* and *achievement.*

To give students extra help and practice in taking standardized tests, you may want to have them take the Review Test for this lesson on pages 46–47. After scoring the tests, return them to students so that they can record their misspelled words in their Word Locker.

After practicing their troublesome words, students can work through the exercises for **Lessons 7–11.** Before they begin each exercise, you may want to go over the spelling rule.

🏠 **Take It Home** Invite students to listen for the List Words in **Lessons 7–11** as they watch TV news and weather programs. For a complete list of the words, encourage them to take their *Spelling Workout* books home. Students can also use Take It Home Master 2 on pages 48–49 to help them do the activity. Invite students to bring their lists to class and to compare them, noting which words were used most frequently.

Name _____

Time Out

Some words are spelled differently than you expect. The letter **s**, the letters **sc**, and the letters **ear** can stand for more than one sound. In addition, one sound, like /er/ or /ē/ may be spelled in many different ways.

Check Your Word Locker
Look at the words in your Word Locker. Write your most troublesome words from Lessons 7 through 11.

_____

_____

Practice writing your troublesome words with a partner. Erase certain letters from the words, trade papers with your partner, and fill in the missing letters.

Lesson 7

The letter **s** can spell the /s/ sound, as in <u>instruments</u>; the /z/ sound, as in <u>husband</u>; and the /zh/ sound, as in <u>treasury</u>.

List Words	
composure	
diseases	
casual	
seasonal	
resemble	
husband	
desirable	
leisurely	
deserving	
usually	

Write a List Word that means the opposite of the word given.

1. differ — resemble
2. never — usually
3. health — diseases
4. year-round — seasonal
5. quickly — leisurely
6. unworthy — deserving
7. formal — casual
8. wife — husband
9. unwanted — desirable
10. nervousness — composure

49

Lesson 8

The /sh/ sound can be spelled with **sh**, as in <u>nourish</u>; **su**, as in <u>assure</u>; **ti**, as in <u>invention</u>; **ci**, as in <u>social</u>; and **ch**, as in <u>brochure</u>.

List Words	
insure	
ashamed	
partial	
nourish	
brochure	
invention	
assure	
facial	
machinery	
parachute	

Write five List Words that could be found listed between each set of dictionary guide words given. Write the words in alphabetical order.

able/intact	interest/patio
1. ashamed	6. invention
2. assure	7. machinery
3. brochure	8. nourish
4. facial	9. parachute
5. insure	10. partial

Lesson 9

The letters **sc** can stand for three different sounds: the /sk/ sound, as in <u>scalding</u>; the /s/ sound, as in <u>muscles</u>; and the /sh/ sound, as in <u>luscious</u>.

List Words	
scented	
scattered	
scissors	
screaming	
muscles	
scalding	
crescent	
descending	
escape	
luscious	

Study the relationship between the first two underlined words. Then write a List Word that has the same relationship with the third underlined word.

1. <u>Throw</u> is to <u>catch</u> as <u>capture</u> is to — escape
2. <u>Draw</u> is to <u>sketch</u> as <u>tasty</u> is to — luscious
3. <u>Sew</u> is to <u>needle</u> as <u>cut</u> is to — scissors
4. <u>Reading</u> is to your <u>mind</u> as <u>exercise</u> is to your — muscles
5. <u>Cool</u> is to <u>chilly</u> as <u>boiling</u> is to — scalding
6. <u>Up</u> is to <u>down</u> as <u>climbing</u> is to — descending
7. <u>Whispering</u> is to <u>murmuring</u> as <u>yelling</u> is to — screaming
8. <u>Whole</u> is to <u>part</u> as <u>full moon</u> is to — crescent moon.
9. <u>Food</u> is to <u>flavored</u> as <u>flower</u> is to — scented
10. <u>Gathered</u> is to <u>spread</u> as <u>joined</u> is to — scattered

Lesson 10

The letters **ear** make the /ir/ sound, as in <u>ear</u>rings, and the /ur/ sound, as in res<u>ear</u>ch. The /er/ sound is sometimes spelled **are**, as in unaw<u>are</u>, or **air**, as in unf<u>air</u>ly.

List Words

searching
appeared
millionaire
carefully
squares
gears
earning
unfairly
despair
rehearsal

Each word below is hidden in a List Word. Write the List Words.

1. mill ___millionaire___
2. fully ___carefully___
3. earn ___earning___
4. fair ___unfairly___
5. hear ___rehearsal___
6. pair ___despair___
7. ears ___gears___
8. arch ___searching___
9. pear ___appeared___
10. are ___squares___

Lesson 11

The /ē/ sound can be spelled several ways: **e, ee, ea, ie, e_e, y,** and **ey,** as in <u>e</u>cology, est<u>ee</u>m, rev<u>ea</u>led, bel<u>ie</u>vable, del<u>e</u>t<u>e</u>, deliver<u>y</u>, and troll<u>ey</u>.

List Words

trolley
delivery
delete
greasy
revealed
concealed
squeezed
succeeded
repeated
achievement

Write a List Word to complete each sentence.

1. These dirty dishes are ___greasy___.
2. What an ___achievement___ it was to win first prize!
3. We can ride on the ___trolley___.
4. After many falls, my baby sister finally ___succeeded___ in walking.
5. No one heard, so I ___repeated___ the question.
6. Send it by special ___delivery___.
7. Just ___delete___ the extra names.
8. The magician ___revealed___ a rabbit that had been hiding under the hat.
9. Jon ___squeezed___ the sponge dry.
10. The actor's face was ___concealed___ by a beard.

Lesson 12 ■ Instant Replay   51

Lessons 7–11

List Words

delete
scented
repeated
scalding
ashamed
resemble
partial
luscious
leisurely
appeared
usually
searching
brochure
scattered
nourish

Write a List Word to solve each definition clue. Then use the letters in the shaded box to solve the riddle.

1. a piece of — P A R T I A L
2. booklet — B R O C H U R E
3. very hot — S C A L D I N G
4. fragrant — S C E N T E D
5. looking for — S E A R C H I N G
6. without hurry — L E I S U R E L Y
7. spread all over — S C A T T E R E D
8. did it again — R E P E A T E D
9. not proud — A S H A M E D
10. look like — R E S E M B L E
11. delicious — L U S C I O U S
12. showed itself — A P P E A R E D
13. feed — N O U R I S H
14. take out, erase — D E L E T E

Riddle: What did the leopard say when the rain started?

Answer: THAT HIT THE SPOT!

Go for the Goal

Take your Final Replay Test. Then fill in your Scoreboard. Send any misspelled words to your Word Locker.

SCOREBOARD
number correct   number wrong

Clean Out Your Word Locker
Look in your Word Locker. Cross out each word you spelled correctly on your Final Replay Test. Circle the words you're still having trouble with. Add the words you circled to your Spelling Notebook. What do you notice about the words? Watch for those words as you write.

desirable
appreciate
adolescent
rehearsal
achievement

52   Lesson 12 ■ Instant Replay

Go for the Goal/Final Replay Test   *Page 52*

1. Uncle Max is Aunt Mollie's **husband.**
2. This style of car is **desirable** in snowy climates.
3. Let's take a **leisurely** walk through the garden.
4. Both contestants are **deserving** of a prize.
5. Doesn't Elena **usually** walk home with you?
6. The **invention** of computers changed the world.
7. We **assure** you that there are seats left.
8. An actor's **facial** expressions are important.
9. Be very careful around this **machinery.**
10. The soldier learned how to fold a **parachute.**
11. That water is **scalding,** so let it cool.
12. There is a **crescent**-shaped moon tonight.
13. Going up the hill may be easier than **descending.**
14. The magician could **escape** from any trap.
15. Those berries we picked are **luscious!**
16. This car has four forward **gears.**
17. The money I am **earning** will pay for a bike.
18. Did you think the other team played **unfairly?**
19. Their **despair** lifted when they spotted the ship.
20. Today we are having a **rehearsal** for our play.
21. My parents are proud of my **achievement.**
22. Finally, the judges **revealed** the winning poster.
23. Tom **succeeded** at swimming ten laps.
24. The chef **squeezed** all the juice from the lemon.
25. How easily the disguise **concealed** my identity!
26. Some **diseases** are found mainly in the tropics.
27. We are having a **casual** get-together after school.
28. These cabins are rented on a **seasonal** basis.
29. Yes, your dog does **resemble** the one on TV.
30. Don't lose your **composure** over one mistake.
31. Did you **insure** your belongings yet?
32. No one should be **ashamed** of an honest mistake.
33. I need **partial** payment now and the rest later.
34. This plant food will **nourish** your flowers.
35. This **brochure** explains how to use the appliance.
36. The smell of fresh bread **scented** the apartment.
37. The newspaper was **scattered** around the room.
38. Don't use those **scissors** for cutting paper.
39. The children are **screaming** with delight.
40. Seth's **muscles** were sore after the race.
41. The rescue ship began **searching** at once.
42. When the people **appeared,** the deer vanished.
43. That mansion must belong to a **millionaire!**
44. Make sure you pack that fragile vase **carefully.**
45. The quilt was made from small **squares.**
46. Did you enjoy riding the old **trolley?**
47. Make sure this **delivery** is made before noon.
48. Remember to **delete** the extra word in the title.
49. When we **repeated** the song, we did a better job.
50. Don't touch the sofa with those **greasy** hands!

Clean Out Your Word Locker   Before writing the words, students can pronounce them and listen for the various consonant and vowel sounds they learned in **Lessons 7–11.**

45

Instant Replay Test

Side A

Read each set of phrases. Fill in the circle next to the phrase
with an underlined word that is spelled correctly.

1. (a) two <u>deserving</u> applicants   (c) the <u>desserveing</u> students
   (b) a <u>deserveing</u> graduate   (d) one <u>desserving</u> candidate

2. (a) this ingenious <u>inventian</u>   (c) a modern <u>invension</u>
   (b) his clever <u>invencion</u>   (d) that incredible <u>invention</u>

3. (a) her caring <u>huzband</u>   (c) your tired <u>husband</u>
   (b) my talented <u>husbend</u>   (d) her concerned <u>huzbend</u>

4. (a) many childhood <u>diseases</u>   (c) some tropical <u>diseazes</u>
   (b) these curable <u>dizeases</u>   (d) those contagious <u>deseases</u>

5. (a) special <u>delivary</u>   (c) daily <u>dellivary</u>
   (b) weekly <u>delivery</u>   (d) monthly <u>deliverry</u>

6. (a) these <u>lusious</u> grapes   (c) one <u>luscious</u> honeydew
   (b) those <u>lucious</u> pears   (d) some <u>luscous</u> strawberries

7. (a) treated <u>unfarely</u>   (c) scolded <u>unfarly</u>
   (b) handled <u>unfairley</u>   (d) punished <u>unfairly</u>

8. (a) this free <u>broshure</u>   (c) a promotional <u>brochure</u>
   (b) their detailed <u>brosure</u>   (d) a colorful <u>brossure</u>

9. (a) the <u>skreming</u> monkeys   (c) excited, <u>skreaming</u> fans
   (b) those <u>screeming</u> arguers   (d) the <u>screaming</u> infant

10. (a) maintained her <u>composure</u>   (c) weakening my <u>cumpossure</u>
    (b) testing his <u>cumposure</u>   (d) lost their <u>compossure</u>

11. (a) his courageous <u>excape</u>   (c) their ingenious <u>escape</u>
    (b) her daring <u>escaipe</u>   (d) an unsuccessful <u>eskape</u>

12. (a) these sharp <u>scisors</u>   (c) the tailor's <u>scissors</u>
    (b) those children's <u>scissers</u>   (d) these blunt <u>sissors</u>

13. (a) frantically <u>serching</u>   (c) <u>sertching</u> the area
    (b) <u>seartching</u> for clues   (d) intensely <u>searching</u>

Instant Replay Test

Side B

ead each set of phrases. Fill in the circle next to the phrase
th an underlined word that is spelled correctly.

4. (a) appeared at dawn   (c) suddenly appeered
   (b) quietly apeered   (d) mysteriously apeared

5. (a) your outstanding acheivement   (c) their extraordinary achievment
   (b) my academic acheivment   (d) this incredible achievement

6. (a) squeezed the orange   (c) squeased the handle
   (b) squezed the pillow   (d) squeesed between them

7. (a) deleat this word   (c) dellete one paragraph
   (b) delete that letter   (d) delleat that phrase

8. (a) my greasy hands   (c) greasey bicycle chain
   (b) this gresey pizza   (d) gresy cooking utensils

9. (a) inshure for fire   (c) insure for damage
   (b) inssure for theft   (d) inchure for hospitalization

0. (a) those scattered toys   (c) the skattered crumbs
   (b) the scaterred pages   (d) these skatered documents

1. (a) parcial acceptance   (c) receive parsial payment
   (b) this partial shipment   (d) parshal completion

2. (a) many engine geers   (c) the airplane's gears
   (b) these bicycle geares   (d) my wristwatch's geres

3. (a) the ashaimmed thief   (c) the ashaimed puppy
   (b) an ashammed liar   (d) his ashamed expression

4. (a) her casuel clothing   (c) his cashuel invitation
   (b) a cashual reunion   (d) a casual acquaintance

5. (a) these quilted squares   (c) those wooden scuairs
   (b) some plastic squars   (d) the orange scuares

TAKE IT HOME

Your child has learned to spell many ne[w]
words and would like to share them wit[h]
you and your family. Here are some ide[as]
for having family fun as you help your
child review the words in Lessons 7–11.

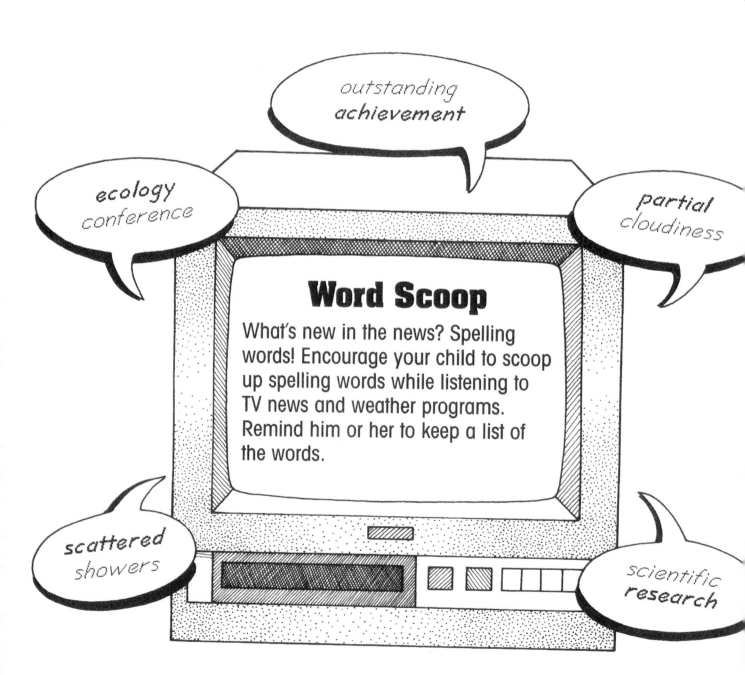

outstanding achievement

ecology conference

partial cloudiness

Word Scoop

What's new in the news? Spelling words! Encourage your child to scoop up spelling words while listening to TV news and weather programs. Remind him or her to keep a list of the words.

scattered showers

scientific research

Crossword Puzzle Challenge

See how fast you and your child can complete this crossword puzzle.

proceed	concealed	scenic	composure	despair
accomplish	earnest	gymnasium	gears	instruments

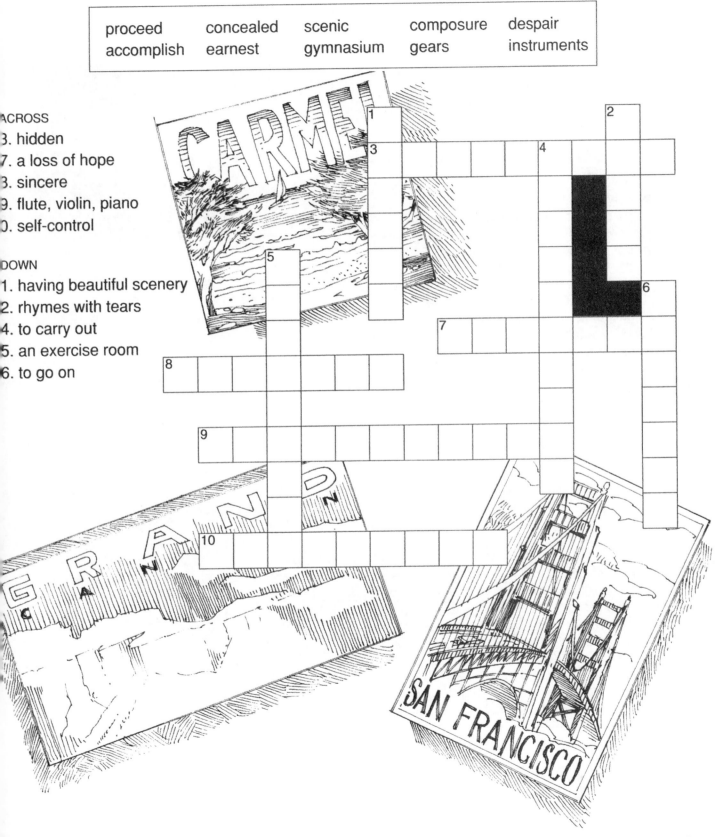

ACROSS

3. hidden
7. a loss of hope
8. sincere
9. flute, violin, piano
10. self-control

DOWN

1. having beautiful scenery
2. rhymes with tears
4. to carry out
5. an exercise room
6. to go on

Lesson 13

Objective
To spell words in which *oa, oe, ou,* and *ow* spell /ō/

Correlated Phonics Lesson
MCP Phonics, Level F, Lesson 16

Warm Up   *Page 53*
In this selection, students read about a small musical instrument that makes a big sound—the harmonica. Ask students if they play any musical instruments and whether they would like to play the harmonica.

Encourage students to look back at the boldfaced words. Ask volunteers to say the words and identify the different ways to spell the /ō/ sound.

On Your Mark/Warm Up Test
1. The *borrower* promptly paid back the debt.
2. Gloria mixed the *doughnut* batter in a big bowl.
3. *Although* Peg got off to a bad start, she won.
4. My uncle raises *poultry* on his farm.
5. The school *bowling* team meets every Saturday.
6. Mr. Earl planted ten acres and left ten *fallow.*
7. The berries on *mistletoe* plants are poisonous.
8. Did you know that some fire engines are *yellow?*
9. I record my yearly *growth* on the kitchen door.
10. As winter *approaches,* the birds fly south.
11. They used oxen to move the heavy *boulders.*
12. I read a story about a *stowaway* on a ship.
13. Please rinse the dishes *thoroughly.*
14. Chocolate and *cocoa* come from the cacao bean.
15. What a beautiful sound the *oboe* makes!
16. I live in a *bungalow* on Crescent Avenue.
17. We *tiptoed* because the baby was sleeping.
18. What color did you paint the *rowboat?*
19. For dessert, we'll have chilled *cantaloupe.*
20. The god Atlas held the world on his *shoulders.*

Pep Talk/Game Plan   *Pages 54–55*
Introduce the spelling rule and have students read the List Words aloud. You may also wish to point out that *rowboat* contains both the *ow* and the *oa* spelling of /ō/. Then encourage students to look back at their Warm Up Tests and apply the spelling rule to any misspelled words.

As students work through the **Spelling Lineup, Vocabulary,** and **Classification** exercises, remind them to look back at their List Words or in their dictionaries if they need help.

 See **Variant Spellings,** page 14

Warm Up
What musical instrument weighs very little but makes a big sound?

Your Own Kind of Music
A harmonica is **thoroughly** enjoyable to listen to, easy to play, and a lot easier to carry than a piano! You can keep it in your pocket and reach for it anytime you feel a song coming on.

This little music-maker was invented over one hundred years ago by a man named Sir Charles Wheatstone. **Although** no one is sure exactly why, Wheatstone named his instrument the *aeolina.* Since then, it has been known as a French harp, a mouth organ, and of course, a harmonica.

Its **growth** in popularity is certainly understandable. Depending upon how you play it, the sound of a harmonica **approaches** that of a bagpipe, piccolo, or **oboe.** Even though there are books on how to play, harmonica musicians usually learn by trial and error. With the harmonica, the errors generally aren't all that bad. With a little practice, you too can curve your hands around it and give it a sound all your own!

In his novel *The Grapes of Wrath,* John Steinbeck talks about the pride of harmonica ownership. Breaking or losing a harmonica "is no great loss," he says, "You can always buy another for a quarter." While that may not be true today, harmonicas are still inexpensive. It's a small price to play to make your own kind of music.

 Say the boldfaced words in the selection. What vowel sound do you hear in each word? How many ways can you find to spell that vowel sound?

On Your Mark
Take your Warm Up Test. Then check your spelling with the List Words on the next page.

53

Pep Talk
The /ō/ sound can be spelled many ways:
oa, as in <u>row</u>boat
oe, as in <u>oboe</u>
ou, as in d<u>ough</u>nut
ow, as in gr<u>ow</u>th

LIST WORDS
1. borrower
2. doughnut
3. although
4. poultry
5. bowling
6. fallow
7. mistletoe
8. yellow
9. growth
10. approaches
11. boulders
12. stowaway
13. thoroughly
14. cocoa
15. oboe
16. bungalow
17. tiptoed
18. rowboat
19. cantaloupe
20. shoulders

Game Plan
Spelling Lineup
Write each List Word under the spelling of its /ō/ sound. One word will be used twice.

/ō/, as in <u>throw</u>	/ō/, as in <u>dough</u>
1. borrower	12. doughnut
2. bowling	13. although
3. fallow	14. poultry
4. yellow	15. boulders
5. growth	16. thoroughly
6. stowaway	17. cantaloupe
7. bungalow	18. shoulders
8. rowboat	

/ō/, as in <u>boat</u>	/ō/, as in <u>toe</u>
9. approaches	19. mistletoe
10. cocoa	20. oboe
11. rowboat	21. tiptoed

54   Lesson 13 ■ /ō/: **oa, oe, ou,** and **ow**

Vocabulary

The underlined word in each sentence does not make sense. Replace the word with a List Word that does make sense. Write that word on the line.

1. Would you like a steaming cup of boulders? _cocoa_
2. Jim plays the rowboat in the high school band. _oboe_
3. The tiptoed is a melon with light orange flesh. _cantaloupe_
4. The farmer made a wall out of cocoa. _boulders_
5. Bungalow is a sport the whole family enjoys. _Bowling_
6. Stand back when the train shoulders the station. _approaches_
7. We hung poultry over the door during the holidays. _mistletoe_
8. Thoroughly I tried, I couldn't lift the rock. _Although_
9. The doughnut paid back the money I loaned her. _borrower_
10. He shoulders down the hall. _tiptoed_

Classification

Write the List Word that belongs in each group.

1. red, blue, _yellow_
2. increase, development, _growth_
3. barren, unplanted, _fallow_
4. ranch, townhouse, _bungalow_
5. watermelon, honeydew, _cantaloupe_
6. hen, rooster, _poultry_
7. completely, totally, _thoroughly_
8. holly, cactus, _mistletoe_
9. elbows, knees, _shoulders_
10. bread, waffle, _doughnut_
11. flute, clarinet, _oboe_
12. canoe, sailboat, _rowboat_

Lesson 13 ∎ /ō/: **oa, oe, ou,** and **ow**   55

Flex Your Spelling Muscles

Writing

Create a silly song using as many List Words as you can. Write words to a familiar tune or create one of your own. Have a Silly Song Contest. Perhaps a partner would like to accompany you on a harmonica or other musical instrument.

Proofreading

The words to this silly song, sung to the tune of "On Top of Old Smokey," have ten mistakes. Use the proofreading marks to correct them. Then write the misspelled List Words correctly on the lines.

Proofreading Marks
◯ spelling mistake
≡ capital letter
∧ add something

1. on top of a doenut
   All filled with cream,
   I spilled my hot cocoe
   When I heard a scream.

2. I left my buhngalo
   And tiptowed around.
   I wanted to find out
   Who had made that sound.

3. i looked in a rouboat
   And what did I see?
   A stoaway owl
   Looking right back at me.

Now proofread your own lyrics. Fix any mistakes.

1. _doughnut_
2. _cocoa_
3. _bungalow_
4. _tiptoed_
5. _rowboat_
6. _stowaway_

Go for the Goal

Take your Final Test. Then fill in your Scoreboard. Send your mistakes to the Word Locker.

SCOREBOARD

number correct	number wrong

★ ★ ★ ★ ★ ★ ★ ★ **All-Star Words** ★ ★ ★ ★ ★ ★ ★ ★

overgrown   woeful   approach   borough   mellow

Write a sentence for each All-Star Word. Then, erase the letters that make the /ō/ sound in each word. Trade papers with a partner and fill in the missing letters in each other's words.

56   Lesson 13 ∎ /ō/: **oa, oe, ou,** and **ow**

◎ **Spelling Strategy**   Write each List Word on the board. Then ask a volunteer to come to the front of the class and
• pronounce the word
• circle the letters that spell the /ō/ sound
• suggest another word in which the same letter pair spells long _o_.

Flex Your Spelling Muscles   *Page 56*

As students complete the **Writing** activity, encourage them to brainstorm ideas, write a first draft, revise, and proofread their work. The **Proofreading** exercise will help them prepare to proofread their lyrics. To publish their writing, students may want to
• record their songs
• present a performance for another class.

✍ Writer's Corner

> You might want to bring in recordings of harmonica music and play them for the class. Invite students to draw pictures and to write about their feelings as they listen to the music.

Go for the Goal/Final Test

1. Columbus introduced Europeans to **cocoa.**
2. The seeds of the **cantaloupe** are white.
3. What store sells the freshest **poultry?**
4. Look at all the new **growth** since the last rain.
5. The **oboe** was developed in France.
6. My **shoulders** got sunburned at the beach.
7. Let's go **bowling** on Saturday.
8. As spring **approaches,** the flowers bloom.
9. During the fall, the leaves turn red and **yellow.**
10. We pulled the **rowboat** up on the shore.
11. **Although** it is sunny now, it may rain later.
12. Jennifer cleaned her room **thoroughly** last night.
13. The family rented a **bungalow** near the sea.
14. Last year the farmer let that field lie **fallow.**
15. A **borrower** pays monthly interest on a loan.
16. Just look at the size of those **boulders!**
17. Where on the ship was the **stowaway** hiding?
18. She made a bouquet of holly and **mistletoe.**
19. Grandfather fed **doughnut** crumbs to the birds.
20. We **tiptoed** up to the window to surprise Ebony.

Remind students to complete the Scoreboard and write any misspelled words in their Word Locker.

★★ **All-Star Words**   You may want to point out that the All-Star Words follow the spelling rule and model writing a sentence using a List Word.

Lesson 14

Objective
To spell words with the /ô/ sound spelled *au* and *aw*

Correlated Phonics Lesson
MCP Phonics, Level F, Lesson 20

Warm Up   *Page 57*
In "A New Wave," students read about a new sport called *boardsailing,* which is a combination of sailing and surfboarding. After reading, invite students to tell why they would or would not like to try this sport.

Encourage students to look back at the boldfaced words. Ask volunteers to say each word and identify the vowel sound they hear.

On Your Mark/Warm Up Test
1. The *brawny* athlete raised the barbells.
2. Chang helped me fold the clean *laundry.*
3. Rosa *taught* the alphabet to her little brother.
4. He *paused* when he came to an unfamiliar word.
5. Why do leaves change color in *autumn?*
6. We stood in the shade of the striped *awning.*
7. Climbing Mt. Everest is an *awesome* task!
8. Soon the shuttle will be *launched.*
9. In space, *astronauts* experience weightlessness.
10. The farmer heard the chickens *squawking.*
11. Being small is not a *drawback* for gymnasts.
12. After the relay race, the team was *exhausted.*
13. Marty heated the soup in the *saucepan.*
14. Does the fire alarm go off *automatically?*
15. No one is sure why the *dinosaur* became extinct.
16. Is this old coin *authentic?*
17. Her *withdrawal* from the race caused surprise.
18. A *thesaurus* contains synonyms and antonyms.
19. Careful drivers take *precautions* in bad weather.
20. We gave the dancers a round of *applause.*

Pep Talk/Game Plan   *Pages 58–59*
Introduce the spelling rule and have students read the List Words aloud. Discuss the meanings of unfamiliar words (*brawny, awning, authentic*). Then encourage students to look back at their Warm Up Tests and apply the spelling rule to any misspelled words.

As students work through the **Spelling Lineup, Vocabulary,** and **Puzzle** exercises, remind them to look back at their List Words or in their dictionaries if they need help.

 See **Student Dictation,** page 14

---

au and aw   LESSON 14

Warm Up
For what sport do you need a board and a sail?

A New Wave
First, there was sailboating. Then there was surfboarding. Now, there's "boardsailing," or "windsurfing," a sport that combines the thrills and spills of both sailing and surfing.

On the water, boardsailors feel the **awesome** power of the wind and waves. They guide their boards by carefully adjusting the sail's mast. Steady, smooth movements allow the wind to catch the sail. Any quick, awkward movements could overturn the board.

Although boardsailing was **launched** only a few decades ago, it has risen in popularity due to a few dedicated boardsailors. One daredevil boardsailed across the Atlantic Ocean in just 37 days. Another, a 13-year-old, 103-pound boy, won the world championship.

For people who are afraid to try boardsailing on the water, there are schools for landlubbers where they can be **taught** to boardsail. Would-be boardsailors practice on a simulator. That's a surfboard mounted on a mechanical arm. The simulator duplicates the feel of ocean waves under a board. Although the waves aren't **authentic,** the excitement is real! The simulator has one big **drawback,** however. When a person falls, he or she "splashes" onto the floor. A few hard landings like that encourage people to take a chance and try the water!

 Look back at the boldfaced words in the selection. What vowel sound do you hear in each word?

On Your Mark
Take your Warm Up Test. Then check your spelling with the List Words on the next page.

57

Pep Talk
The vowel digraphs au and aw sound alike. They both spell the /ô/ sound you hear in paused and awesome.

LIST WORDS
1. brawny
2. laundry
3. taught
4. paused
5. autumn
6. awning
7. awesome
8. launched
9. astronauts
10. squawking
11. drawback
12. exhausted
13. saucepan
14. automatically
15. dinosaur
16. authentic
17. withdrawal
18. thesaurus
19. precautions
20. applause

Game Plan
Spelling Lineup
Write the List Words in the correct category to show how the /ô/ sound is spelled.

au spells /ô/	aw spells /ô/
1. laundry	15. brawny
2. taught	16. awning
3. paused	17. awesome
4. autumn	18. squawking
5. launched	19. drawback
6. astronauts	20. withdrawal
7. exhausted	
8. saucepan	
9. automatically	
10. dinosaur	
11. authentic	
12. thesaurus	
13. precautions	
14. applause	

58   Lesson 14 ▪ au and aw

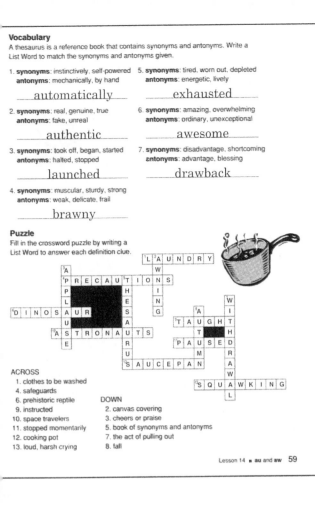

Vocabulary

A thesaurus is a reference book that contains synonyms and antonyms. Write a List Word to match the synonyms and antonyms given.

1. **synonyms**: instinctively, self-powered
   antonyms: mechanically, by hand
   <u>automatically</u>

2. **synonyms**: real, genuine, true
   antonyms: fake, unreal
   <u>authentic</u>

3. **synonyms**: took off, began, started
   antonyms: halted, stopped
   <u>launched</u>

4. **synonyms**: muscular, sturdy, strong
   antonyms: weak, delicate, frail
   <u>brawny</u>

5. **synonyms**: tired, worn out, depleted
   antonyms: energetic, lively
   <u>exhausted</u>

6. **synonyms**: amazing, overwhelming
   antonyms: ordinary, unexceptional
   <u>awesome</u>

7. **synonyms**: disadvantage, shortcoming
   antonyms: advantage, blessing
   <u>drawback</u>

Puzzle

Fill in the crossword puzzle by writing a List Word to answer each definition clue.

ACROSS
1. clothes to be washed
4. safeguards
6. prehistoric reptile
9. instructed
10. space travelers
11. stopped momentarily
12. cooking pot
13. loud, harsh crying

DOWN
2. canvas covering
3. cheers or praise
5. book of synonyms and antonyms
7. the act of pulling out
8. fall

Lesson 14 ■ au and aw   59

Flex Your Spelling Muscles

Writing

You have just been asked to interview a daredevil. Write a series of questions to ask during the interview. Find out as many details as possible about that person's most recent adventure.

Proofreading

The course description that follows has ten mistakes. Use the proofreading marks to correct them. Then write the misspelled List Words correctly on the lines.

Proofreading Marks
- ◯ spelling mistake
- ⊙ add period
- ∧ add something

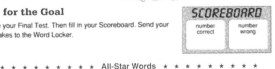

Semester at Sea—Spend an entire semester aboard a sailboat. Sail from Boston, Massachusetts to the Bahamas aboard an (awthentick) 19th century sailing vessel. Students are (tougt) navigation, maritime history, literature of the sea, and marine biology. You'll come back (exshawsted) but filled with stories about an (awsume) experience. If you pass, you are (automatically) enrolled in the advanced marine biology class. This course is available both (awtum) and spring terms. *15 credits*

1. <u>authentic</u>
2. <u>taught</u>
3. <u>exhausted</u>
4. <u>awesome</u>
5. <u>automatically</u>
6. <u>autumn</u>

Now proofread your interview questions. Fix any mistakes.

Go for the Goal

Take your Final Test. Then fill in your Scoreboard. Send your mistakes to the Word Locker.

SCOREBOARD
| number correct | number wrong |

★ ★ ★ ★ ★ ★ ★ **All-Star Words** ★ ★ ★ ★ ★ ★ ★

clause   auction   law-abiding   nausea   gawk

Write a sentence for each All-Star Word. Then erase each All-Star Word. Trade papers with a partner. Can you correctly fill in each other's All-Star Words?

60 Lesson 14 ■ au and aw

◉ **Spelling Strategy**   Write each List Word on the board, leaving out the digraph *au* or *aw*. For each word, ask a volunteer to come to the board, name the missing letters, and complete the word by filling in the digraph. Have the class check each spelling against the List Words in their *Spelling Workout* books.

Flex Your Spelling Muscles   Page 60

As students complete the **Writing** activity, encourage them to brainstorm ideas, write a first draft, revise, and proofread their work. The **Proofreading** exercise will help them prepare to proofread their interview questions. To publish their writing, students may want to get together with a partner to role-play an interview with a daredevil.

✍ Writer's Corner

> Students might enjoy inventing a sport that combines two existing sports. Encourage them to research various sports at the library and to write about their new activity in a style similar to the entries in the book *Sports* by Tim Hammond.

Go for the Goal/Final Test

1. We took **precautions** to avoid the storm.
2. He made a **withdrawal** from his bank.
3. Ken made a **dinosaur** model for the science fair.
4. Lena poured the gravy into the **saucepan.**
5. A poor memory is a **drawback** during a test.
6. The first **astronauts** were considered heroes.
7. Her triple somersault in midair was **awesome!**
8. When was the space shuttle **launched?**
9. Mr. Li unrolled the **awning** in front of his store.
10. She **paused** in the middle of her speech.
11. Does Franny do her own **laundry?**
12. **Applause** is an inspiration to performers.
13. A **thesaurus** is a useful reference book.
14. The chair was an **authentic** antique from 1750.
15. Did you know that the door opens **automatically?**
16. The farmer was **exhausted** after working all day.
17. The **squawking** birds are making a loud racket.
18. How cool and crisp the air is in **autumn!**
19. My mother **taught** me how to weave on a loom.
20. He was once frail, but now he's **brawny.**

Remind students to complete the Scoreboard and write any misspelled words in their Word Locker.

★★ **All-Star Words**   You may want to point out that the All-Star Words follow the spelling rule and model writing a sentence with a List Word.

Lesson 15

Objective
To spell words with /yo͞o/, /o͞o/, /i/ spelled *oo, ew, ue, ui*

Correlated Phonics Lessons
MCP Phonics, Level F, Lessons 22–23, 27

Warm Up   *Page 61*
In this selection, students learn why animals are natural weather forecasters. After reading, invite students to share their own observations of approaching storms.

Encourage students to look back at the boldfaced words. Ask volunteers to say each word and tell whether it has the sound of /o͞o/ in *poodle* or the sound of /i/ in *build.*

On Your Mark/Warm Up Test
1. Dampness can cause *mildew* to form.
2. Stuart played his *guitar* at my sister's party.
3. The rainy day made the old house look *gloomy.*
4. Grandma is going on an ocean *cruise.*
5. The jury found the defendant *guilty* as charged.
6. What time is *curfew* at summer camp?
7. These old spoons are made from *pewter.*
8. What a *juicy* hamburger that was!
9. Use fine sandpaper to make the wood *smoother.*
10. Maria *bruised* her knee sliding into first base.
11. Bonnie made a *quilted* bedspread from scraps.
12. The bank *building* is behind the post office.
13. The parents' committee had a *fruitful* meeting.
14. Is this *shampoo* good for sun-damaged hair?
15. Soft music can be *soothing* after a busy day.
16. In summer, a cotton blanket is a *suitable* cover.
17. The dog *pursued* the cat around the house.
18. Daryl enjoyed the *biscuit* my mother baked.
19. Earth's *circuit* around the sun takes a year.
20. That ringing phone upstairs is a real *nuisance!*

Pep Talk/Game Plan   *Pages 62–63*
Introduce the spelling rule and have students read the List Words aloud. Encourage students to look back at their Warm Up Tests and apply the spelling rule to any misspelled words.

As students work through the **Spelling Lineup, Missing Words,** and **Puzzle** exercises, remind them to look back at their List Words or in their dictionaries if they need help.

 See **Letter Cards,** page 15

54

Name _____

oo, ew, ue, and ui   LESSON **15**

Warm Up
What do animals do when they sense a storm coming?

Weather Report
Sea crabs are running along the beach, looking for a **suitable** hiding place. Fish are diving deeper and deeper into the sea, escaping into **smoother** waters. What are these sea creatures trying to tell us? A storm is coming!

Sea animals are not the only natural weather forecasters. Before a storm, field mice become more energetic. Rabbits eat more, and squirrels argue with one another. Raccoons and opossums remove their young from nests in carved-out logs. They seem to know that their homes are about to be flooded. Even indoor critters are good weather forecasters. Cockroaches scamper even more than usual before a storm.

Perhaps the best of nature's forecasters are birds. Birds are also the easiest to observe. Long before the first **gloomy** cloud appears overhead, you can see birds preparing for a storm. Since the air pressure always falls before a storm, you'll see birds flying close to the ground. They're trying to escape the low air pressure that is higher in the sky. Some birds will be **building** onto their nests, making sure the nests are strong enough. Though most birds eat early in the morning, some will catch insects even into the evening. Just before the rain begins to fall, you'll see few robins in the sky. They've all **pursued** a place to hide.

> Say the boldfaced words in the selection. Which words have the /o͞o/ sound you hear in *poodle*? Which words have the /i/ sound you hear in *build*?

On Your Mark
Take your Warm Up Test. Then check your spelling with the List Words on the next page.

61

Pep Talk
The /yo͞o/ sound, as in *curfew*, can be spelled **ew**.
The /o͞o/ sound, as in *smoother*, can be spelled in the following ways:
ew, as in *mildew*   **oo**, as in *gloomy*
ue, as in *pursued*   **ui**, as in *fruitful*
The letters **ui** can spell the /i/ sound as in *biscuit*.

LIST WORDS
1. mildew
2. guitar
3. gloomy
4. cruise
5. guilty
6. curfew
7. pewter
8. juicy
9. smoother
10. bruised
11. quilted
12. building
13. fruitful
14. shampoo
15. soothing
16. suitable
17. pursued
18. biscuit
19. circuit
20. nuisance

Game Plan
Spelling Lineup
Write each List Word under the correct heading.

ew spells /o͞o/ or /yo͞o/
1. mildew
2. curfew
3. pewter

ui spells /o͞o/
4. cruise
5. juicy
6. bruised
7. fruitful
8. suitable
9. nuisance

ue spells /o͞o/
10. pursued

oo spells /o͞o/
11. gloomy
12. smoother
13. shampoo
14. soothing

ui spells /i/
15. guitar
16. guilty
17. quilted
18. building
19. biscuit
20. circuit

62   Lesson 15 ■ oo, ew, ue, and ui

Missing Words

Write the List Word that completes each sentence.

1. A __guitar__ is an instrument that typically has six strings.

2. __Pewter__ is a grayish metal alloy made with tin and lead, brass, or copper.

3. He had no broken bones, but he was badly __bruised__ from the fall.

4. The lioness __pursued__ her prey skillfully, never letting it out of her sight.

Puzzle

This is a crossword puzzle without definition clues. Use the length of the word and the letters provided as clues to figure out which List Words fit in the spaces. Then fill in the puzzle.

Flex Your Spelling Muscles

Writing

Write a script for a TV weather report that is both factual and entertaining. For example, you can give the temperature and describe what kinds of clothes would be suitable for viewers to wear. Use as many List Words as you can.

Proofreading

This naturalist's journal entry has nine mistakes. Use the proofreading marks to fix the mistakes. Write the misspelled List Words correctly on the lines.

Proofreading Marks
◯ spelling mistake
ℓ take out something

March 13: I spotted a prairie dog being (persooed) by a ~~a~~ coyote. Warning barks could be heard all over the town. One prairie dog carrying grass (sootable) for a nest it was was (bilding) dove head-first into its burrow. Within seconds the the ~~the~~ entire town was deserted as if a (curfue) had been set. I noticed that the soil is richer and more fertile in prairie dog towns. I must collect evidence to prove that prairie dogs are a help and not a ~~a~~ (newsance) to ranchers.

1. __pursued__
2. __suitable__
3. __building__
4. __curfew__
5. __nuisance__

Now proofread your weather report. Fix any mistakes.

Go for the Goal

Take your Final Test. Then fill in your Scoreboard. Send your mistakes to the Word Locker.

SCOREBOARD	
number correct	number wrong

★ ★ ★ ★ ★ ★ ★ ★ All-Star Words ★ ★ ★ ★ ★ ★ ★ ★

steward   typhoon   undue   recruit   monsoon

Write a clue for each All-Star Word. Trade papers with a partner. Write the All-Star Words that match the clues.

◎ **Spelling Strategy**   To help students practice spelling the List Words, invite them to get together with a partner and take turns
• writing the List Words
• pronouncing the word they write
• circling the letters *ew, ue, oo,* or *ui*
• telling the sound the letters stand for.

Flex Your Spelling Muscles   *Page 64*

As students complete the **Writing** activity, encourage them to brainstorm ideas, write a first draft, revise, and proofread their work. The **Proofreading** exercise will help them prepare to proofread their weather reports. To publish their writing, students may want to
• read their reports aloud as television broadcasts
• use their reports to create a classroom display.

✍ **Writer's Corner** _____

At the beginning of each day for a week, write the weather forecast in your local newspaper on the board. Have students observe the weather during the day and take notes. The following morning, invite students to refer to their notes to check the accuracy of the previous day's forecast.

Go for the Goal/Final Test

1. Please buy a bottle of *shampoo* at the store.
2. Each year, my parents and I agree on a *curfew.*
3. Linda is taking *guitar* lessons after school.
4. People stopped to stare at the strange *building.*
5. Don't feel *guilty,* because it wasn't your fault.
6. Those insects are beginning to be a *nuisance.*
7. The lawyer *pursued* one line of questioning.
8. *Mildew* grows in warm, damp places.
9. This *juicy* orange is delicious!
10. Steam rose from the *biscuit* as I cut it.
11. The coat was made of a blue, *quilted* material.
12. That restaurant serves salads on *pewter* dishes.
13. Our trip to the library was most *fruitful.*
14. Did the lights go out when the *circuit* failed?
15. Some of the music by Brahms is very *soothing.*
16. Stir the batter until it's a little *smoother.*
17. This weekend, let's take a *cruise* on the bay.
18. The house sure looks *gloomy* without a light!
19. I *bruised* my ankle when I tripped over a branch.
20. Did you wear *suitable* shoes for walking?

Remind students to complete the Scoreboard and write any misspelled words in their Word Locker.

★★ **All-Star Words**   You may want to point out that the All-Star Words follow the spelling rule and model writing a clue for a List Word.

Lesson 16

Objective
To spell words in which *ay* or *ai* spells /ā/; *oi* or *oy* spells /ȯi/

Correlated Phonics Lessons
MCP Phonics, Level F, Lessons 14, 25

Warm Up   **Page 65**
In this selection, students discover that the eggshell is the world's best-designed container. Afterward, invite students to discuss other facts they know about eggs and to share their favorite ways to eat eggs.

Ask volunteers to say the boldfaced words and to compare the vowel sounds they hear.

On Your Mark/Warm Up Test
1. Ralph Waldo Emerson wrote many *essays.*
2. Donna *boiled* two eggs for her breakfast.
3. Pearls are sometimes found in *oysters.*
4. Is the crew responsible for road *maintenance?*
5. Juanita is searching for summer *employment.*
6. She decorated the pillow with *embroidery.*
7. Would you like to borrow my *crayons?*
8. The hero had one daring *exploit* after another.
9. At rush hour, the station is in *turmoil.*
10. The nurse put *ointment* on my poison ivy.
11. Please rinse the strawberries in a *strainer.*
12. The principal *praised* us for our hard work.
13. What *disappointment* I felt when I lost!
14. Put the *container* of milk into the refrigerator.
15. Taking six from eight leaves a *remainder* of two.
16. Franklin Roosevelt had a *faithful* dog, Fala.
17. By wearing seat belts, they *avoided* injury.
18. We are *rejoicing* because Alicia won the election.
19. I'd like a ham sandwich with *mayonnaise,* please.
20. He is a business *acquaintance* of my father.

Pep Talk/Game Plan   **Pages 66–67**
Introduce the spelling rule and have students read the List Words aloud. Point out that *mayonnaise* contains both *ay* and *ai* and call students' attention to the double *p* in *disappointment* and the double *n* in *mayonnaise.* Then encourage students to look back at their Warm Up Tests and apply the spelling rule to any misspelled words.

As students work through the **Spelling Lineup, Classification, Antonyms,** and **Missing Words** exercises, remind them to look back at their List Words or in their dictionaries if they need help.

 See **Charades/Pantomime,** page 15

Name _____

ai, ay, oi, and oy
LESSON 16

Warm Up
What is the world's most naturally well-designed container?

A Half-Dozen Egg Facts

The world's most **praised** and well-designed **container** is not a gift-wrapped box from a department store. It's an eggshell. An eggshell may seem fragile, but it's able to withstand a lot of pressure. Try holding an egg in the palm of your hand and squeezing it tightly. It usually won't break.

Have you ever tried to balance an egg on its smaller end? Most of the time, you can't do it, but during the vernal equinox, the time in the spring when the sun crosses the equator, an egg will stand on end. A hard-boiled egg will spin on its side. An uncooked egg will barely spin.

Today's chickens are really super chickens. Two hundred years ago, before scientists got involved in egg breeding, an average chicken laid only about 15 eggs a year. Today they produce more than 300 yearly, which is what the average American eats every year. Therefore, one chicken provides enough eggs for one person. Not all the eggs are **boiled,** fried, or scrambled. Some are in soufflés, eggnog, **mayonnaise,** or baked into breads.

Egg breeding provides steady **employment** in the leading egg-producing states: California, Georgia, Arkansas, and Pennsylvania.

 Say the boldfaced words in the selection. What vowel sound do you hear in each word? How are the vowel sounds alike? How are they different?

On Your Mark
Take your Warm Up Test. Then check your spelling with the List Words on the next page.

65

Pep Talk
The letters **ay** and **ai** make the /ā/ sound you hear in crayons and praised.

The letters **oy** and **oi** make the /ȯi/ sound you hear in oysters and rejoicing.

LIST WORDS
1. essays
2. boiled
3. oysters
4. maintenance
5. employment
6. embroidery
7. crayons
8. exploit
9. turmoil
10. ointment
11. strainer
12. praised
13. disappointment
14. container
15. remainder
16. faithful
17. avoided
18. rejoicing
19. mayonnaise
20. acquaintance

Game Plan
Spelling Lineup
Write each List Word under the spelling of its /ā/ or /ȯi/ sound. One word is used twice.

/ā/, as in train	/ȯi/, as in oil
1. maintenance	12. boiled
2. strainer	13. embroidery
3. praised	14. exploit
4. container	15. turmoil
5. remainder	16. ointment
6. faithful	17. disappointment
7. mayonnaise	18. avoided
8. acquaintance	19. rejoicing

/ā/, as in play	/ȯi/, as in toy
9. essays	20. oysters
10. crayons	21. employment
11. mayonnaise	

66 Lesson 16 ▪ ai, ay, oi, and oy

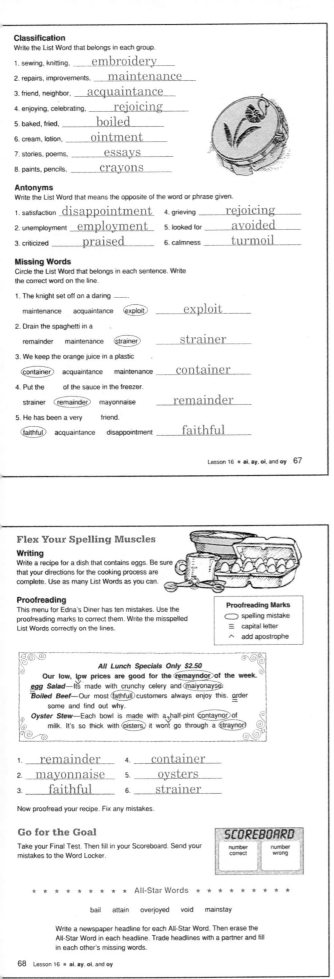

Classification
Write the List Word that belongs in each group.

1. sewing, knitting, _embroidery_
2. repairs, improvements, _maintenance_
3. friend, neighbor, _acquaintance_
4. enjoying, celebrating, _rejoicing_
5. baked, fried, _boiled_
6. cream, lotion, _ointment_
7. stories, poems, _essays_
8. paints, pencils, _crayons_

Antonyms
Write the List Word that means the opposite of the word or phrase given.

1. satisfaction _disappointment_
2. unemployment _employment_
3. criticized _praised_
4. grieving _rejoicing_
5. looked for _avoided_
6. calmness _turmoil_

Missing Words
Circle the List Word that belongs in each sentence. Write the correct word on the line.

1. The knight set off on a daring ____.

maintenance   acquaintance   (exploit)   _exploit_

2. Drain the spaghetti in a ____

remainder   maintenance   (strainer)   _strainer_

3. We keep the orange juice in a plastic ____

(container)   acquaintance   maintenance   _container_

4. Put the ____ of the sauce in the freezer.

strainer   (remainder)   mayonnaise   _remainder_

5. He has been a very ____ friend.

(faithful)   acquaintance   disappointment   _faithful_

Lesson 16 ■ ai, ay, oi, and oy   67

Flex Your Spelling Muscles

Writing
Write a recipe for a dish that contains eggs. Be sure that your directions for the cooking process are complete. Use as many List Words as you can.

Proofreading
This menu for Edna's Diner has ten mistakes. Use the proofreading marks to correct them. Write the misspelled List Words correctly on the lines.

Proofreading Marks
◯ spelling mistake
≡ capital letter
∧ add apostrophe

> *All Lunch Specials Only $2.50*
> Our low, low prices are good for the (remayndor) of the week.
> *egg Salad*—It's made with crunchy celery and (maiyonayse)
> *Boiled Beef*—Our most (faithull) customers always enjoy this. order some and find out why.
> *Oyster Stew*—Each bowl is made with a half-pint (contaynor) of milk. It's so thick with (oisters) it wont go through a (straynor)

1. _remainder_   4. _container_
2. _mayonnaise_   5. _oysters_
3. _faithful_   6. _strainer_

Now proofread your recipe. Fix any mistakes.

Go for the Goal
Take your Final Test. Then fill in your Scoreboard. Send your mistakes to the Word Locker.

SCOREBOARD

number correct	number wrong

★ ★ ★ ★ ★ ★ ★ All-Star Words ★ ★ ★ ★ ★ ★ ★ ★

bail   attain   overjoyed   void   mainstay

Write a newspaper headline for each All-Star Word. Then erase the All-Star Word in each headline. Trade headlines with a partner and fill in each other's missing words.

68   Lesson 16 ■ ai, ay, oi, and oy

⊙ **Spelling Strategy**   With a partner, students can fold a piece of paper in half lengthwise to make two columns. Have them label the columns /ā/ and /oi/ and write each List Word in the appropriate column, circling the letters that stand for the /ā/ or /oi/ sound. Encourage students to exchange papers with another set of partners and check one another's work.

Flex Your Spelling Muscles   *Page 68*
As students complete the **Writing** activity, encourage them to brainstorm ideas, write a first draft, revise, and proofread their work. The **Proofreading** exercise will help them prepare to proofread their recipes. To publish their writing, students may want to
• use their recipes to create a cookbook
• take their recipes home and try them, with adult supervision.

✎ Writer's Corner

Students might enjoy conducting some of the experiments in *Science Experiments* by Robert Gardner, or a similar book. Encourage students to work with a group and to take notes as they do the experiments.

Go for the Goal/Final Test
1. The crowds at the sale created ***turmoil.***
2. My aunt has a recipe for ***mayonnaise.***
3. Jim bought a small ***container*** of sardines.
4. Is ***maintenance*** of your car expensive?
5. I put the ***remainder*** of the salad on a plate.
6. Mother found ***employment*** at the new law firm.
7. The veterinarian put ***ointment*** in the cat's ears.
8. Kim is an ***acquaintance*** of mine from Chicago.
9. The astronaut told about his exciting ***exploit.***
10. I felt ***disappointment*** when we lost the game.
11. Try the ***oysters*** when you visit Key West.
12. The fans were ***rejoicing*** after the game.
13. Henry David Thoreau wrote many ***essays.***
14. Will you pour the broth through a ***strainer?***
15. How thankful I am for my ***faithful*** friends!
16. We saw a beautiful exhibit of old ***embroidery.***
17. Grandfather ***boiled*** the lobsters in a big pot.
18. Each child at the party got a box of ***crayons.***
19. The driver barely ***avoided*** an accident.
20. The teacher ***praised*** Nicole for her fine report.

Remind students to complete the Scoreboard and write any misspelled words in their Word Locker.

★★ All-Star Words   You may want to point out that the All-Star Words follow the spelling rule and show newspaper headlines as examples.

Lesson 17

Objective
To spell words with the /ou/ sound spelled by the diphthongs *ou* and *ow*

Correlated Phonics Lesson
MCP Phonics, Level F, Lesson 26

Warm Up   **Page 69**
In this selection, students learn fascinating facts about the ocean's most ferocious fish—the great white shark. After reading, invite students to share other facts they may know about sharks or other fish.

Encourage students to look back at the boldfaced words. Ask volunteers to say the words and compare the sounds that *ou* and *ow* stand for.

On Your Mark/Warm Up Test
1. A ***coward*** lacks courage in the face of danger.
2. Al ***drowsily*** climbed into bed after a busy day.
3. Heavy snow weighed down a ***bough*** of the tree.
4. The rich woman will ***endow*** a new school.
5. Don't talk when you have a ***mouthful*** of food.
6. Two words are joined to form a ***compound*** word.
7. A ***pronoun*** takes the place of a noun.
8. The entire ***household*** was awake at seven.
9. The swift current carried the canoe ***downstream***.
10. Is that store offering a ***discount*** on TV sets?
11. We like to hike in the hills ***surrounding*** the town.
12. Laura carefully ***pronounced*** each syllable.
13. The log cabin has a stone ***foundation***.
14. A ***resounding*** cheer came from the fans!
15. On Saturdays, I ***lounge*** around the house.
16. Will Mr. Lee ***announce*** the winner of the contest?
17. Leroy opened his own bank ***account***.
18. Night is the ***counterpart*** of day.
19. One customer thought the price was ***outrageous***.
20. A long ***drought*** can cause great damage to crops.

Pep Talk/Game Plan   **Pages 70–71**
Introduce the spelling rule and define the word *diphthong:* "two vowels blended together to form one sound." Then have students read the List Words aloud. Encourage them to look back at their Warm Up Tests and apply the spelling rule to any misspelled words.

As students work through the **Spelling Lineup,** **Missing Letters,** and **Puzzle** exercises, remind them to look back at their List Words or in their dictionaries if they need help.

 for ESL students See **Tape Recording,** page 15

---

ou and ow

Warm Up
What is the sea's most ferocious fish?

Great White

The white shark is known as a dangerous, man-eating monster. In fact, anyone who ran into one would probably feel like a **coward.** Much of what is said about this shark, however, isn't true. For one thing, the "white" shark is mostly grayish-brown. Only its underside is white. This shark isn't a man-eater, either. What is true about the white shark is that it's the sea's most ferocious fish.

Though not too smart, this fish seems programmed to rule the oceans. It can smell its prey—fish, squid, seals, sea lions, porpoises, and other sharks—in its **surrounding** area from as far as a quarter-mile away. Once attacked, few creatures can escape its steel-trap jaws. Its **mouthful** of teeth, serrated like a knife's blade, are as sharp as a razor's edge. When a tooth falls out, it is immediately replaced by another, equally powerful tooth.

Because few white sharks have been caught, no one is really sure how big they are. The smallest white shark ever found was just four feet long. The longest brought to shore was nearly 25 feet long and weighed more than an **outrageous** 7,000 pounds. That's larger than most houseboats. There has been more than one **account** of a white shark over 40 feet long. But that's probably just a fish story.

Look back at the boldfaced words in the selection. Say the words. Compare the sounds made by the letters **ou** and **ow.**

On Your Mark
Take your Warm Up Test. Then check your spelling with the List Words on the next page.

69

Pep Talk
The diphthongs **ou** and **ow** spell the /ou/ sound you hear in <u>bough</u> and <u>coward</u>.

Listen for the /ou/ sound in the List Words. Notice the letters that spell the /ou/ sound in each word.

LIST WORDS

1. coward
2. drowsily
3. bough
4. endow
5. mouthful
6. compound
7. pronoun
8. household
9. downstream
10. discount
11. surrounding
12. pronounced
13. foundation
14. resounding
15. lounge
16. announce
17. account
18. counterpart
19. outrageous
20. drought

Game Plan
Spelling Lineup
Write the List Words in the correct category to show how the /ou/ sound is spelled.

ou spells /ou/

1. bough
2. mouthful
3. compound
4. pronoun
5. household
6. discount
7. surrounding
8. pronounced
9. foundation
10. resounding
11. lounge
12. announce
13. account
14. counterpart
15. outrageous
16. drought

ow spells /ou/

17. coward
18. drowsily
19. endow
20. downstream

70   Lesson 17 ▪ ou and ow

Missing Letters

Fill in the missing letters to form List Words. Then
write the List Words on the lines.

1. d r o w sily   drowsily
2. c o w a rd   coward
3. b o u g h   bough
4. dis c o u nt   discount
5. dr o u g ht   drought
6. h o u s ehold   household

Puzzle

Fill in the crossword puzzle by writing a List Word to
answer each definition clue.

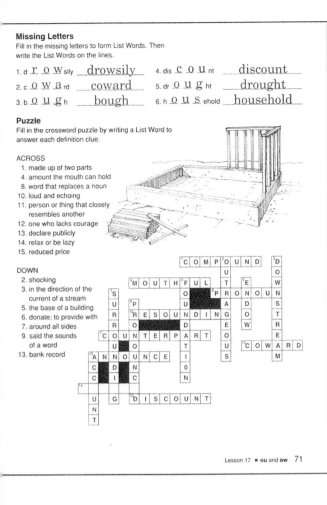

ACROSS
1. made up of two parts
4. amount the mouth can hold
8. word that replaces a noun
10. loud and echoing
11. person or thing that closely
   resembles another
12. one who lacks courage
13. declare publicly
14. relax or be lazy
15. reduced price

DOWN
2. shocking
3. in the direction of the
   current of a stream
5. the base of a building
6. donate; to provide with
7. around all sides
9. said the sounds
   of a word
13. bank record

Lesson 17 ■ ou and ow   71

Flex Your Spelling Muscles

Writing

Write a tall tale that features a shark. Make yourself the hero. The more
 your exaggerations, the better your tale will be. Try to use as
many List Words as you can.

Proofreading

This flyer for the Verne Aquarium has ten mistakes. Use the
proofreading marks to correct them. Write the misspelled
List Words correctly on the lines.

Proofreading Marks	
◯	spelling mistake
∧	add something

     Where can you have your picture taken with a white shark,
a penguin, or a seal? Where can everyone in your howshold
have outrajous fun watching a dolphin do tricks? Where can
you follow a river donstreem in a glass-bottomed boat? Where
can you lownge around and enjoy the ocean view? The
answer is at the Verne Aquarium. We are pleased to
announse that we now give a discownt to students, senior
citizens, and aquarium members.

1. household   4. lounge
2. outrageous   5. announce
3. downstream   6. discount

Now proofread your tall tale. Fix any mistakes.

Go for the Goal

Take your Final Test. Then fill in your Scoreboard. Send your
mistakes to the Word Locker.

SCOREBOARD
number correct	number wrong

★ ★ ★ ★ ★ ★ ★ ★ **All-Star Words** ★ ★ ★ ★ ★ ★ ★ ★

profound   counsel   founder   cauliflower   scowl

Create a crossword puzzle using the All-Star Words. Write clues and
draw an empty grid. Trade puzzles with a partner. Are you both able
to solve the puzzles?

◎ **Spelling Strategy**   Write *touch, flower, shout,
soup, tour, frown, dough, flown,* and *mountain* on the
board. Ask students to identify the words that contain
the same vowel sound as the List Words *account* and
coward (*flower, shout, frown, mountain*). As each word
is said, call students' attention to the /ou/ sound
spelled by *ou* or *ow*. Then invite students to call out
List Words, stressing the /ou/ sound and identifying
the diphthong that spells the sound.

Flex Your Spelling Muscles   *Page 72*
As students complete the **Writing** activity, encourage
them to brainstorm ideas, write a first draft, revise,
and proofread their work. The **Proofreading** exercise
will help them prepare to proofread their tall tales. To
publish their writing, students may want to plan a
"Festival of Tall Tales" and invite their families or
another class to be the audience.

✎ **Writer's Corner**

For information about "adopting" an animal, the
class can write to the American Association of
Zoological Parks and Aquariums, 4550 Montgomery
Ave., Suite 940N, Bethesda, MD 20814.

Go for the Goal/Final Test
1. Due to the **drought**, there is a water ban.
2. What an **outrageous** costume Sue wore!
3. I'd like to thank my **counterpart** for his help.
4. Only a **coward** would have run away like that.
5. The cat sat **drowsily** in the sun.
6. The **bough** of the tree is covered with flowers.
7. Will you put that check into a savings **account**?
8. Nature may **endow** any of us with special talents.
9. I will **announce** the names of the winners.
10. She took a big **mouthful** of pizza.
11. When I'm feeling lazy, I **lounge** in the hammock.
12. Are there two subjects in a **compound** sentence?
13. We gave Jerry a **resounding** round of applause.
14. Please replace that noun with a **pro.ioun**.
15. This house was built on a concrete **foundation**.
16. Every member of our **household** has chores.
17. Santos **pronounced** each word slowly and clearly.
18. We stopped rowing and drifted **downstream.**
19. **Surrounding** the grassy yard was a white fence.
20. Does this store sell shoes at **discount** prices?

Remind students to complete the Scoreboard and
write any misspelled words in their Word Locker.

★★ **All-Star Words**   You may want to point out
that the All-Star Words follow the spelling rule.
Suggest that students begin their puzzles by
arranging the All-Star Words, then drawing a blank
grid based on that arrangement.

Lesson 18 • Instant Replay

Objective
To review spelling words with /ō/: *oa, oe, ou,* and *ow; au* and *aw; oo, ew, ue, ui; ai, ay, oi,* and *oy; ou* and *ow*

Time Out   *Pages 73–76*
Check Your Word Locker Based on your observations, note which words are giving students the most difficulty and offer assistance for spelling them correctly. Here are some frequently misspelled words to watch for: *although, shoulders, exhausted, pursued, biscuit, maintenance, outrageous,* and *drought.*

To give students extra help and practice in taking standardized tests, you may want to have them take the Review Test for this lesson on pages 62–63. After scoring the tests, return them to students so that they can record their misspelled words in their Word Locker.

After practicing their troublesome words, students can work through the exercises for **Lessons 13–17.** Before they begin each exercise, you may want to go over the spelling rule.

Take It Home Invite students to choose a List Word from **Lessons 13–17** for each day of the week. Students can tell their families that they are going to use a "secret word" in conversation each day. At night, students can ask their family members to name the word. For a complete list of the words, encourage students to take their *Spelling Workout* books home. They can also use Take It Home Master 3 on pages 64–65 to help them do the activity. In class, students can share their experiences and discuss which List Words were easy and which were difficult to use in conversation.

Instant Replay • Lessons 13–17   LESSON 18

Time Out
Look again at the spelling of vowel sounds in words. Some vowel sounds can be spelled many different ways.

Check Your Word Locker
Look at the words in your Word Locker. Write your most troublesome words from Lessons 13 through 17.

_____

Practice writing your troublesome words with a partner. Write the words on slips of paper and put them in a container. Take turns drawing a word, illustrating it, and having the other person guess the word.

Lesson 13
The /ō/ sound can be spelled in more than one way: **oa,** as in cocoa; **oe,** as in mistletoe; **ou,** as in boulders; and **ow,** as in bowling.

List Words

bowling
yellow
growth
approaches
boulders
thoroughly
cocoa
oboe
rowboat
shoulders

Write a List Word to complete each sentence.

1. School buses are often ___ yellow ___.
2. That jacket is tight across your ___ shoulders ___
3. If a dog ___ approaches ___ with its tail wagging, you don't have to worry.
4. Wear a life jacket in the ___ rowboat ___
5. An ___ oboe ___ is a woodwind instrument.
6. These ___ boulders ___ are blocking the path.
7. Make sure the ___ cocoa ___ is not too hot.
8. I'm getting better at ___ bowling ___ with our team.
9. Plant ___ growth ___ depends upon light and water.
10. Mix the batter ___ thoroughly ___ to make it smooth.

73

Lesson 14
The /ô/ sound can be spelled with **au,** as in dinosaur, and **aw,** as in drawback.

List Words

brawny
paused
autumn
awesome
exhausted
squawking
drawback
authentic
withdrawal
applause

Write a List Word that means the same or almost the same as the word given.

1. fatigued ___ exhausted ___
2. waited ___ paused ___
3. clapping ___ applause ___
4. muscular ___ brawny ___
5. clucking ___ squawking ___
6. genuine ___ authentic ___
7. fall ___ autumn ___
8. removal ___ withdrawal ___
9. wonderful ___ awesome ___
10. shortcoming ___ drawback ___

Lesson 15
The /yo͞o/ sound can be spelled **ew,** as in pewter. The /o͞o/ sound can be spelled in several ways: **ew,** as in mildew; **ue,** as in pursued; **oo,** as in smoother; **ui,** as in juicy. The /i/ sound can also be spelled with **ui,** as in circuit.

List Words

mildew
guitar
pewter
quilted
cruise
shampoo
biscuit
pursued
nuisance
soothing

Write the List Word that belongs in each group.

1. bother, annoyance, ___ nuisance ___
2. copper, bronze, ___ pewter ___
3. mold, fungus, ___ mildew ___
4. soap, detergent, ___ shampoo ___
5. sewed, stitched, ___ quilted ___
6. chased, followed, ___ pursued ___
7. banjo, mandolin, ___ guitar ___
8. muffin, toast, ___ biscuit ___
9. calming, quieting, ___ soothing ___
10. voyage, trip, ___ cruise ___

74 Lesson 18 ■ Instant Replay

60

The /ā/ sound can be spelled with **ay**, as in crayons, and **ai**, as in strainer. The /oi/ sound can be spelled with **oy**, as in employment, and **oi**, as in exploit.

List Words

essays
boiled
oysters
maintenance
employment
ointment
praised
container
faithful
avoided

Write the List Words that fit each description.

1. What the people did who turned down every job:

  avoided   employment

2. What the teacher who liked my writing did:

  praised my essays

3. What you could call a jar for a creamy medicine:

  an ointment container

4. One kind of cooked shellfish:

  boiled   oysters

5. What you could call regular painting of a house:

  faithful maintenance

Lesson 17

The /ou/ sound can be spelled two ways: **ou**, as in surrounding, and **ow**, as in drowsily.

List Words

coward
bough
mouthful
compound
pronoun
discount
foundation
lounge
announce
outrageous

Write a List Word to match each clue.

1. tree part _____ bough
2. a room to relax in _____ lounge
3. a bargain price _____ discount
4. base of a house _____ foundation
5. shocking; excessive _____ outrageous
6. proclaim, make known _____ announce
7. don't talk with this _____ mouthful
8. he, she, it, or they _____ pronoun
9. mixture made of two or more parts _____ compound
10. a person who lacks courage _____ coward

Lesson 18 ■ Instant Replay 75

Lessons 13–17

List Words

maintenance
autumn
essays
guitar
thoroughly
exhausted
authentic
container
mouthful
shampoo
avoided
boulders
nuisance
cocoa
lounge

Write a List Word to answer each definition clue.

1. extremely tired exhausted
2. warm drink made with milk cocoa
3. hair cleaner shampoo
4. stayed away from avoided
5. upkeep maintenance
6. a season of the year autumn
7. real and genuine authentic
8. lie around lounge
9. completely thoroughly
10. musical instrument guitar
11. written works essays
12. big rocks boulders
13. jar, box, carton container
14. more than a taste mouthful
15. pest nuisance

Go for the Goal

Take your Final Replay Test. Then fill in your Scoreboard.
Send any misspelled words to your Word Locker.

SCOREBOARD

number correct	number wrong

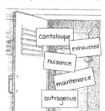

Clean Out Your Word Locker
Look in your Word Locker. Cross out each word you spelled correctly on your Final Replay Test. Circle the words you're still having trouble with. Add the words you circled to your Spelling Notebook. What do you notice about the words? Watch for those words as you write.

76 Lesson 18 ■ Instant Replay

Go for the Goal/Final Replay Test   *Page 76*

1. The book's ending left me ***thoroughly*** confused.
2. After skiing, this ***cocoa*** will warm you up.
3. An ***oboe*** makes a soft, mellow sound.
4. We pulled the ***rowboat*** onto the dock to paint it.
5. I wear pads on my ***shoulders*** for football.
6. The ***brawny*** workers moved the heavy boxes.
7. We ***paused*** at the door to speak to Pedro.
8. Will those flowers bloom until ***autumn?***
9. The Grand Canyon is ***awesome*** to see.
10. The chickens' ***squawking*** woke us early.
11. I think that bottle of ***shampoo*** is empty.
12. Don't eat that ***biscuit*** because it's burned.
13. The dog ***pursued*** the cat across the field.
14. These tiny buttons are a ***nuisance*** to use!
15. Don't you find the sound of waves ***soothing?***
16. Everyone wrote ***essays*** on different topics.
17. We are having ***boiled*** potatoes with chicken.
18. Only very fresh raw ***oysters*** are safe to eat.
19. Cars run better with regular ***maintenance.***
20. The ads were run by ***employment*** agencies.
21. The ***foundation*** of a house must be strong.
22. Please carry that ***lounge*** chair into the shade.
23. Do you have some news to ***announce?***
24. Some ***compound*** words are hyphenated.
25. What an ***outrageous*** thing to say!
26. On Saturdays my friends and I go ***bowling.***
27. Let's paint the room a cheerful ***yellow.***
28. This city's ***growth*** has been very rapid.
29. Watch as the bird ***approaches*** the feeder.
30. Aren't those ***boulders*** too large to move?
31. I can find only one ***drawback*** to your plan.
32. Everyone was ***exhausted*** after the soccer game.
33. At the museum we saw an ***authentic*** Ming vase.
34. Judy made a cash ***withdrawal*** from the bank.
35. The symphony ended and the ***applause*** began.
36. Use chlorine bleach to remove that ***mildew.***
37. Would you please play your ***guitar*** for me?
38. These old plates are made of ***pewter.***
39. A beautiful ***quilted*** bedspread hung on the wall.
40. The travel agent told us about a weekend ***cruise.***
41. You can buy that ***ointment*** in a tube or a jar.
42. Everyone ***praised*** the lasagna that I made.
43. Carry the juice in a ***container*** with a lid.
44. Jody was a ***faithful*** companion during the trip.
45. We ***avoided*** standing near the edge of the cliff.
46. Alan was careful, but he was no ***coward.***
47. During the storm, a ***bough*** fell from the tree.
48. Lawanda took a ***mouthful*** of spinach soup.
49. A singular ***pronoun*** replaces a singular noun.
50. Why don't you buy a radio at a ***discount*** store?

Clean Out Your Word Locker   Encourage students to say each word, emphasizing the vowel sound they hear, and to identify the letters that spell the sound.

61

Instant Replay Test

Side A

Read each sentence and set of words. Fill in the circle next to the word that is spelled correctly to complete the sentence.

1. This applicant is seeking _____ in the engineering department.
   - ⓐ emploiment
   - ⓒ employement
   - ⓑ employmint
   - ⓓ employment

2. Autumn foliage is an _____ sight in Vermont.
   - ⓐ ausome
   - ⓒ awsome
   - ⓑ awesome
   - ⓓ auesome

3. Jellyfish and seaweed are both _____ words.
   - ⓐ compounde
   - ⓒ compound
   - ⓑ compownde
   - ⓓ compownd

4. Hot _____ is a popular beverage in the wintertime.
   - ⓐ coacoe
   - ⓒ cocoa
   - ⓑ cocoe
   - ⓓ coaco

5. A damp cellar provides favorable conditions for _____ growth.
   - ⓐ mildew
   - ⓒ mildue
   - ⓑ milldew
   - ⓓ milldue

6. Tomorrow the principal will _____ the winning contestants' names.
   - ⓐ anownce
   - ⓒ anounce
   - ⓑ announce
   - ⓓ annonce

7. When the basement for our house was excavated, huge _____ were uncovered.
   - ⓐ boalders
   - ⓒ bolders
   - ⓑ boulders
   - ⓓ boleders

8. The hurricane caused a gigantic _____ from our willow tree to fall.
   - ⓐ bough
   - ⓒ bowgh
   - ⓑ bugh
   - ⓓ bogh

Instant Replay Test

Side B

ead each sentence and set of words. Fill in the circle next to the word that is
elled correctly to complete the sentence.

9. Some of the town's historic buildings require costly _____.
   - (a) maintenence
   - (c) maintanence
   - (b) maintenance
   - (d) maintainance

0. An infant's _____ is carefully recorded by a physician.
   - (a) growthe
   - (c) groth
   - (b) groath
   - (d) growth

1. His sister has _____ a career in dentistry.
   - (a) pursued
   - (c) pursood
   - (b) persood
   - (d) persued

2. Consult a jeweler to determine whether the diamond is _____.
   - (a) authentic
   - (c) authentick
   - (b) awthentick
   - (d) awthentic

3. This _____ is formulated to shield skin from the sun's harmful rays.
   - (a) oyntment
   - (c) ointement
   - (b) ountment
   - (d) ointment

4. That _____ blanket was hand-stitched by my stepmother.
   - (a) quielted
   - (c) cuilted
   - (b) kwuilted
   - (d) quilted

5. The comedian appreciated the audience's exuberant _____.
   - (a) aplause
   - (c) applause
   - (b) applawse
   - (d) aplawse

TAKE IT HOME

Your child has learned to spell many new words and would like to share them with you and your family. Here are some idea that will make reviewing the words in Lessons 13–17 fun for everyone.

Secrets of Spelling

Every day this week, try to guess the secret spelling word that your child has chosen and is using in conversations. After you guess each word, don't keep its spelling to yourself—spell it aloud together!

Sky Spelling

Encourage your child to complete the spelling words that the skywriters have begun.

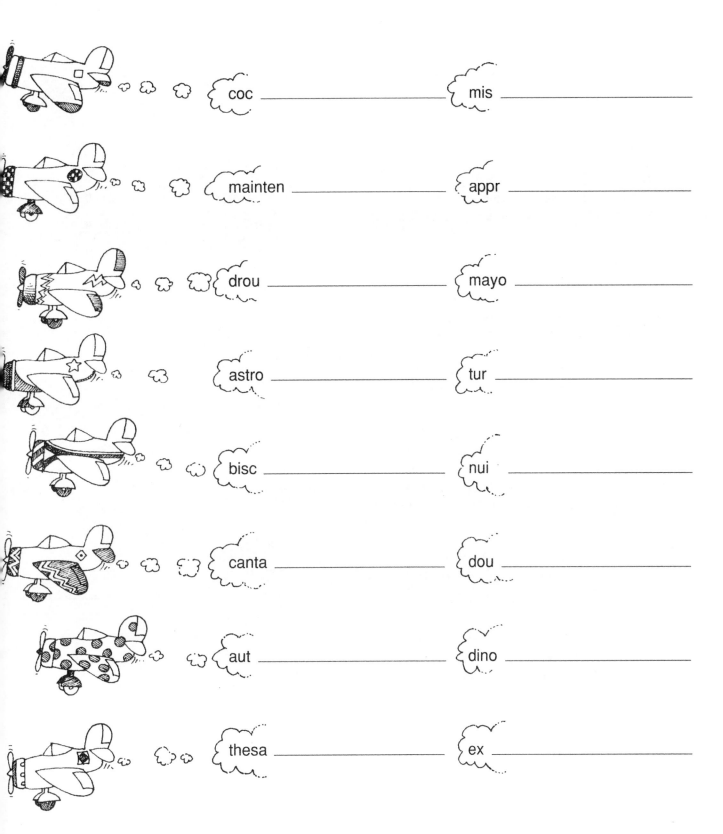

coc _____

mis _____

mainten _____

appr _____

drou _____

mayo _____

astro _____

tur _____

bisc _____

nui _____

canta _____

dou _____

aut _____

dino _____

thesa _____

ex _____

Lesson 19

Objective
To spell words with the digraphs *ei* and *ie*

Correlated Phonics Lessons
MCP Phonics, Level F, Lessons 15, 19–20

Warm Up   *Page 77*
Students may enjoy learning about the Japanese bonsai tree in "Tiny Trees." After reading, ask students why they would or would not like to have a bonsai tree.

Call on volunteers to say each boldfaced word and tell whether it contains *ei* or *ie*.

On Your Mark/ Warm Up Test
1. In the fable, *conceit* caused a lot of trouble.
2. The *sleigh* sped over the snow-covered road.
3. Our school nurse will measure everyone's *height.*
4. A *veil* of clouds hid the mountains.
5. Last night the army *seized* the fort.
6. A careful driver always *yields* the right of way.
7. The explorer saw *weird* shadows in the cave.
8. We promise to stay out of *mischief!*
9. Greeting others warmly is a *neighborly* act.
10. Can *reindeer* pull several hundred pounds?
11. The hurricane winds blew *fiercely* all day long.
12. That character's actions were *unbelievable!*
13. We met *briefly* at a party last week.
14. The knight's armor was never *pierced.*
15. Many cars now have *diesel* engines.
16. Through the window we *perceived* a small fire.
17. I was *relieved* when the long flight was over.
18. Foods high in *protein* must be properly cooked.
19. Were these stones part of an *ancient* castle?
20. Carl must *retrieve* the book he left behind.

Pep Talk/Game Plan   *Pages 78–79*
Introduce the spelling rule and have students read the List Words aloud. Encourage students to look back at their Warm Up Tests and apply the spelling rule to any misspelled words.

As students work through the **Spelling Lineup,** **Comparing Words,** and **Puzzle** exercises, remind them to look back at their List Words or in their dictionaries if they need help. For the **Comparing Words** exercise, review analogies by writing this example on the board: <u>Leaf</u> is to <u>tree</u> as <u>feather</u> is to <u>bird</u>. Help students conclude that a leaf covers a branch of a tree as a feather covers part of a bird.

 See **Picture Clues,** page 15

66

Name _____

ei and ie

 LESSON 19

Warm Up
What is the name of a tiny tree in Japan?

Tiny Trees

Japan is a small country, about the size of Montana. Yet 124 million people—the same number of people that live in America's ten most populated states combined—live there. Because of the limited space, the Japanese have developed smaller versions of many things. Japanese cars, for example, were among the first to come in compact sizes. Japanese houses, too, are small. Likewise, miniature gardens surround houses in Japan.

One of the most remarkable achievements in size reduction is the creation of the bonsai. The word *bonsai* means "trees in pots." When looking at a picture of a bonsai tree on a plain background, it may be **perceived** to be as large as a giant oak. It is perfectly formed. Its branches arch and drape just like a tree in a forest. Yet the picture may deceive you. A bonsai tree is usually no more than two feet in **height.** A bonsai cypress tree, for example, reaches just 19 inches tall. A bonsai maple tree grows red leaves smaller than your fingernail.

Growing bonsai trees is an **ancient** art. Some of the trees, too, are nearly ancient. It may seem **unbelievable,** but a bonsai can live in a small pot for 200 years or more. Some are handed down in families from parent to child. Each generation takes its turn bending and pruning the branches to keep the tree from growing larger. A grower's patience is rewarded with a forest that can fit in the palm of a hand.

Look back at the boldfaced words. Which words contain the vowel digraph **ei**? Which words contain the vowel digraph **ie**?

On Your Mark
Take your Warm Up Test. Then check your spelling with the List Words on the next page.

77

Pep Talk
Here's a helpful rhyme you can use when spelling words that contain the vowel digraphs ie or ei:
I before E except after C
as in retrieved or conceit,
or when sounded like A
as in neighborly or sleigh.
There are exceptions to this rule, as in weird and height.

LIST WORDS
1. conceit
2. sleigh
3. height
4. veil
5. seized
6. yields
7. weird
8. mischief
9. neighborly
10. reindeer
11. fiercely
12. unbelievable
13. briefly
14. pierced
15. diesel
16. perceived
17. relieved
18. protein
19. ancient
20. retrieve

Game Plan
Spelling Lineup
Write each List Word under the correct heading.

ie spells /ē/	ei spells /ā/
1. yields	11. sleigh
2. fiercely	12. veil
3. unbelievable	13. neighborly
4. briefly	14. reindeer
5. pierced	
6. diesel	**ie or ei—no rule**
7. relieved	15. height
8. retrieve	16. seized
	17. weird
ei after c spells /ē/	18. mischief
9. conceit	19. protein
10. perceive	20. ancient

78   Lesson 19 ▪ ei and ie

Comparing Words

Study the relationship between the first two underlined words or phrases. Then write a List Word that has the same relationship with the third underlined word.

1. Orange is to vitamin C as cheese is to _____ protein
2. Gave is to took as provided is to _____ seized
3. Water is to rowboat as snow is to _____ sleigh
4. Heavy is to weight as tall is to _____ height
5. Young is to new as old is to _____ ancient
6. Friend is to neighbor as friendly is to _____ neighborly
7. Knife is to sliced as arrow is to _____ pierced
8. Generosity is to stinginess as modesty is to _____ conceit
9. Happy is to content as strange is to _____ weird
10. Causing problems is to trouble as playing pranks is to _____ mischief
11. Tusk is to elephant as antler is to _____ reindeer
12. Hear is to heard as perceive is to _____ perceived
13. Furniture is to chair as covering is to _____ veil

Puzzle

Fill in the puzzle by writing a List Word to answer each definition clue. Then read across the shaded boxes to find out how these List Words are spelled.

1. for a short time
2. not likely
3. type of engine
4. wildly
5. fetch
6. gives way to
7. eased

Lesson 19 ■ ei and ie 79

Flex Your Spelling Muscles

Writing

You and your neighbors have received a notice that an ancient tree in your neighborhood is about to be cut down. Write a letter to the City Council to protest the action. Use as many List Words as you can.

Proofreading

This myth has eleven mistakes. Use the proofreading marks to correct them. Write the misspelled List Words correctly on the lines.

Proofreading Marks	
⌒	spelling mistake
⌄⌄ ⌄⌄	add quotation marks
¶	indent paragraph

"Your pointy leaves are weard," said Oak Tree. "That's not very naighborley," said Pine Tree. "Mine are ever so much more beautiful," said Oak Tree. "I'd be relived if you found another forest to live in." North Wind did not like Oak Tree's conseit. She blew feersely causing all of Oak Tree's leaves to fall. Oak Tree tried desperately to retreave his leaves, but he couldn't. That is why oak trees lose their leaves every autumn.

1. ___weird___ 4. ___conceit___
2. ___neighborly___ 5. ___fiercely___
3. ___relieved___ 6. ___retrieve___

Now proofread your own letter. Fix any mistakes.

Go for the Goal

Take your Final Test. Then fill in your Scoreboard. Send your mistakes to the Word Locker.

SCOREBOARD	
number correct	number wrong

★ ★ ★ ★ ★ ★ ★ ★ All-Star Words ★ ★ ★ ★ ★ ★ ★ ★

mischievous   receipt   freight   debrief   masterpiece

Write a tongue twister for each All-Star Word, leaving a blank where the word should go. Trade papers and fill in the missing words. Can you read the completed twisters aloud without twisting your tongue?

80 Lesson 19 ■ ei and ie

◎ **Spelling Strategy** Ask the class to identify the List Words in which *i* comes before *e*. Write these words on the board and underline the digraph *ie*. Then repeat the rhyme in the Pep Talk box and ask students to name the List Words in which *ei* spells the long *a* sound or follows *c*. Add the words to the board, underlining *ei*. Point out to students that some of the List Words (*weird, height, ancient, seized, protein*) do not follow the spelling rule.

Flex Your Spelling Muscles   *Page 80*

As students complete the **Writing** activity, encourage them to brainstorm ideas, write a first draft, revise, and proofread their work. The **Proofreading** exercise will help them prepare to proofread their letters. To publish their writing, students may want to use their letters to develop a play called "Spare That Tree!"

✍ Writer's Corner

Explain to students that origami, or paper-folding, is a popular art form in Japan. Encourage students to read a book such as *Easy Origami* by Dokuihtei Nakano and to make their own origami figures. Students can write a verse or a short poem to display with their artwork.

Go for the Goal/Final Test

1. Yolanda *pierced* the leather with a sharp needle.
2. The dogs get into *mischief* when they're alone.
3. Allen shows self-confidence but no *conceit.*
4. We were *relieved* to hear that you arrived safely.
5. Can Mika *retrieve* the kite from that tree?
6. The *weird* sounds made by the wind scared us.
7. The lion *fiercely* defended her young.
8. The *veil* on this wedding gown is antique lace.
9. My grandfather had an old horse-drawn *sleigh.*
10. Through the fog, the sailor *perceived* a ship.
11. The light flickered *briefly* and then went out.
12. From this *height* you can see the entire city.
13. The car on the left *yields* to the one on the right.
14. Was Pompeii an important city in *ancient* times?
15. Some of the stories Tim told were *unbelievable!*
16. A *diesel* engine uses a special kind of fuel.
17. They were *neighborly* and let us use their phone.
18. Thirsty runners *seized* the cups of water.
19. Meat, dairy products, and eggs contain *protein.*
20. In Lapland, *reindeer* roam in large herds.

Remind students to complete the Scoreboard and write any misspelled words in their Word Locker.

★★ **All-Star Words** You may want to point out that the All-Star Words follow the spelling rule and review the meaning of a tongue twister.

Lesson 20

Objective
To spell words with the prefixes *ir, in, il,* and *im*

Correlated Phonics Lesson
MCP Phonics, Level F, Lesson 30

Warm Up   *Page 81*
In "About Face," students learn about the connection between the ancient Roman god Janus and the modern custom of making New Year's resolutions. Afterward, invite students to discuss New Year's resolutions they have made.

Encourage students to look back at the boldfaced words. Ask volunteers to say the words and to identify the prefixes.

On Your Mark/Warm Up Test
1. No one took the *incredible* story seriously.
2. The work of great artists is *immortal.*
3. Some people are *intolerant* of new ideas.
4. My grandfather was an *immigrant* from England.
5. Doesn't their hasty decision seem *illogical?*
6. *Immature* trees need plenty of water to grow.
7. It is *illegal* to go over the speed limit.
8. I put the model car together *improperly.*
9. Babies are *incapable* of caring for themselves.
10. Some singular nouns have *irregular* plural forms.
11. Did waiting for the bus make you *impatient?*
12. The people in the theater behaved *impolitely.*
13. We were late because we took an *indirect* route.
14. We left our plans *indefinite* so we could relax.
15. A judge ruled that her testimony was *immaterial.*
16. Liz is teaching an *illiterate* man how to read.
17. Why do you think that our plan is *impractical?*
18. Leaving matches near toddlers is *irresponsible!*
19. The man lost his temper and became *irrational.*
20. Please correct any words that are *illegible.*

Pep Talk/Game Plan   *Pages 82–83*
Introduce the spelling rule and ask students to read the List Words aloud, having them define each word using *not* or *to.* Then encourage students to look back at their Warm Up Tests and apply the spelling rule to any misspelled words.

As students work through the **Spelling Lineup, Missing Words,** and **Alphabetical Order** exercises, remind them to look back at their List Words or in their dictionaries if they need help.

 See **Comparing/Contrasting,** page 15

68

Prefixes ir, in, il, and im

Warm Up
Why do we make New Year's resolutions?

About Face

To the ancient Romans, Janus was an **immortal** god who represented new beginnings. Janus was portrayed as a bearded figure with two faces. One face looked west—toward the setting sun. The other face looked east—toward the new day. The face that looked at the past was old. The one facing the dawn was that of an **immature** youth. Janus inspired the Romans to review the past and to look toward the future with hope. We do not worship the god Janus today, but his inspiration, and even his name, are with us. January, the first month of the year, is named in honor of Janus. On January 1st, we, too, review the past and look forward to the new year with hope.

Though it may be **illogical,** people make New Year's resolutions every January 1st. On this day, we become **intolerant** of our imperfections, and we vow never to be **irresponsible** again. We may decide to stop being impolite or **impatient.** Deciding to be perfect is an **impractical** goal, however. No one, not even Janus, can do a complete about-face!

 Look back at the boldfaced words in the selection. These words have prefixes at the beginning of each word. How many prefixes can you find?

On Your Mark
Take your Warm Up Test. Then check your spelling with the List Words on the next page.

81

Pep Talk
The prefixes **ir, in, il,** and **im** usually mean not, as in irregular, incapable, illegal, and immature.
The prefix **im** can also mean to, as in immigrant.
Here are some helpful spelling rules:
- Words that follow the prefix **im** begin with **m** or **p.**
- Words that follow the prefix **il** begin with the letter **l.**
- Words that follow the prefix **ir** begin with the letter **r.**
- Words that follow the prefix **in** begin with several different letters.

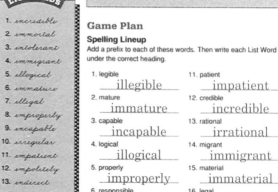

LIST WORDS
1. incredible
2. immortal
3. intolerant
4. immigrant
5. illogical
6. immature
7. illegal
8. improperly
9. incapable
10. irregular
11. impatient
12. impolitely
13. indirect
14. indefinite
15. immaterial
16. illiterate
17. impractical
18. irresponsible
19. irrational
20. illegible

Game Plan
Spelling Lineup
Add a prefix to each of these words. Then write each List Word under the correct heading.

1. legible ___illegible___
2. mature ___immature___
3. capable ___incapable___
4. logical ___illogical___
5. properly ___improperly___
6. responsible ___irresponsible___
7. direct ___indirect___
8. practical ___impractical___
9. tolerant ___intolerant___
10. politely ___impolitely___
11. patient ___impatient___
12. credible ___incredible___
13. rational ___irrational___
14. migrant ___immigrant___
15. material ___immaterial___
16. legal ___illegal___
17. literate ___illiterate___
18. definite ___indefinite___
19. mortal ___immortal___
20. regular ___irregular___

82 Lesson 20 ▪ Prefixes ir, in, il, and im

Missing Words

Write a List Word to complete each sentence.

1. A person who acts childishly is _immature_.
2. A person who has little patience is _impatient_.
3. An _illiterate_ person cannot read and write.
4. Something that is _illegal_ is against the law.
5. A person who moves to a new country is an _immigrant_.
6. Something that will never die is called _immortal_.
7. A piece of writing that is impossible to read is _illegible_.
8. A plan that will not work well is called _impractical_.
9. Something that is difficult to believe is _incredible_.
10. Something that really doesn't matter is _immaterial_.

Alphabetical Order

Write the List Words in alphabetical order.

1.	illegal	15.	indefinite
2.	illegible	16.	indirect
3.	illiterate	17.	intolerant
4.	illogical	18.	irrational
5.	immaterial	19.	irregular
6.	immature	20.	irresponsible
7.	immigrant		
8.	immortal		
9.	impatient		
10.	impolitely		
11.	impractical		
12.	improperly		
13.	incapable		
14.	incredible		

Flex Your Spelling Muscles

Writing
A resolution is something that you resolve or decide to do. Write one or more resolutions that you feel everyone should try to keep. Write an explanation saying why you feel these resolutions are important.

Proofreading
This magazine article has eight mistakes. Use the proofreading marks to correct them. Write the misspelled List Words correctly on the lines.

Proofreading Marks
- ⌒ spelling mistake
- ≡ capital letter
- ⊙ add period
- ∧ add something

Are winter blues making you (inpatiant) for spring? Don't just lie around and moan. Remember, january is a good month to do some new or different things.
- Tutor someone who is (literite)
- Spend the day in bed reading an (imcreditable) adventure story⊙
- Clean out a closet and give away those (inpractical) gadgets that gather dust.
- Try to master something that you assumed you were (ircapible) of learning.

1. _impatient_
2. _illiterate_
3. _incredible_
4. _impractical_
5. _incapable_

Now proofread your resolutions and explanation. Fix any mistakes.

Go for the Goal
Take your Final Test. Then fill in your Scoreboard. Send your mistakes to the Word Locker.

SCOREBOARD

number correct	number wrong

★ ★ ★ ★ ★ ★ ★ ★ **All-Star Words** ★ ★ ★ ★ ★ ★ ★ ★

inability   irrelevant   illuminate   imperfect   imprint

Divide the list of All-Star Words between you and a partner. Write a real and a made-up definition for each of your words. See if you can match each of your partner's words with its correct definition.

Spelling Strategy
With a partner, students can write the List Words and
- circle the prefix in each word
- point to and name the letter that immediately follows the prefix
- orally complete this sentence: "Root words that follow the prefix_____begin with the letter_____."

Flex Your Spelling Muscles   Page 84
As students complete the **Writing** activity, encourage them to brainstorm ideas, write a first draft, revise, and proofread their work. The **Proofreading** exercise will help them prepare to proofread their resolutions and explanations. To publish their writing, students may want to
- have a class discussion based on their resolutions
- take their resolutions home and share them with a family member.

Writer's Corner

Students may enjoy reading a mythology book, such as *Words from the Myths* by Isaac Asimov. Encourage them to take notes as they research and to share the information they gather with their classmates.

Go for the Goal/Final Test
1. The coat of an *immature* deer is spotted.
2. All human beings are born *illiterate.*
3. I become *impatient* when I have to wait.
4. Frank's artistic talents are *incredible!*
5. Did you find the plot of the movie *illogical?*
6. That fact is *immaterial* to the case.
7. Write slowly or your answers may be *illegible.*
8. This strange pumpkin has an *irregular* shape.
9. The child was *incapable* of lifting the trunk.
10. The schedule for our summer trip is *indefinite.*
11. Anger may make a person *irrational.*
12. My neighbor is an *immigrant* from Russia.
13. At first, I held the chopsticks *improperly.*
14. I'm *intolerant* of the barking dog next door.
15. I won't accept an *indirect* answer.
16. It's *irresponsible* to leave the keys in a car.
17. The poems of Emily Dickinson are *immortal.*
18. Is it *illegal* to own an unlicensed dog?
19. Teaching cows to read is totally *impractical!*
20. I'm sorry I acted *impolitely* at lunch.

Remind students to complete the Scoreboard and write any misspelled words in their Word Locker.

★★ **All-Star Words** You may want to point out that the All-Star Words follow the spelling rule. Refer students to their dictionaries so they can follow its style for writing definitions.

Lesson 21

Objective
To spell words with the prefixes *de, pre, pro, con, com,* and *mis*

Correlated Phonics Lessons
MCP Phonics, Level F, Lessons 32, 35

Warm Up   **Page 85**
In this selection, students find out how deadly fights with a sword have evolved into the Olympic sport of fencing. After reading, ask students why they would or wouldn't like to try fencing.

Call on volunteers to say the boldfaced words and identify the different prefixes.

On Your Mark/Warm Up Test
1. Jim uses a pole when ***propelling*** his raft.
2. Did your school send ***competitors*** to the contest?
3. There is a ***provision*** for shelter if it rains.
4. Mrs. Lu met other engineers at the ***conference.***
5. We talked on a ***previous*** occasion.
6. Danita will ***dedicate*** this song to her best friend.
7. The millionaire ***deposited*** cash in many accounts.
8. What a silly ***complaint*** they made!
9. The lion cubs ***depended*** on their mother.
10. I felt better when the humidity ***decreased.***
11. Has the weather forecaster ***predicted*** snow?
12. Computers have helped industry to ***progress.***
13. I ***misunderstood*** the directions and got lost.
14. The driver was ***confused*** about which way to go.
15. I ***presume*** that you are tired after your trip.
16. Some medicines require a doctor's ***prescription.***
17. The French tourist ***mispronounced*** some words.
18. A fence ***prevented*** the cows from wandering off.
19. The witness felt ***compelled*** to tell the truth.
20. We would like a ***confirmation*** of our reservation.

Pep Talk/Game Plan   **Pages 86–87**
Introduce the spelling rule and have students read the List Words aloud. Encourage students to look back at their Warm Up Tests and apply the spelling rule to any misspelled words.

As students work through the **Spelling Lineup, Word Parts,** and **Missing Words** exercises, remind them to look back at their List Words or in their dictionaries if they need help. For the **Word Parts** exercise, remind students that a new word can be formed by using a different prefix. As an example, write *product, induct,* and *conduct* on the board.

 See **Charades/Pantomime,** page 15

70

Warm Up
What Olympic sport involves attacking your opponent with a foil, or sword?

Touché

Imagine yourself in a duel. A fencing sword is just inches from your body. You can't predict your opponent's next move. If you **propel** yourself toward your rival, you may catch him or her off guard. If you make a wrong move, however, you could be jabbed with the point of a foil, a 35-inch blade used in fencing.

Fencing is somewhat of a **misunderstood** sport. Those who **dedicate** their time to the sport do not want their fans to be **confused.** Some fans **presume** that the competitors get hurt. That is not the case today.

Fencing **competitors** used to engage in a duel to settle an argument. Only the winner survived. Today, however, fencing has endured **progress** and is now an Olympic sport; it is practiced just for show. Instead of dueling to the death, each fencer wears protective clothing. This includes a wired face mask, gloves, and a wired vest. If one fencer's foil touches the other's vest, the touch (called *touché*) is recorded electronically. A judge then determines if the touch is valid. The judge makes the decision based on whether or not the fencer used a proper defense, or parry. After all, had you left yourself open to attack while trying to touch your opponent, it wouldn't have been a good defense. The fencer must also be ready for a counterattack, or riposte. In other words, to score a point, your opponent must get the point!

 Say the boldfaced words in the selection. These words have prefixes at the beginning of each word. How many prefixes can you find?

On Your Mark
Take your Warm Up Test. Then check your spelling with the List Words on the next page.

85

Pep Talk
The prefixes **pre** and **pro** usually mean <u>before</u>. **Pro** can also mean <u>forward.</u>
The prefix **de** means <u>down</u>, <u>not</u>, or <u>reverse.</u> **De** can also mean <u>apart</u> or <u>aside.</u>
The prefixes **con** and **com** mean <u>with</u> or <u>together.</u>
The prefix **mis** usually means <u>bad</u> or <u>badly.</u>

LIST WORDS

1. propelling
2. competitors
3. provision
4. conference
5. previous
6. dedicate
7. deposited
8. complaint
9. depended
10. decreased
11. predicted
12. progress
13. misunderstood
14. confused
15. presume
16. prescription
17. mispronounced
18. prevented
19. compelled
20. confirmation

Game Plan
Spelling Lineup
Write the List Words under the correct category.

Words with the prefix **pre** or **pro**	Words with the prefix **con** or **com**
1. propelling	13. competitors
2. provision	14. conference
3. previous	15. complaint
4. predicted	16. confused
5. progress	17. compelled
6. presume	18. confirmation
7. prescription	
8. prevented	Words with the prefix **mis**
	19. misunderstood
Words with the prefix **de**	20. mispronounced
9. dedicate	
10. deposited	
11. depended	
12. decreased	

 complaints

86 Lesson 21 ■ Prefixes **de, pre, pro, con, com,** and **mis**

Word Parts

Write a List Word that contains the same root as the word given.

1. increase __decreased__
2. refuse __confused__
3. invented __prevented__
4. devious __previous__
5. compelling __propelling__
6. inference __conference__
7. indicate __dedicate__
8. division __provision__
9. inscription __prescription__
10. announce __mispronounced__
11. assume __presume__
12. suspended __depended__
13. affirmation __confirmation__
14. digress __progress__

Missing Words

Write a List Word to complete each sentence.

1. The meteorologist __predicted__ that it would rain today.
2. We are here to __dedicate__ this statue to the memory of a great hero.
3. There were many __competitors__ trying for first place.
4. Kathy filed a __complaint__ against her employer when he refused to pay her.
5. Jon __misunderstood__ you and drove to the wrong address.
6. They __deposited__ all their money into a joint savings account.
7. Louisa __depended__ on her brother to drive her to work.
8. Manny felt __compelled__ to tell his mother about his low test grade.

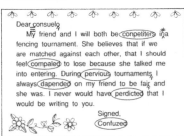

Lesson 21 ■ Prefixes **de**, **pre**, **pro**, **con**, **com**, and **mis** 87

Flex Your Spelling Muscles

Writing

Don't settle an argument by fencing. Instead, write a letter asking Consuelo, the advice columnist, to settle it for you. Once you write your letter, write Consuelo's answer. Use as many List Words as you can.

Proofreading

This letter has eleven mistakes. Use the proofreading marks to correct them. Write the misspelled List Words correctly on the lines.

Proofreading Marks
- ⬭ spelling mistake
- ≡ capital letter
- ∧ add something

Dear consuelo,
My friend and I will both be ⬭competiters⬭ in a fencing tournament. She believes that if we are matched against each other, that I should feel ⬭compaled⬭ to lose because she talked me into entering. During ⬭pervious⬭ tournaments I always ⬭dapended⬭ on my friend to be fair and she was. I never would have ⬭perdicted⬭ that I would be writing to you.

Signed,
⬭Confuzed⬭

1. __competitors__
2. __compelled__
3. __previous__
4. __depended__
5. __predicted__
6. __Confused__

Now proofread your letter. Fix any mistakes.

Go for the Goal

Take your Final Test. Then fill in your Scoreboard. Send your mistakes to the Word Locker.

SCOREBOARD
| number correct | number wrong |

★ ★ ★ ★ ★ ★ ★ ★ **All-Star Words** ★ ★ ★ ★ ★ ★ ★ ★

miscalculate   commotion   provoke   prelude   decline

Write a definition for each All-Star Word. Then, write a question for each All-Star Word. Refer to your definitions if you need to. Trade papers with a partner. Answer each question repeating the All-Star Word in your response.

◎ **Spelling Strategy**   Write several sentences containing List Words on the board, but leave blanks for the prefixes. For example:

- "She _____ dicted what would happen."
- "I _____ pronounced the word."

Then invite the class to read each sentence aloud, completing the List Word. Ask a volunteer to come to the board and fill in the missing prefix.

Flex Your Spelling Muscles   *Page 88*

As students complete the **Writing** activity, encourage them to brainstorm ideas, write a first draft, revise, and proofread their work. The **Proofreading** exercise will help them prepare to proofread their letters. To publish their writing, students may want to use their letters to create a radio show called "Ask Consuelo," in which listeners call in for on-the-air advice.

✍ Writer's Corner

Students might enjoy learning more about fencing by reading *Fencing Is for Me* by Art Thomas, or a similar book. Encourage them to write a compare-and-contrast paragraph telling what they thought about fencing before and after they read the book.

Go for the Goal/Final Test

1. Theo's complicated explanation **confused** me.
2. The wind is **propelling** debris across the road.
3. I received **confirmation** that my letter arrived.
4. **Competitors** from ten countries came to race.
5. I **presume** that you have an excuse for being late.
6. We felt **compelled** to tell you the news.
7. A **provision** for a garage is in the house plans.
8. Sherelle **misunderstood** what I said.
9. Will the **conference** focus on health issues?
10. We discussed our plans at a **previous** meeting.
11. Bad weather **prevented** us from having a picnic.
12. We'd like to **dedicate** this song to our parents.
13. My baby brother **mispronounced** my name.
14. Jill **deposited** half her allowance in the bank.
15. Will Dr. Saka write a **prescription** for you?
16. We made a **complaint** about the poor service.
17. Gramps **predicted** rain whenever his knee hurt.
18. She **decreased** the car's speed on the curve.
19. The farmer **depended** on rain for a good crop.
20. What **progress** we've made on this project!

Remind students to complete the Scoreboard and write any misspelled words in their Word Locker.

★★ **All-Star Words**   You may want to point out that the All-Star Words follow the spelling rule and model completing the activity with a List Word.

Lesson 22

Objective

To spell words with the prefixes *em, en, fore, post,* and *over*

Correlated Phonics Lessons

MCP Phonics, Level F, Lessons 31, 36, 38

Warm Up   *Page 89*

In this selection, students find out how the people of Boston coped with a flood of molasses in 1919. After reading, ask students what they would have done to help clean up the mess if they had been there.

Call on volunteers to say the boldfaced words, identify the different prefixes, and suggest how the prefixes change the meanings of the root words.

On Your Mark/Warm Up Test

1. Are those sounds the ***forewarning*** of a storm?
2. Janelle added a ***postscript*** to her letter.
3. The generals agreed to a ***postwar*** treaty.
4. Phil tries to ***encourage*** his brother to study.
5. Passengers paid extra for ***overweight*** baggage.
6. Turn off the water or the sink will ***overflow.***
7. A leader must have ***foresight*** to govern well.
8. Cindy will ***embellish*** her story with a few jokes.
9. We will ***emblazon*** our ties with the team emblem.
10. A jeweler can ***engrave*** your name on the bracelet.
11. Don't ***endanger*** your life by skating on thin ice!
12. The man in the ***foreground*** of the photo is Dad.
13. A life of hardship can ***embitter*** a person.
14. Your library books are three days ***overdue.***
15. The principal had ***foreknowledge*** of the scores.
16. Parents sometimes ***overprotect*** their children.
17. Rosa fished from the river ***embankment.***
18. We must ***embattle*** our village against attack.
19. How long is the ***enlistment*** period for the Navy?
20. An atlas can ***enlighten*** you about faraway lands.

Pep Talk/Game Plan   *Pages 90–91*

Introduce the spelling rule and have students read the List Words aloud. Discuss the meanings of less familiar words, such as *embellish, emblazon, embankment,* and *embattle.* Then encourage students to look back at their Warm Up Tests and apply the spelling rule to any misspelled words.

As students work through the **Spelling Lineup, Comparing Words,** and **Definitions** exercises, remind them to look back at their List Words or in their dictionaries if they need help.

 See **Words in Context,** page 14

Prefixes em, en, fore, post, and over

LESSON
22

Warm Up

How would you stop a flood of sticky molasses?

The Molasses Flood

It was a cold day in Boston, but not as cold as it usually was in January. The year was 1919. The city famous for its baked beans was about to become known for something else.

At around noontime, without any **forewarning**, a storage tank holding 14,000 tons of molasses began to split apart. The loose rivets that held the tank together popped out, and the molasses began to **overflow** onto the street. An enormous gooey wave nearly 15 feet high swept down the streets, traveling almost 35 miles per hour. It began to **endanger** everything in its path. It destroyed houses and even hit one of the supports for the elevated train. Luckily, the engineer saw the disaster ahead. The train screeched to a halt just before the tracks dropped down into the brown muck.

The cleanup effort lasted for weeks. Workers hired to **embattle** the sticky substance were knee deep in molasses and tracked the mess everywhere. Boots and clothing carried it as far as fifty miles away! Eventually nearby fireboats were employed to hose down the area. Boston Harbor turned a brown color as the syrup was washed into the bay. Wishing they had had the **foresight** to do it earlier, the streets were later covered with sand, so that people could walk without sticking to the ground.

 Say the boldfaced words in the selection. Each boldfaced word has a prefix. How many prefixes can you find? How do the prefixes change the meanings of the root words?

On Your Mark

Take your Warm Up Test. Then check your spelling with the List Words on the next page.

Pep Talk

The prefixes **em** and **en** mean <u>in</u>, <u>into</u>, <u>cause to be</u>, or <u>to make</u>.
The prefix **fore** means <u>before</u>.
The prefix **post** means <u>after</u>.
The prefix **over** usually means <u>too much</u> or <u>above</u>.

LIST WORDS

1. forewarning
2. postscript
3. postwar
4. encourage
5. overweight
6. overflow
7. foresight
8. embellish
9. emblazon
10. engrave
11. endanger
12. foreground
13. embitter
14. overdue
15. foreknowledge
16. overprotect
17. embankment
18. embattle
19. enlistment
20. enlighten

Game Plan

Spelling Lineup

Write the List Word under the correct category.

Words with the prefix **em** or **en**

1. encourage
2. embellish
3. emblazon
4. engrave
5. endanger
6. embitter
7. embankment
8. embattle
9. enlistment
10. enlighten

Words with the prefix **fore**

11. forewarning
12. foresight
13. foreground
14. foreknowledge

Words with the prefix **post**

15. postscript
16. postwar

Words with the prefix **over**

17. overweight
18. overflow
19. overdue
20. overprotect

Comparing Words

Study the relationship between the first two underlined words. Then write a List Word that has the same relationship with the third underlined word.

1. Curb is to roadway as __embankment__ is to river.
2. Underweight is to thin as __overweight__ is to chubby.
3. Discourage is to hinder as __encourage__ is to help.
4. Flood is to lake as __overflow__ is to bathtub.
5. Careless is to careful as __endanger__ is to protect.
6. Carve is to wood as __engrave__ is to metal.
7. Period is to sentence as __postscript__ is to letter.
8. Near is to far as __foreground__ is to background.

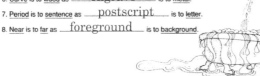

Definitions

Write a List Word to answer each definition clue.

1. to make better or improve — embellish
2. to make bitter — embitter
3. to know beforehand — foreknowledge
4. after war — postwar
5. being enrolled for service — enlistment
6. warning ahead of time — forewarning
7. to mark with an emblem — emblazon
8. to make clear — enlighten
9. power to look ahead — foresight
10. to protect more than necessary — overprotect
11. delayed past expected date — overdue
12. to prepare to fight — embattle

Lesson 22 ■ Prefixes em, en, fore, post, and over 91

Flex Your Spelling Muscles

Writing

What do you think people who were on the train that nearly plunged into the molasses flood might have said? Write quotations for several different people who may have experienced this train ride. Use as many List Words as you can.

Proofreading

This pamphlet on storm safety tips has ten mistakes. Use the proofreading marks to correct them. Write the misspelled List Words correctly on the lines.

Proofreading Marks
- ◯ spelling mistake
- ≡ capital letter
- ∧ add something
- ⌄ add apostrophe

When a storm is coming, you cant overpertect yourself. With forsite and planning you can remain safe. If you don't have a portable radio, you're overdew to get one. Follow any forwoning about flooding if you live in a low-lying area. Keep batteries, bottled water, and candles on hand. During the storm, encaurage everyone to keep away from windows, electrical appliances, and telephones. after the storm, don't emdanger yourself by going near downed wires.

1. overprotect
2. foresight
3. overdue
4. forewarning
5. encourage
6. endanger

Now proofread your quotations. Fix any mistakes.

Go for the Goal

Take your Final Test. Then fill in your Scoreboard. Send your mistakes to the Word Locker.

SCOREBOARD
number correct	number wrong

★ ★ ★ ★ ★ ★ ★ **All-Star Words** ★ ★ ★ ★ ★ ★ ★

empower   encompass   foremost   oversensitive   overemotional

Write a question for each All-Star Word that you will use to interview a person who survived the molasses flood. With a partner, take turns role-playing the parts of interviewer and survivor.

92 Lesson 22 ■ Prefixes em, en, fore, post, and over

◉ **Spelling Strategy**   You may want to write the definitions in the Pep Talk box on the board and ask students to name the prefix or prefixes that go with each definition. Then challenge students to
- name List Words for each prefix
- define each word based on the prefix's meaning
- spell each word.

Flex Your Spelling Muscles   *Page 92*

As students complete the **Writing** activity, encourage them to brainstorm ideas, write a first draft, revise, and proofread their work. The **Proofreading** exercise will help them prepare to proofread their quotations. To publish their writing, students may want to use their quotations to create a TV "person-on-the-scene" news report.

✍ Writer's Corner

> To receive a collection of stories about young people who have helped clean up the environment, the class can write to Renew America, Suite 710, 1400 16th St. NW, Washington, DC 20036.

Go for the Goal/Final Test

1. Mr. Chi will *enlighten* us about the election.
2. I received *forewarning* that I was failing math.
3. What did the soldiers do after *enlistment?*
4. Celeste signed the letter and added a *postscript.*
5. The *postwar* calm was a relief to the villagers.
6. They will *embattle* themselves against the enemy.
7. We slid down the *embankment* to the river.
8. I want to *encourage* everyone to attend the play.
9. A mother dog will *overprotect* her newborn pups.
10. *Foreknowledge* of the hurricane reduced injuries.
11. Was the *overweight* wrestler disqualified?
12. Don't let the tub *overflow!*
13. With *foresight,* we may avoid many problems.
14. Pat will *embellish* her tales with scary noises.
15. What is the fine on these *overdue* books?
16. His harsh words may *embitter* his audience.
17. We will *emblazon* the walls with our paintings.
18. She'll *engrave* the date on the silver plate.
19. Chemical waste can *endanger* public health.
20. I stood in the *foreground,* with Mom in back.

Remind students to complete the Scoreboard and write any misspelled words in their Word Locker.

★★ **All-Star Words**   You may want to point out that the All-Star Words follow the spelling rule. Model writing a question using a List Word and ask a volunteer to role-play a survivor as you ask the question.

Lesson 23

Objective
To spell words with the prefixes *uni, mono, bi, tri,* and *mid*

Correlated Phonics Lessons
MCP Phonics, Level F, Lessons 40–41

Warm Up   *Page 93*
The meaning of *barnstorming* becomes clear in this selection about the hazardous early days of "flying machines." After reading, invite students to read aloud the part of the selection they liked the best.

Encourage students to look back at the boldfaced words. Ask volunteers to say the words, identify the different prefixes, and suggest their meanings.

On Your Mark/Warm Up Test
1. The flag of Italy is **tricolor.**
2. Illinois is one of America's **midwestern** states.
3. Membership in the science club has **tripled.**
4. Wittenberg is a **university** in Springfield, Ohio.
5. Where did you go on your **midsummer** trip?
6. The committee meets on a **biweekly** basis.
7. The clown rode a **unicycle** in the circus parade.
8. A high-speed **monorail** runs through Japan.
9. Each staff member wears an identical **uniform.**
10. The diameter line **bisects** a circle into halves.
11. One of the earliest airplanes was the **biplane.**
12. Mother cut the meat pie into **triangular** pieces.
13. I enjoy watching birds through my **binoculars.**
14. How well the chorus sings in **unison!**
15. Three books in a series make up a **trilogy.**
16. Was driving across the desert **monotonous?**
17. The word **monosyllable** means "one syllable."
18. The students worked for **universal** peace.
19. Please fill out the application in **triplicate.**
20. The reunion is a **biannual** event.

Pep Talk/Game Plan   *Pages 94–95*
Introduce the spelling rule and have students read the List Words aloud. Encourage students to look back at their Warm Up Tests and apply the spelling rule to any misspelled words.

As students work through the **Spelling Lineup, Definitions,** and **Alphabetical Order** exercises, remind them to look back at their List Words or in their dictionaries if they need help.

 See **Questions/Answers,** page 15

74

Warm Up
What does "barnstorming" mean?

Barnstorming
Picture yourself on a **midsummer** afternoon in the 1920s. It is more than a decade since the Wright brothers made their first airplane flight. You've just heard that some of those new flying machines would be landing at Farmer Jones' field. You've never seen an airplane, so you hop in your brand-new Model-T and drive off.

There they are—half a dozen biplanes sitting on the field. Then you hear an announcer's voice coming over the loudspeaker.

You take a seat on the newly built bleachers. The **biplane** speeds down the grassy "runway." It lifts off, carrying a pilot and one passenger. It seems impossible that this machine can travel in midair. Then, as you sit there in amazement, you see the passenger step out onto the wing. You're glad you brought your **binoculars** to get a close-up look. Everyone gasps in **unison** as the passenger, a stuntman, walks the length of the wing. He's holding on to nothing but a thin crossbar with a **triangular** shape.

Another plane takes off, and then another. They fly in a **uniform** pattern, zigzagging through the clouds. Then the engine of one of the planes starts to make a sputtering sound. It's losing power. It's falling in a spiral down toward the earth. The pilot leaps out and safely floats to the ground in his parachute. The plane, however, crashes through the farmer's barn. You've heard the word "barnstorming" before. Now you know what it means.

 Look back at the boldfaced words in the selection. Find the different prefixes in the words. Try coming up with the meaning for each prefix.

On Your Mark
Take your Warm Up Test. Then check your spelling with the List Words on the next page.

Pep Talk
The prefixes **uni** and **mono** mean one or <u>single</u>.
The prefix **bi** means <u>two</u>, or <u>twice</u>.
The prefix **tri** means <u>three</u>, or <u>three times</u>.
The prefix **mid** means <u>in the middle of</u>.

LIST WORDS
1. tricolor
2. midwestern
3. tripled
4. university
5. midsummer
6. biweekly
7. unicycle
8. monorail
9. uniform
10. bisects
11. biplane
12. triangular
13. binoculars
14. unison
15. trilogy
16. monotonous
17. monosyllable
18. universal
19. triplicate
20. biannual

Game Plan

Spelling Lineup
Write each List Word in the correct category to show the prefix it contains.

uni
1. university
2. unicycle
3. uniform
4. unison
5. universal

bi
11. biweekly
12. bisects
13. biplane
14. binoculars
15. biannual

mono
6. monorail
7. monotonous
8. monosyllable

tri
16. tricolor
17. tripled
18. triangular
19. trilogy
20. triplicate

mid
9. midwestern
10. midsummer

94   Lesson 23 ▪Prefixes **uni, mono, bi, tri,** and **mid**

Definitions

Write a List Word to solve each definition clue.

1. once every two weeks   __biweekly__
2. multiplied by three   __tripled__
3. magnifying glasses   __binoculars__
4. twice a year   __biannual__
5. having three sides   __triangular__
6. train with one track   __monorail__
7. flag with three stripes   __tricolor__
8. boring and repetitive   __monotonous__
9. in the middle of the west   __midwest__
10. in three copies   __triplicate__
11. divides into two parts   __bisects__

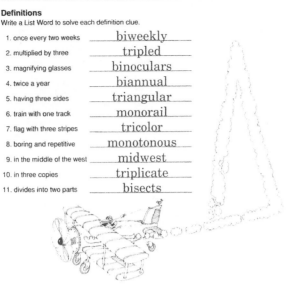

Alphabetical Order

Write this group of List Words in alphabetical order.

midsummer	unison	biplane	university	universal
trilogy	unicycle	uniform	monosyllable	

1. __biplane__
2. __midsummer__
3. __monosyllable__
4. __trilogy__
5. __unicycle__
6. __uniform__
7. __unison__
8. __universal__
9. __university__

Lesson 23 ■ Prefixes **uni, mono, bi, tri,** and **mid**   95

Flex Your Spelling Muscles

Writing

Write a paragraph comparing and contrasting the following means of transportation: a <u>biplane</u>, a <u>monorail</u>, a <u>unicycle</u>. Be sure to include the advantages and disadvantages of each of these.

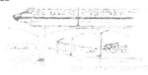

Proofreading

This biography has ten mistakes. Use the proofreading marks to correct them. Write the misspelled List Words correctly on the lines.

Bessie Coleman was the first African American woman to become a pilot. Tired of monotenus work, Coleman wanted to fly a a biplane Prejudice nearly stopped her, but she earned a license in Europe. Her first exhibition was in a middwesdern city in 1922. Her stunts won her unaversil acclaim. Can you imagine Coleman in her Pilot's unaforme standing before a cheering crowd? If only we had a pair of magic binoculars that would enable us to see her as she bisecks the sky.

Now proofread your paragraph. Fix any mistakes.

Proofreading Marks
- ◯ spelling mistake
- ∧ add something
- ℒ take out something
- / make small letter

1. __monotonous__
2. __biplane__
3. __midwestern__
4. __universal__
5. __uniform__
6. __bisects__

Go for the Goal

Take your Final Test. Then fill in your Scoreboard. Send your mistakes to the Word Locker.

SCOREBOARD

number correct	number wrong

★ ★ ★ ★ ★ ★ ★ ★ ★ **All-Star Words** ★ ★ ★ ★ ★ ★ ★ ★ ★

unilateral   monogram   bifocals   trilingual   midpoint

Write a definition or draw a simple sketch for each All-Star Word. Use your dictionary if you need help with a meaning. Then trade papers with a partner. Can you write the word that fits each clue?

96   Lesson 23 ■ Prefixes **uni, mono, bi, tri,** and **mid**

Flex Your Spelling Muscles   *Page 96*

As students complete the **Writing** activity, encourage them to brainstorm ideas, write a first draft, revise, and proofread their work. The **Proofreading** exercise will help them prepare to proofread their paragraphs. To publish their writing, students may want to illustrate or draw a diagram of each type of transportation and display their paragraphs with their artwork.

✍ Writer's Corner

You may want to bring in newspaper clippings about events such as air shows, bicycle races, or truck rallies. Invite students to write a paragraph telling which event they would have liked to attend, and why.

Go for the Goal/Final Test

1. The theater presented a *trilogy* of plays.
2. Our family gathered for the *biannual* reunion.
3. This line *bisects* the square into two triangles.
4. Where shall we have our *midsummer* picnic?
5. Does France have a *tricolor* flag?
6. The call of the catbird is somewhat *monotonous.*
7. The museum has a model of an early *biplane.*
8. We clean the apartment on a *biweekly* schedule.
9. Chicago is a lovely *midwestern* city.
10. The acrobat stood on his head on a *unicycle.*
11. The word *monosyllable* contains five syllables.
12. How many *triangular* patches are in the quilt?
13. The police officer wore a bright blue *uniform.*
14. What a great *university* Harvard is!
15. The students recited the poem in *unison.*
16. She filled out the order form in *triplicate.*
17. We'll take the *monorail* from Paris to Nice.
18. Our annual profits have *tripled* over five years.
19. We can look ahead to *universal* space travel.
20. I used *binoculars* to watch the fielder's catch.

Remind students to complete the Scoreboard and write any misspelled words in their Word Locker.

★★ **All-Star Words**   You may want to point out that the All-Star Words follow the spelling rule and model writing or drawing a clue for a List Word.

Lesson 24 • Instant Replay

Objective
To review spelling words with *ei* and *ie*; prefixes *ir, in, il, im, de, pre, pro, con, com, mis, em, en, fore, post, over, uni, mono, bi, tri,* and *mid*

Time Out   *Pages 97–100*
Check Your Word Locker Based on your observations, note which words are giving students the most difficulty and offer assistance for spelling them correctly. Here are some frequently misspelled words to watch for: *conceit, weird, incredible, illiterate, irresponsible, compelled,* and *encourage.*

To give students extra help and practice in taking standardized tests, you may want to have them take the Review Test for this lesson on pages 78–79. After scoring the tests, return them to students so that they can record their misspelled words in their Word Locker.

After practicing their troublesome words, students can work through the exercises for **Lessons 19–23.** Before they begin each exercise, you may want to go over the spelling rule.

🏠 **Take It Home** Invite students to locate List Words from **Lessons 19–23** in books, magazines, and newspapers they read at home. For a complete list of the words, encourage students to take their *Spelling Workout* books home. Students can also use Take It Home Master 4 on pages 80–81 to help them do the activity. Invite students to share their lists with the class.

Name_____

Time Out
Look again at the spelling of vowel sounds in words. Also look at the words with prefixes added to the root word. Think about what the prefixes mean.

Check Your Word Locker
Look at the words in your Word Locker. Write your most troublesome words from Lessons 19 through 23.

_____

_____

Practice writing your troublesome words with a partner. Say a sentence for each troublesome word and spell the word aloud for your partner.

◄ Lesson 19 ►
Use the spelling rule you learned when spelling words with **ie** or **ei**. It will help you spell words, such as <u>pierce</u>, <u>ceiling</u>, and <u>weigh</u>. Remember that some words, such as <u>ancient</u>, are exceptions to the rule.

List Words

retrieve
yields
conceit
veil
height
fiercely
briefly
perceived
neighborly
weird

Write a List Word that means the opposite of the word given.

1. normal		weird
2. expose		veil
3. width		height
4. lengthily		briefly
5. throw		retrieve
6. sweetly		fiercely
7. unfriendly		neighborly
8. modesty		conceit
9. overlooked		perceived
10. continues		yields

97

◄ Lesson 20 ►
The prefixes ir, in, il, and im usually mean not, as in <u>irresponsible</u>, <u>indirect</u>, <u>illogical</u>, and <u>immaterial</u>. The prefix im can also mean to, as in <u>immigrant</u>.

List Words

immortal
irregular
intolerant
indirect
illegal
illegible
immigrant
incapable
impatient
indefinite

Write the List Word that has the same root as the word given.

1. definitely		indefinite
2. migrate		immigrant
3. capability		incapable
4. mortality		immortal
5. legalize		illegal
6. tolerate		intolerant
7. patience		impatient
8. regulate		irregular
9. direction		indirect
10. legibility		illegible

◄ Lesson 21 ►
Prefixes and Their Meanings

pre, pro = <u>before</u>	con, com = <u>with</u> or <u>together</u>
pro = <u>forward</u>	mis = <u>bad</u> or <u>badly</u>
de = <u>down</u>, <u>not</u>, <u>reverse</u>, <u>apart</u>, <u>aside</u>	

List Words

prevented
depended
confused
predicted
complaint
conference
prescription
decreased
progress
misunderstood

Write five List Words that could be found listed between each set of dictionary guide words given. Write the words in alphabetical order.

comma/deposit		mistake/protect	
1. complaint	6.	misunderstood
2. conference	7.	predicted
3. confused	8.	prescription
4. decreased	9.	prevented
5. depended	10.	progress

98 Lesson 24 ■ Instant Replay

Lesson 22

Prefixes and Their Meanings

em, en = in, into, cause to be, to make
fore = before   **post** = after   **over** = too much or above

List Words

postscript
foresight
overweight
overdue
embattle
engrave
embitter
encourage
embankment
overflow

Make List Words by choosing a prefix from the chart above to add to each root or root word. Write the words on the lines.

1. sight ___foresight___
2. script ___postscript___
3. bitter ___embitter___
4. bankment ___embankment___
5. grave ___engrave___
6. weight ___overweight___
7. courage ___encourage___
8. flow ___overflow___
9. battle ___embattle___
10. due ___overdue___

Lesson 23

Prefixes and Their Meanings

uni, mono = one, single   **bi** = two, twice
tri = three, three times   **mid** = in the middle of

List Words

unicycle
bisects
biplane
triangular
binoculars
monotonous
midsummer
triplicate
universal
trilogy

Write a List Word to match each clue.

1. Wednesday is to midweek as July is to ___midsummer___
2. Unites is to joins as divides is to ___bisects___
3. Balloon is to circular as pennant is to ___triangular___
4. Pogo stick is to stilts as ___unicycle___ is to bicycle.
5. Three artists are to trio as three books are to ___trilogy___
6. Double is to triple as duplicate is to ___triplicate___
7. 1990s are to jet as 1920s are to ___biplane___
8. Telescopes are to astonomers as ___binoculars___ are to bird watchers.
9. Illegal is to unlawful as global is to ___universal___
10. Interesting is to captivating as boring is to ___monotonous___

Lesson 24 ■ Instant Replay   **99**

Lessons 19–23

List Words

foresight
binoculars
conceit
irregular
predicted
overweight
monotonous
neighborly
indefinite
confused
encourage
retrieve
intolerant
complaint
incapable

Missing Words

Complete each sentence with a List Word.

1. We're not sure we'll move; our plans are ___indefinite___.
2. Lena used ___binoculars___ to see the animals up close.
3. If we ___encourage___ him to try harder, he will win the next race.
4. She can ___retrieve___ the information from the computer.
5. My ___complaint___ was about the bad service.
6. No one had ___predicted___ the storm would be so intense.
7. The owner became ___intolerant___ of his dog's bad behavior.
8. He does not show any ___conceit___ about his incredible talents.
9. We all wish for ___foresight___ to know what we're getting into.
10. He is ___incapable___ of doing that task until he is trained.
11. I'm ___confused___ about this; the directions are unclear.
12. Being friendly and ___neighborly___, she introduced herself.
13. The speaker's ___monotonous___ voice bored us.
14. The shape of some volcanoes is ___irregular___.
15. The scale says he is ___overweight___, but he's in good shape.

Go for the Goal

Take your Final Replay Test. Then fill in your Scoreboard.
Send any misspelled words to your Word Locker.

SCOREBOARD

number correct	number wrong

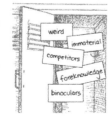

Clean Out Your Word Locker
Look in your Word Locker. Cross out each word you spelled correctly on your Final Replay Test. Circle the words you're still having trouble with. Add the words you circled to your Spelling Notebook. What do you notice about the words? Watch for those words as you write.

Go for the Goal/Final Replay Test   *Page 100*

1. The lion was *fiercely* protective of its cubs.
2. Rain fell *briefly,* but then it was sunny again.
3. The scout *perceived* movement in the bushes.
4. People in this area are very *neighborly.*
5. The sky changed to a *weird* shade of gray.
6. Books can make an author's ideas *immortal.*
7. Don't be *intolerant* of ideas that are different.
8. A natural pond has an *irregular* shape.
9. That route is *indirect,* but it's beautiful.
10. It is *illegal* to go through a stop sign.
11. You have made a lot of *progress* in your work.
12. I'm sorry that I *misunderstood* your message.
13. Jamal was *confused* by the mass of traffic signs.
14. The drugstore has your *prescription* ready.
15. What *prevented* you from being here earlier?
16. Mom added a *postscript* to Dad's letter.
17. I had the *foresight* to pack a warm coat.
18. I paid extra because my bag was *overweight.*
19. Your library books are a week *overdue.*
20. We will *embattle* the fort against the invaders.
21. How *monotonous* the speaker's voice is!
22. My family is having a *midsummer* party in July.
23. Please fill out this form in *triplicate.*
24. Our goal is *universal* literacy.
25. Did you read the last book in the *trilogy?.*
26. I need to *retrieve* the suitcase I left behind.
27. If their team *yields* one goal, we will win.
28. Elise's *conceit* about her work is unfortunate.
29. A beekeeper wears a hat with a big *veil.*
30. Make sure the *height* of the fence is six feet.
31. The signature on that contract is *illegible.*
32. My father came to this country as an *immigrant.*
33. They seem *incapable* of learning to swim.
34. Please don't be so *impatient!*
35. Are your weekend plans still *indefinite?*
36. My mother is at a business *conference* this week.
37. Put your *complaint* in writing and give it to me.
38. The symphony orchestra *depended* on donations.
39. The number of students in school has *decreased.*
40. No one *predicted* that the score would be tied.
41. I want you to *engrave* my name on this cup.
42. The rain-swollen river overran its *embankment.*
43. Paul's bad luck did not *embitter* him.
44. Will you *encourage* your friend to see the movie?
45. Watch out or the water in the sink will *overflow!*
46. Look at Camille ride that *unicycle!*
47. The bicycle path *bisects* the park.
48. At the air show, they watched a *biplane* do stunts.
49. Use a *triangular* piece of cloth to make a sling.
50. With these new *binoculars* I can see the islands.

Clean Out Your Word Locker   After writing each word, students can circle the vowel digraph *ei* or *ie* or underline the prefix.

Instant Replay Test

Side A

Read each set of words. Fill in the circle next to the word that
is spelled wrong.

1. ⓐ illegible   ⓒ prevented
   ⓑ enbankment   ⓓ impatient

2. ⓐ midsummer   ⓒ intolerent
   ⓑ retrieve   ⓓ embattle

3. ⓐ binolculers   ⓒ unicycle
   ⓑ perceived   ⓓ indirect

4. ⓐ hight   ⓒ predicted
   ⓑ progress   ⓓ conceit

5. ⓐ yields   ⓒ bisect
   ⓑ overdue   ⓓ unniversal

6. ⓐ biplane   ⓒ misunderstood
   ⓑ immortle   ⓓ postscript

7. ⓐ overflow   ⓒ deposited
   ⓑ indefinite   ⓓ perscription

8. ⓐ illegal   ⓒ complant
   ⓑ biweekly   ⓓ engrave

9. ⓐ uniform   ⓒ enlighten
   ⓑ fiersely   ⓓ triplicate

10. ⓐ depended   ⓒ provision
    ⓑ overanxious   ⓓ triology

11. ⓐ mispronounced   ⓒ retrieve
    ⓑ conferance   ⓓ midsummer

12. ⓐ predicted   ⓒ imigrant
    ⓑ illegible   ⓓ impatient

13. ⓐ illegal   ⓒ perceived
    ⓑ monotanous   ⓓ engrave

Instant Replay Test

Side B

ead each set of words. Fill in the circle next to the word that
spelled wrong.

4. (a) unicycle   (c) conceit
   (b) vayl   (d) embattle

5. (a) overflow   (c) forsight
   (b) yields   (d) prevented

6. (a) triplicate   (c) decresed
   (b) indefinite   (d) bisect

7. (a) incapeble   (c) predicted
   (b) postscript   (d) illegible

8. (a) impatient   (c) overdue
   (b) midsummer   (d) overwieght

9. (a) wierd   (c) illogical
   (b) retrieve   (d) depended

0. (a) briefly   (c) uniform
   (b) progress   (d) imbitter

1. (a) indirect   (c) ancient
   (b) endanger   (d) irreguler

2. (a) overanxious   (c) biplane
   (b) confuesed   (d) misunderstood

3. (a) neighberly   (c) tricolor
   (b) engrave   (d) overflow

4. (a) prevented   (c) encurage
   (b) conceit   (d) impractical

5. (a) bisect   (c) indefinite
   (b) trianglar   (d) postscript

TAKE IT HOME

You and your family can have fun sharing the new words that your child has learned to spell at school. You'll find some ideas on these pages for helping your child review the words in Lessons 19–23.

Read All About It!

Keep a piece of paper and a pencil handy in the room where your family usually gathers to read. Encourage your child to look for spelling words while reading books, magazines, and newspapers and to write each one he or she finds on the paper.

Word Search

There are twelve spelling words hidden in this puzzle. How many can you and your child find? Remember to look horizontally, vertically, and diagonally.

unison	trilogy	reindeer	diesel	uniform	yields
unicycle	weird	biplane	protein	indirect	illegal

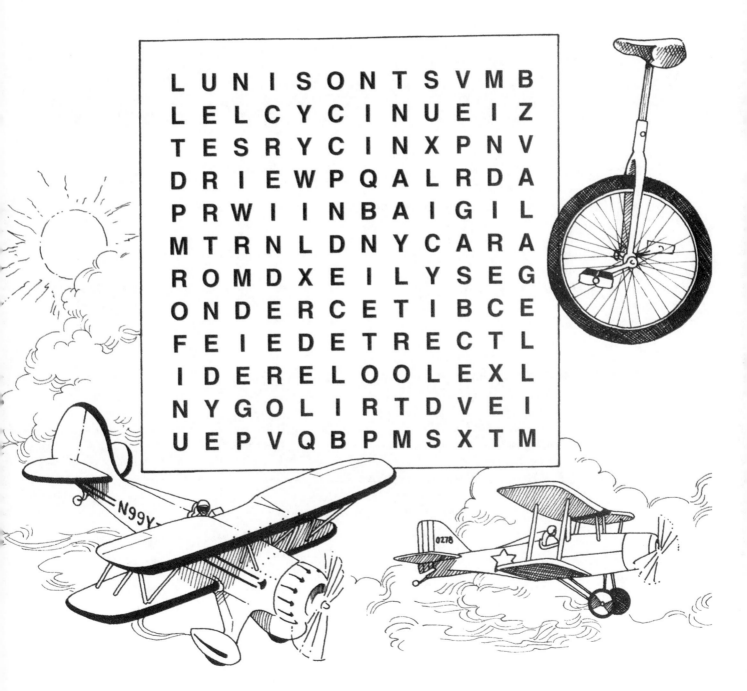

```
L U N I S O N T S V M B
L E L C Y C I N U E I Z
T E S R Y C I N X P N V
D R I E W P Q A L R D A
P R W I I N B A I G I L
M T R N L D N Y C A R A
R O M D X E I L Y S E G
O N D E R C E T I B C E
F E I E D E T R E C T L
I D E R E L O O L E X L
N Y G O L I R T D V E I
U E P V Q B P M S X T M
```

Lesson 25

Objective
To spell words with the prefixes *anti, counter, super, sub, ultra, trans,* and *semi*

Correlated Phonics Lessons
MCP Phonics, Level F, Lessons 34, 38–40

Warm Up   Page 101
In this selection, students learn not only how robots may make people's lives easier, but also how one robot made a family's life more difficult. Invite students to share what they know about robots and to tell what kind of personal robot they would like to have.

Ask volunteers to say the boldfaced words and identify the different prefixes.

On Your Mark/Warm Up Test
1. Mark put *antifreeze* in the car.
2. Who will *supervise* the building of the house?
3. Our team played in the *semifinal* tournament.
4. Rita applied an *antiseptic* to her scraped knee.
5. Window glass is a *transparent* material.
6. My *substitution* of ingredients improved the pie.
7. For some poisons, milk is an *antidote.*
8. Radar helped the ship locate the *submarine.*
9. The cut looked bad, but it was only *superficial.*
10. Did you get a magazine *subscription* as a gift?
11. The boys sat in a *semicircle* around the fire.
12. Aspirin is often used to *counteract* pain.
13. What a clever *counterattack* the army staged!
14. The proofreader put a *semicolon* in the sentence.
15. Do *supersonic* jets exceed the speed of sound?
16. A *transistor* is an electronic device in radios.
17. The sun's *ultraviolet* rays are invisible.
18. Keneesha *transferred* to a new school.
19. The FBI investigates *counterfeit* money.
20. Blood produces *antibodies* to destroy bacteria.

Pep Talk/Game Plan   Pages 102–103
Introduce the spelling rule and have students read the List Words aloud. Encourage students to look back at their Warm Up Tests and apply the spelling rule to any misspelled words.

As students work through the **Spelling Lineup, Word Parts,** and **Definitions** exercises, remind them to look back at their List Words or in their dictionaries if they need help.

 See **Spelling Aloud,** page 14

Prefixes anti, counter, super, sub, ultra, trans, and semi
LESSON 25

Warm Up
How can a robot improve your life?

Mechanical Marvel

The ultramodern robot is on its way. Although it is not yet a **substitute** for a human being, it can do some remarkable things. A personal robot can be programmed to teach you how to speak a foreign language. It can protect your house at night, wake you in the morning, and then do the housework. It can even follow you around and drill you on your spelling words. Unlike pets, you do not need to **supervise** a robot. It will even recharge itself.

One futuristic family attracted attention for being the first on the block with an android (robot). One day, the two teenaged sons decided to take the family robot for a walk. It was rush hour when they set the robot free on the freeway. The boys did not anticipate it, but traffic came to a halt. Drivers formed a **semicircle** around the machine. Eventually, the police arrived. The boys had planned on that. They had programmed their robot to run and shout, "Help me! Help me! They are trying to take me apart!" The boys were amused. The police weren't. They did **counteract** what the boys had done and carried the powerless robot off to jail.

The story ends happily, however. The android was **transferred** back to its owners. According to all reports, the robot has since managed to stay within the law.

 Look back at the boldfaced words in the selection. Each word has a prefix at the beginning of the word. How many different prefixes can you find?

On Your Mark
Take your Warm Up Test. Then check your spelling with the List Words on the next page.

Pep Talk
Prefixes and Their Meanings

anti = against   counter = against
ultra = beyond   super = above; over
sub = below   trans = across; through
semi = half

LIST WORDS
1. antifreeze
2. supervise
3. semifinal
4. antiseptic
5. transparent
6. substitution
7. antidote
8. submarine
9. superficial
10. subscription
11. semicircle
12. counteract
13. counterattack
14. semicolon
15. supersonic
16. transistor
17. ultraviolet
18. transferred
19. counterfeit
20. antibodies

Game Plan
Spelling Lineup
Write each List Word under the correct heading.

words with the prefixes **anti** and **counter**
1. antifreeze
2. antiseptic
3. antidote
4. counteract
5. counterattack
6. counterfeit
7. antibodies

words with the prefix **super**
8. supervise
9. superficial
10. supersonic

word with the prefix **ultra**
11. ultraviolet

words with the prefix **sub**
12. substitution
13. submarine
14. subscription

words with the prefix **trans**
15. transparent
16. transistor
17. transferred

words with the prefix **semi**
18. semifinal
19. semicircle
20. semicolon

Word Parts

Add a prefix to each root given to form a List Word. Write the word on the line.

1. violet   ultraviolet
2. colon   semicolon
3. act   counteract
4. circle   semicircle
5. final   semifinal
6. marine   submarine
7. attack   counterattack
8. sonic   supersonic
9. freeze   antifreeze
10. septic   antiseptic
11. bodies   antibodies

Definitions

Write a List Word to match each definition.

1. something that works against a poison   antidote
2. something that is false   counterfeit
3. limited to the surface area   superficial
4. electronic device that allows electrical impulses to travel across the air without any resistance   transistor
5. able to see through   transparent
6. to oversee or direct work   supervise
7. moved from one person, place, or thing to another   transferred
8. the act of putting one thing in place of another   substitution
9. agreement to receive and pay for magazines, books, theater tickets for a specified period of time   subscription
10. beyond the speed of sound   supersonic
11. half of a round shape   semicircle
12. something that acts against germs   antiseptic
13. to act directly against   counteract

Flex Your Spelling Muscles

Writing

A robot could be a handy thing to have around. What do you think it would be like to have a robot? Write a description of your robot and tell what jobs you would have it do.

Proofreading

The following poem has twelve mistakes. Use the proofreading marks to fix each mistake. Write the misspelled List Words correctly on the lines.

Proofreading Marks
◯ spelling mistake
௧ take out something
∧ add something
⍘ add apostrophe

Most robots appear official,
But surely it is superfisial
I've heard they can suppervize
And act in ways most wise.
But are they a real solution
As a human substitushon?
There's a transeestor in every space
And less on a robots transparant face.
Their antiseptic forms forms appear
To lack a comfort some hold dear.

1. superficial
2. supervise
3. substitution
4. transistor
5. transparent
6. antiseptic

Proofread your description of a robot. Fix any mistakes.

Go for the Goal

Take your Final Test. Then fill in your Scoreboard. Send your mistakes to the Word Locker.

SCOREBOARD

number correct	number wrong

★ ★ ★ ★ ★ ★ ★ All-Star Words ★ ★ ★ ★ ★ ★ ★

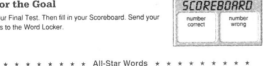

antisocial   counterbalance   subcontract   transaction   semiprecious

Write a sentence for each All-Star Word. Then, erase the prefixes. Trade papers with a partner and rewrite each other's sentences, adding the prefixes. Talk about how the prefixes change the meanings of the words.

⊚ **Spelling Strategy**   Write *anti, counter, sub, super, ultra, trans,* and *semi* on the board as separate column headings. Then tell students a root or root word (in a List Word) and ask which prefix they would add to it to form a List Word. Ask a volunteer to write the complete word on the board in the correct column and to give its meaning. Continue this procedure until all the List Words have been written.

Flex Your Spelling Muscles   *Page 104*

As students complete the **Writing** activity, encourage them to brainstorm ideas, write a first draft, revise, and proofread their work. The **Proofreading** exercise will help them prepare to proofread their descriptions. To publish their writing, students may want to make illustrations of their robots and combine their drawings and descriptions into a robot catalog.

✍ Writer's Corner

Invite students' grandparents or guests from a senior center to talk about how they envisioned the future when they were young. Have students compare their speculations of the future with those of their guests by writing two paragraphs: "Today's Future" and "Yesterday's Future."

Go for the Goal/Final Test

1. Vaccines cause the blood to produce **antibodies.**
2. Bo **transferred** money into his checking account.
3. **Transistor** radios were popular in the 1960s.
4. This sentence does not need a **semicolon.**
5. Your smiling face may **counteract** Jan's sadness.
6. When does this magazine **subscription** expire?
7. Waves surrounded the **submarine** as it surfaced.
8. The **substitution** of salt for sugar was horrible!
9. An **antiseptic** will prevent infection.
10. Roland will **supervise** the children.
11. We bought **antifreeze** at the gas station.
12. Mom attended our **semifinal** chess tournament.
13. The silky curtain material is **transparent.**
14. The doctor carried an **antidote** for snake bites.
15. The accident caused only a **superficial** wound.
16. Draw a full circle, and then draw a **semicircle.**
17. The chess player pondered his **counterattack.**
18. Some pilots are trained to fly **supersonic** jets.
19. The sun's **ultraviolet** rays may damage the skin.
20. Were you fooled by those **counterfeit** paintings?

Remind students to complete the Scoreboard and write any misspelled words in their Word Locker.

★★ **All-Star Words**   Point out that the All-Star Words follow the spelling rule and review the meanings of *anti, counter, sub, trans,* and *semi.*

Lesson 26

Objective

To spell words with the suffixes *or, er, ist, logy,* and *ology*

Correlated Phonics Lesson

MCP Phonics, Level F, Lesson 52

Warm Up   *Page 105*

In this selection, students learn about the amazing history of a common substance—salt. Ask students why they think salt used to be so valuable.

Ask volunteers to say the boldfaced words, identify the suffixes, and tell how many different suffixes there are.

On Your Mark/Warm Up Test

1. A *juror* became ill during the trial.
2. A *consumer* should inspect products carefully.
3. *Biology* is the study of plants and animals.
4. Sam asked the *jeweler* to repair his watch.
5. Charles Lindbergh was a famous *aviator.*
6. Would you rather be a *spectator* or a player?
7. An *insulator* does not conduct electricity.
8. The lawyer asked the *typist* to compose a letter.
9. A *transformer* alters the voltage of electricity.
10. We put up the *projector* to view our slides.
11. The *machinist* repaired the printing press.
12. Aretha is a *geologist* who works in Greenland.
13. The *florist* created a beautiful bridal bouquet.
14. The *divisor* is a number divided into another.
15. What humorous columns that *journalist* writes!
16. Modern *technology* has brought us computers.
17. Achilles is a hero of Greek *mythology.*
18. Let's take the *escalator* to the fifth floor.
19. Which *manufacturer* made that video game?
20. My mother is a police *investigator.*

Pep Talk/Game Plan   *Pages 106–107*

Introduce the spelling rule and have students read the List Words aloud. Call on volunteers to look up such difficult words as *technology, insulator,* and *transformer* and read the definitions aloud. Then encourage students to look back at their Warm Up Tests and apply the spelling rule to any misspelled words.

As students work through the **Spelling Lineup, Comparing Words, Classification,** and **Vocabulary** exercises, remind them to look back at their List Words or in their dictionaries if they need help.

 See **Student Dictation,** page 14

Suffixes or, er, ist, logy, and ology   LESSON 26

Warm Up

What mineral used to be as valuable as gold?

Salt of the Earth

You can preserve food with it. You can ease sore throat pain by gargling with it. You can even use it to melt snow or to flavor your popcorn. In case you haven't guessed, "it" is that marvelous mineral we call salt. As much as we need air and water, we need salt to live. If you are a **consumer** of packaged food, you probably get enough salt in your diet, so there's no need to sprinkle on any more. Besides, doctors warn that too much salt is just as bad as not enough.

Salt has played an interesting role in history. In ancient Rome, salt was so valuable that soldiers were paid handfuls of salt instead of money. Our word *salary* comes from the Latin word *sal,* which means *salt.* Salt also had a part in the American Civil War. The Northern forces had large supplies of salt. The Southern fighters, however, had very little. As a result, the Southerners could not preserve the food they needed.

Salt can be obtained by two different methods. Using modern **technology,** it can be mined from the earth, much like mining coal. It can also be collected by evaporating ocean water, which contains most of the world's salt. In fact, any **geologist** will tell you that there is enough salt in the sea to cover North America with a mile-thick layer of salt. Think of all the popcorn you could spice up with that!

 Look back at the boldfaced words in the selection. These words have word parts, called suffixes, at the end of each word. How many suffixes can you find?

On Your Mark

Take your Warm Up Test. Then check your spelling with the List Words on the next page.

Pep Talk

The suffixes **or, er,** and **ist** mean <u>one who</u> or <u>something that,</u> as in <u>jeweler, typist, projector,</u> and <u>juror.</u>

The suffixes **logy** and **ology** mean <u>the study of,</u> as in <u>biology.</u>

LIST WORDS

1. juror
2. consumer
3. biology
4. jeweler
5. aviator
6. spectator
7. insulator
8. typist
9. transformer
10. projector
11. machinist
12. geologist
13. florist
14. divisor
15. journalist
16. technology
17. mythology
18. escalator
19. manufacturer
20. investigator

Game Plan

Spelling Lineup

Write a List Word that has the same root as the word given.

1. mythical
   mythology
2. consume
   consumer
3. geology
   geologist
4. escalate
   escalator
5. inspect
   spectator
6. aviation
   aviator
7. journal
   journalist
8. technique
   technology
9. factory
   manufacturer
10. project
    projector
11. biosphere
    biology
12. machine
    machinist
13. investigate
    investigator
14. type
    typist
15. jewel
    jeweler
16. flower
    florist
17. jury
    juror
18. divide
    divisor
19. form
    transformer
20. insulate
    insulator

Comparing Words

Study the relationship between the first two underlined words. Then write a List Word that has the same relationship with the third underlined word or phrase.

1. Dishwasher is to sink as ___escalator___ is to stairs.
2. Poet is to poem as ___journalist___ is to news story.
3. Classroom is to student as courtroom is to ___juror___.
4. CD is to CD player as film is to ___projector___.
5. Pianist is to piano as ___typist___ is to typewriter.
6. Listener is to radio as ___spectator___ is to sporting event.
7. Wood is to carpenter as gold is to ___jeweler___.
8. Sailor is to boat as ___aviator___ is to plane.
9. Competing is to athlete as buying is to ___consumer___.
10. Wetsuit is to diver as ___insulator___ is to electric wire.

Classification

Write the List Word that belongs in each group.

1. legends, poetry, ___mythology___
2. dividend, quotient, ___divisor___
3. reporter, editor, ___journalist___
4. plants, animals, ___biology___
5. science, industry, ___technology___
6. maker, producer, ___manufacturer___
7. ramp, elevator, ___escalator___

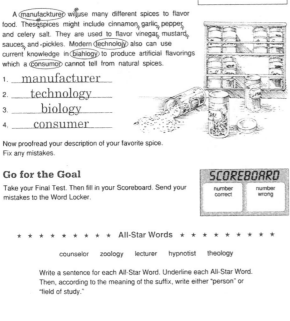

Vocabulary

Write a List Word to name the person whose work involves the items given.

1. rocks and minerals ___geologist___
2. bracelets and pins ___jeweler___
3. flowers ___florist___
4. machines and wrenches ___machinist___
5. clues and fingerprints ___investigator___

Flex Your Spelling Muscles

Writing

Millions of Americans love spices. What is your favorite spice? Research how your favorite spice is made by the manufacturer. What kind of technology is used? Write a description of this process.

Proofreading

This article has twelve mistakes. Use the proofreading marks to fix each mistake. Write the misspelled List Words correctly on the lines.

Proofreading Marks	
◯	spelling mistake
∧	add something

A manufackturer wiljuse many different spices to flavor food. Theseᴬspices might include cinnamon, garlic, pepper, and celery salt. They are used to flavor vinegar, mustard, sauces, and ·pickles. Modern technology also can use current knowledge in biahlogy to produce artificial flavorings which a consumor cannot tell from natural spices.

1. ___manufacturer___
2. ___technology___
3. ___biology___
4. ___consumer___

Now proofread your description of your favorite spice. Fix any mistakes.

Go for the Goal

Take your Final Test. Then fill in your Scoreboard. Send your mistakes to the Word Locker.

SCOREBOARD

number correct	number wrong

★ ★ ★ ★ ★ ★ ★ All-Star Words ★ ★ ★ ★ ★ ★ ★ ★

counselor zoology lecturer hypnotist theology

Write a sentence for each All-Star Word. Underline each All-Star Word. Then, according to the meaning of the suffix, write either "person" or "field of study."

◉ **Spelling Strategy** Use the definitions in the Pep Talk box to help create clues for several of the List Words. For example:
- *"something that* insulates"
- *"one who* works with machines"

Say each clue aloud and invite the class to guess the matching List Word. Call on a volunteer to write the word on the board, circle the suffix, and give the meaning of the suffix.

Flex Your Spelling Muscles   *Page 108*

As students complete the **Writing** activity, encourage them to brainstorm ideas, write a first draft, revise, and proofread their work. The **Proofreading** exercise will help them prepare to proofread their descriptions. To publish their writing, students may want to use their descriptions to create a bulletin-board display called "Something Spicy."

✍ Writer's Corner

You may wish to bring in containers of spices and pass them around so that students can read the labels as well as discover what the contents smell and look like. Invite students to jot down words or phrases to describe their favorite spices.

Go for the Goal/Final Test

1. The **jeweler** repaired Grandmother's ring.
2. The **divisor** seven goes into fourteen twice.
3. We had no power when the **transformer** broke.
4. My uncle is a **manufacturer** of cardboard boxes.
5. The movie **projector** needs a new lightbulb.
6. What a courageous **aviator** Amelia Earhart was!
7. Russell Baker is a famous American **journalist.**
8. Mr. Flynn is an **investigator** for the FBI.
9. The **biology** professor conducted an experiment.
10. Did a **florist** arrange that bouquet?
11. We took the **escalator** up to the third floor.
12. A secretary needs to be an excellent **typist.**
13. Will each **consumer** receive a refund?
14. Glass is an effective **insulator** for electric wires.
15. I read about the Trojan War in Greek **mythology.**
16. A **geologist** studies the earth's composition.
17. Was your mother picked as a **juror** on that case?
18. My aunt worked as a **machinist** in Toledo.
19. A computer is an example of high **technology.**
20. Every **spectator** cheered when the race began.

Remind students to complete the Scoreboard and write any misspelled words in their Word Locker.

★★ **All-Star Words** You may want to point out that the All-Star Words follow the spelling rule and review the meanings of the suffixes used.

Lesson 27

Objective
To spell words with the suffixes *er*, *est*, and *ness*

Correlated Phonics Lessons
MCP Phonics, Level F, Lessons 53, 56

Warm Up   *Page 109*
After reading this selection about a talented storyteller, students may decide to tell some stories of their own. Call on volunteers to give brief summaries of stories they would like to tell or of favorite stories they have heard.

Ask volunteers to say the boldfaced words, identify the root words, and describe any spelling changes that occurred in the root words when the suffixes were added.

On Your Mark/Warm Up Test
1. The children's **happiness** was clearly evident.
2. The river is **muddiest** after a severe rainstorm.
3. Is this pair of shoes **tighter** than that pair?
4. The **cruelest** winter storms are often in January.
5. The **noisiest** part of the school day is recess.
6. This TV show is even **crazier** than the last one!
7. Earl felt some **stiffness** in his legs after the race.
8. The **dampness** of the air makes me sneeze.
9. The chef checked the **sharpness** of her knives.
10. Her sergeant was the **strictest** on the army base.
11. The **brightest** star is often the North Star.
12. Barry wants the **thickest** jacket he can buy.
13. Our voices echoed in the **emptiness** of the room.
14. The second puppy was even **tinier** than the first.
15. The **firmest** cucumbers will be the freshest.
16. When writing jokes, **cleverness** is important.
17. Those plants are **healthier** under Lenny's care.
18. Always answer the **simplest** test questions first.
19. **Cleanliness** is important to good health.
20. Do you value the quality of **promptness?**

Pep Talk/Game Plan   *Pages 110–111*
Introduce the spelling rule and have students read the List Words aloud. Encourage students to look back at their Warm Up Tests and apply the spelling rule to any misspelled words.

As students work through the **Spelling Lineup, Word Parts,** and **Synonyms** exercises, remind them to look back at their List Words or in their dictionaries if they need help.

 See **Change or No Change,** page 15

Suffixes <u>er</u>, <u>est</u>, and <u>ness</u>

Warm Up
If you were a storyteller, what kind of stories would you tell?

Storyteller
Joseph Bruchac is a storyteller. With just his voice, a drum, and a little dash of **cleverness,** he can turn the **simplest** tale into a fascinating event. His talents have taken him across the United States and Europe, spreading **happiness** through storytelling.

Joseph believes that a good storyteller helps people by getting them so involved in a story that they forget about their everyday problems and walk away with **healthier** outlooks. "When you hear a story for the first time," he says, "you often take it in with the mind of a child. You see things differently and you go away refreshed."

Joseph also thinks that old stories can give us answers to the problems we face in the future. He believes that we should look to the paths we followed when human beings were in harmony with the earth.

Storytelling events are held all over the country. Check with your local library. Who knows, maybe Joseph will be visiting your neighborhood library. Or you could read some of the folk tales in his book, *Thirteen Moons on Turtle's Back,* and maybe start to be a storyteller yoursel

 Say the boldfaced words in the selection. These words have suffixes. What are the root words to which the suffixes are added? See if you notice any spelling changes in the root words when the suffixes are added.

On Your Mark
Take your Warm Up Test. Then check your spelling with the List Words on the next page.

109

Pep Talk
The suffix **er** means <u>more</u>. The suffix **est** means <u>most</u>. The suffix **ness** changes an adjective into a noun, as in damp— dampness.

For adding suffixes to words that end in y, change the **y** to **i**, as in tiny— tinier; noisy—noisier; empty— emptiness. For adding suffixes to words that end in **e**, drop the **e**, as in simple— simplest.

LIST WORDS
1. happiness
2. muddiest
3. tighter
4. cruelest
5. noisiest
6. crazier
7. stiffness
8. dampness
9. sharpness
10. strictest
11. brightest
12. thickest
13. emptiness
14. tinier
15. firmest
16. cleverness
17. healthier
18. simplest
19. cleanliness
20. promptness

Game Plan
Spelling Lineup
Write a List Word under the correct heading.

words with the suffix **er**
1. tighter
2. crazier
3. tinier
4. healthier

words with the suffix **est**
5. muddiest
6. cruelest
7. noisiest
8. strictest
9. brightest
10. thickest
11. firmest
12. simplest

words that were changed from adjectives to nouns with the suffix **ness**
13. happiness
14. stiffness
15. dampness
16. sharpness
17. emptiness
18. cleverness
19. cleanliness
20. promptness

110 Lesson 27 ■ Suffixes **er**, **est**, and **ness**

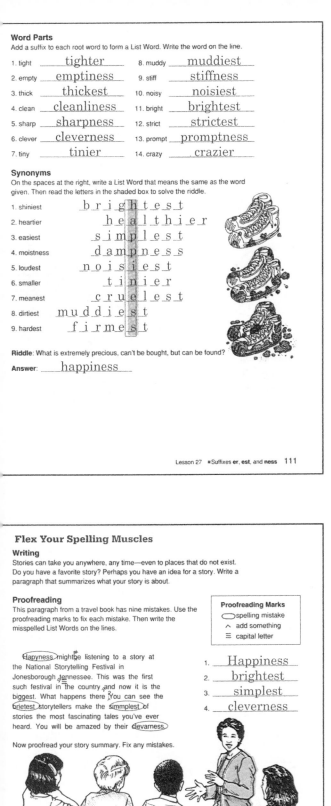

Word Parts
Add a suffix to each root word to form a List Word. Write the word on the line.

1. tight	tighter	8. muddy	muddiest	
2. empty	emptiness	9. stiff	stiffness	
3. thick	thickest	10. noisy	noisiest	
4. clean	cleanliness	11. bright	brightest	
5. sharp	sharpness	12. strict	strictest	
6. clever	cleverness	13. prompt	promptness	
7. tiny	tinier	14. crazy	crazier	

Synonyms
On the spaces at the right, write a List Word that means the same as the word given. Then read the letters in the shaded box to solve the riddle.

1. shiniest   b r i g h t e s t
2. heartier   h e a l t h i e r
3. easiest   s i m p l e s t
4. moistness   d a m p n e s s
5. loudest   n o i s i e s t
6. smaller   t i n i e r
7. meanest   c r u e l e s t
8. dirtiest   m u d d i e s t
9. hardest   f i r m e s t

Riddle: What is extremely precious, can't be bought, but can be found?

Answer: happiness

Flex Your Spelling Muscles

Writing
Stories can take you anywhere, any time—even to places that do not exist. Do you have a favorite story? Perhaps you have an idea for a story. Write a paragraph that summarizes what your story is about.

Proofreading
This paragraph from a travel book has nine mistakes. Use the proofreading marks to fix each mistake. Then write the misspelled List Words on the lines.

Proofreading Marks
◯ spelling mistake
∧ add something
≡ capital letter

Hapyness mightbe listening to a story at the National Storytelling Festival in Jonesborough, Tennessee. This was the first such festival in the country and now it is the biggest. What happens there? You can see the brietest storytellers make the simmplest of stories the most fascinating tales you've ever heard. You will be amazed by their clevarness.

1. Happiness
2. brightest
3. simplest
4. cleverness

Now proofread your story summary. Fix any mistakes.

Go for the Goal
Take your Final Test. Then fill in your Scoreboard. Send your mistakes to the Word Locker.

SCOREBOARD

number correct	number wrong

★ ★ ★ ★ ★ ★ ★ **All-Star Words** ★ ★ ★ ★ ★ ★ ★

bitterness   coarsest   filthier   gentler   painfulness

Write a paragraph using the All-Star Words. Then erase the suffixes. Trade papers with a partner. Read your partner's paragraph, adding the correct suffixes to the All-Star Words.

112   Lesson 27 ▪ Suffixes er, est, and ness

◎ **Spelling Strategy**   Ask the class to identify each List Word in which the root word changed when the suffix was added. Write students' responses on the board. Then call on volunteers to write each word as an equation (*noisy - y + i + est = noisiest/simple - e + est = simplest*), explaining the rule that applies to the spelling change as they do so.

Flex Your Spelling Muscles   *Page 112*

As students complete the **Writing** activity, encourage them to brainstorm ideas, write a first draft, revise, and proofread their work. The **Proofreading** exercise will help them prepare to proofread their summaries. To publish their writing, students may want to use their summaries to create a dust jacket for a book that features their story.

✎ **Writer's Corner**

You may wish to read students a story by Joseph Bruchac, having them take notes as they listen. Encourage students to study their notes to help them retell the story to a friend or to family members.

Go for the Goal/Final Test

1. Some people believe that **cleanliness** is a virtue.
2. He is exercising and eating **healthier** foods.
3. Did you use your **firmest** voice to scold her?
4. When my friend left, I felt an **emptiness** inside.
5. This red shirt is the **brightest** thing in my closet.
6. After falling, Ann had a **stiffness** in her arm.
7. Monkeys are the **noisiest** animals in the zoo.
8. Joey used the wrench to make the screw **tighter.**
9. My parents' greatest concern is my **happiness.**
10. The car is stuck in the **muddiest** part of the road.
11. Snow in May is the **cruelest** of nature's jokes.
12. I had never heard a **crazier** idea, but it worked!
13. A warm fire will get rid of the **dampness.**
14. The **strictest** rules were made for our safety.
15. This cafe serves the **thickest** steaks in town.
16. The sliver of ice got **tinier** as it melted.
17. His invention is an example of his **cleverness.**
18. Which problem did you think was the **simplest?**
19. Jane won an award because of her **promptness.**
20. We heard a **sharpness** in her voice.

Remind students to complete the Scoreboard and write any misspelled words in their Word Locker.

★★ **All-Star Words**   You may want to point out that the All-Star Words follow the spelling rule and help students brainstorm ideas for their paragraphs.

87

Lesson 28

Objective
To spell words with the suffixes *able, ible, ful, hood, ship,* and *ment*

Correlated Phonics Lessons
MCP Phonics, Level F, Lessons 56, 58–59

Warm Up   *Page 113*
In this selection, students learn how freckles help protect the skin from the sun. Invite students to share facts they may know about freckles or the skin.

Ask volunteers to say the boldfaced words and point out any spelling changes that occurred in the root words when the suffixes were added.

On Your Mark/Warm Up Test
1. Is Victor's new dog friendly and *likable?*
2. I have an *appointment* with the dentist tomorrow.
3. The rewards of *parenthood* are many.
4. Good *sportsmanship* means playing fair.
5. The weather in Boston is extremely *changeable.*
6. When you reach *adulthood,* you can vote.
7. The contents of that box are highly *breakable.*
8. Is *enrollment* in college one of your goals?
9. Listening to music puts me in a *fanciful* mood.
10. There are *noticeable* stains on the tablecloth.
11. What a *successful* writer he has become!
12. Sharing tasks will make the project *manageable.*
13. Your *assignment* is to write a poem.
14. My seat was too low and required *adjustment.*
15. The lawyer gave her final *argument* in the case.
16. The delay of the plane was *unavoidable.*
17. A great feature of the coat is that it's *reversible.*
18. Elise really enjoys her old red *convertible.*
19. The apple harvest was so *bountiful* this year!
20. Brenda was awarded a college *scholarship.*

Pep Talk/Game Plan   *Pages 114–115*
Introduce the spelling rule and have students read the List Words aloud. Encourage students to look back at their Warm Up Tests and apply the spelling rule to any misspelled words.

As students work through the **Spelling Lineup,** **Missing Words,** and **Classification** exercises, remind them to look back at their List Words or in their dictionaries if they need help. For the **Spelling Lineup,** review the rules for changing root words (*bounty, reverse*). Point out that *manage, change,* and *notice* do not drop the final *e* when the suffix is added.

 See **Words in Context,** page 14

Suffixes able, ible, ful, hood, ship, and ment   LESSON 28

Warm Up
Do you think that freckles really help protect your skin?

Sun Spots
The chances are good that you or someone you know has freckles. Throughout history, freckles have been a mark of distinction. In the 1700s, a famous English poet named John Dryden referred to "sprinkled freckles" as a sign of beauty. At about the same time, some people in Great Britain were hoping for a "freckle-faced" king. They believed that such a king would provide the best leadership to conquer their enemies.

Freckles are spots of dark skin pigments that help protect the skin from the sun's harmful rays. They're most **noticeable** on the face and arms. These pigments absorb more of the sun's burning and tanning rays than the rest of the skin surrounding them.

You may think that getting freckles is **unavoidable.** That's not entirely true. A person who is prone to freckling can be somewhat **successful** in protecting skin with a sunscreen. Freckles are not fully **reversible.** People who have freckles but wish they didn't can wait for a natural **adjustment.** Freckles will often fade when people reach **adulthood.** What's more, a person who is over 20 probably won't get any new freckles, either.

 Say the boldfaced words in the selection. Each boldfaced word has a prefix. What are the root words? What spelling changes in the root words occur when the suffixes are added?

On Your Mark
Take your Warm Up Test. Then check your spelling with the List Words on the next page.

113

Pep Talk
The suffixes **able** and **ible** usually mean can, or able to be. The suffix **ful** means full of. The suffix **hood** usually means the state or condition of being. The suffix **ship** means having the qualities of. The suffix **ment** means act of, state of.

Before adding the suffix to some words that end in e or y, drop the e or change y to i, as in like + able = likable, and fancy + ful = fanciful.

LIST WORDS

1. likable
2. appointment
3. parenthood
4. sportsmanship
5. changeable
6. adulthood
7. breakable
8. enrollment
9. fanciful
10. noticeable
11. successful
12. manageable
13. assignment
14. adjustment
15. argument
16. unavoidable
17. reversible
18. convertible
19. bountiful
20. scholarship

Game Plan
Spelling Lineup
Write each List Word in the correct category to show the suffix it contains.

able	ment
1. likable	11. appointment
2. changeable	12. enrollment
3. breakable	13. assignment
4. noticeable	14. adjustment
5. manageable	15. argument
6. unavoidable	

ible	**ful**
7. reversible	16. fanciful
8. convertible	17. successful
	18. bountiful

hood	**ship**
9. parenthood	19. sportsmanship
10. adulthood	20. scholarship

114   Lesson 28 ■ Suffixes **able, ible, ful, hood, ship,** and **ment**

Missing Words
Write a List Word to complete each sentence.

1. With the loan and the _____scholarship_____ she received, she'll be able to afford the college tuition.
2. If you purchase a _____reversible_____ shirt, it's like having two shirts in one.
3. Sometimes people raise their voices when they have an _____argument_____.
4. If the brakes are too tight, you'll need to make an _____adjustment_____.
5. After the animal trainer works with the lions, they will be _____manageable_____.
6. She has a whimsical, _____fanciful_____ imagination.
7. The _____enrollment_____ has increased; the school has 500 more students.
8. That is a very _____breakable_____ pitcher; please handle it with care.
9. When a bear cub reaches _____adulthood_____ it can hunt on its own.
10. There are many magazines available to mothers and fathers that have articles about all aspects of _____parenthood_____.

Classification
Write the List Word that belongs in each group.

1. inescapable, unmistakable, _____unavoidable_____
2. fairness, generosity, _____sportsmanship_____
3. visible, remarkable, _____noticeable_____
4. friendly, kind, _____likable_____
5. homework, book report, _____assignment_____
6. date, meeting, _____appointment_____
7. victorious, excellent, _____successful_____
8. unreliable, shifting, _____changeable_____
9. sedan, station wagon, _____convertible_____
10. abundant, rich, _____bountiful_____

Lesson 28 ■ Suffixes **able, ible, ful, hood, ship,** and **ment** 115

Flex Your Spelling Muscles

Writing
Write a paragraph that tells how to take care of your skin. You may want to mention the importance of moisturizers and sunscreens.

Proofreading
This article has twelve mistakes. Use the proofreading marks to fix each mistake. Then write the misspelled List Words correctly on the lines.

Proofreading Marks
- ⌒ spelling mistake
- ⊙ add period
- ⌄ add apostrophe

The earths atmosphere can be changable. The most noticeable change is the widening hole in the ozone layer. Pollutants are causing the ozone to break down. This exposes the earth to more ultraviolet radiation, which can harm peoples skin ⊙ Some people feel this problem is unavoydable. Others believe it's reversable if there's an adjusment in the levels of pollution. We'll be suksessful in doing so only if everyone makes this their own personal assienment.

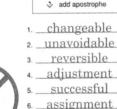

1. _____changeable_____
2. _____unavoidable_____
3. _____reversible_____
4. _____adjustment_____
5. _____successful_____
6. _____assignment_____

Now proofread your paragraph about skin care. Fix any mistakes.

Go for the Goal
Take your Final Test. Then fill in your Scoreboard. Send your mistakes to the Word Locker.

SCOREBOARD
number correct	number wrong

★ ★ ★ ★ ★ ★ ★ All-Star Words ★ ★ ★ ★ ★ ★ ★

digestible   inflatable   livelihood   fellowship   ailment

Write a newspaper headline for each All-Star Word. Trade papers with a partner. Make up a brief story to go with one of the headlines.

116 Lesson 28 ■ Suffixes **able, ible, ful, hood, ship,** and **ment**

⊚ **Spelling Strategy** With a partner, students can fold a piece of paper in half lengthwise, write the root word for each List Word in the first column, and write the List Word in the second column. Point out to students that in the case of *unavoidable* they will be adding not only a suffix, but also a prefix *(un)* to form the List Word. Then have students
- circle the List Words in which a spelling change occurred in the root word when the suffix was added
- discuss the rule that applies to each spelling change.

Flex Your Spelling Muscles   *Page 116*
As students complete the **Writing** activity, encourage them to brainstorm ideas, write a first draft, revise, and proofread their work. The **Proofreading** exercise will help them prepare to proofread their paragraphs. To publish their writing, students may want to use their paragraphs to make a poster about skin care to hang in the doctor's or nurse's office at their school.

✍ **Writer's Corner**

You may want to invite a local dermatologist to speak to the class about skin care. Before the visit, students can prepare a list of questions they would like to ask.

Go for the Goal/Final Test
1. **Changeable** winds made sailing difficult.
2. I overheard an **argument** about the baseball game.
3. The fresh paint made a **noticeable** improvement.
4. Did you apply for a **scholarship** to nursing school?
5. Your grandmother is a very **likable** person.
6. I know you'll be **successful** in your career.
7. When I reached **adulthood,** I moved to Tucson.
8. Some mistakes are totally **unavoidable.**
9. This book discusses **parenthood.**
10. What a relief to finish my homework **assignment!**
11. Jay applied for **enrollment** at the university.
12. Becky drove her **convertible** in the parade.
13. Dad made an **adjustment** on my bicycle.
14. The **fanciful** story told about a timid dragon.
15. The losing team showed good **sportsmanship.**
16. **Bountiful** rainfall helped the crops.
17. Plan ahead to make the project **manageable.**
18. Pack the **breakable** goods in plenty of newspaper.
19. When is your doctor's **appointment?**
20. Miguel's new jacket is **reversible.**

Remind students to complete the Scoreboard and write any misspelled words in their Word Locker.

★★ **All-Star Words** You may want to point out that the All-Star Words follow the spelling rule and display newspaper headlines as examples.

Lesson 29

Objective
To spell words with the suffixes *ion, ation, ition, ance, ence, ive,* and *ity*

Correlated Phonics Lessons
MCP Phonics, Level F, Lessons 60–61

Warm Up   Page 117
In "Twister!," students read about tornadoes and find out what to do if they encounter one. Invite students to share any facts they may know about powerful storms and to discuss their own experiences in them.

Ask volunteers to say the boldfaced words, identify the root words, and point out any spelling changes that occurred in the roots when the suffixes were added.

On Your Mark/ Warm Up Test
1. I know the **difference** between snow and sleet.
2. Coretta wrote a **composition** about her family.
3. Many homes are heated by **electricity.**
4. Our country has an **abundance** of resources.
5. Yesterday I had a **conversation** with Dr. Winter.
6. Do you believe in the **existence** of unicorns?
7. Reading is a relaxing **activity.**
8. **Communication** has been improved by satellites.
9. The **excellence** of that restaurant is well known.
10. In **addition** to swimming, I enjoy baseball.
11. Peanut butter and jelly is a famous **combination.**
12. In my spare time, I enjoy **creative** writing.
13. Was the teacher's **explanation** clear?
14. Spectator sports provide **passive** recreation.
15. I learned a **quotation** by Benjamin Franklin.
16. Fans provided for the **circulation** of fresh air.
17. That **destructive** dog just chewed up my glove!
18. The howling cat created a **disturbance.**
19. Observing a wild animal is a thrilling **experience.**
20. I was firm in my **resistance** to breaking rules.

Pep Talk/Game Plan   Pages 118–119
Introduce the spelling rule and have students read the List Words aloud. Encourage students to look back at their Warm Up Tests and apply the spelling rule to any misspelled words.

As students work through the **Spelling Lineup, Missing Words,** and **Antonyms** exercises, remind them to look back at their List Words or in their dictionaries if they need help. For the **Spelling Lineup,** you may wish to point out that the suffix *ion,* not *ation,* is used for words ending in *ate.*

 See **Tape Recording,** page 15

90

Name _____

Suffixes *ion, ation, ition, ance, ence, ive,* and *ity*   LESSON 29

Warm Up
What is the best thing to do if you see dark clouds coiling like a snake in the sky?

Twister!

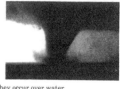

The storm began near Havre, Montana, on February 23, 1925. For thirty days, swirling winds blew, destroying everything in their path. The winds didn't die down until they had completely circled the globe—a distance of nearly 22,000 miles. This was no ordinary tornado. It was the longest-lasting cyclone in **existence.**

The word *cyclone* is borrowed from the folklore of ancient India. Cyclone means "coil of a snake." Tornadoes are also called twisters or waterspouts if they occur over water.

A tornado is formed when a quantity of cool, dry air collides with a massive stream of warm, moist air. When the two air masses collide, the warm air rises rapidly and more warm air rushes in beneath it. The warm rushing air also rises and, in **addition,** may begin to rotate, or turn. The rotating air may form a tornado. Soon a funnel forms as the **combination** of cool and warm air actively changes position.

In North America the winds of a tornado spin in a counterclockwise direction. The winds may be whirling around the center of the storm at speeds of more than 300 miles per hour. Most tornadoes last just an hour or two. They can travel up to 200 miles before exhausting themselves. Despite the short duration of a tornado, these storms can be extremely **destructive.**

If you ever see dark clouds coiling like a snake, take cover. A twister is on its way!

 Look back at the boldfaced words in the selection. What are the root words? What spelling changes in the root words occur when the suffixes are added?

On Your Mark
Take your Warm Up Test. Then check your spelling with the List Words on the next page.

117

Pep Talk
Suffixes and Their Meanings

ion, ation, and **ition** = the act of or the condition of being, as in *conversation* and *composition*

ance, ence, and **ity** = quality or fact of being, as in *resistance, experience,* and *activity*

ive = likely to or having to do with, as in *destructive* and *creative*

LIST WORDS
1. difference
2. composition
3. electricity
4. abundance
5. conversation
6. existence
7. activity
8. communication
9. excellence
10. addition
11. combination
12. creative
13. explanation
14. passive
15. quotation
16. circulation
17. destructive
18. disturbance
19. experience
20. resistance

Game Plan
Spelling Lineup
Write the List Words that contain the suffixes given.

ence
1. difference
2. existence
3. excellence
4. experience

ation
5. conversation
6. combination
7. explanation
8. quotation

ance
9. abundance
10. disturbance
11. resistance

ion
12. communication
13. circulation

ive
14. creative
15. passive
16. destructive

ition
17. composition
18. addition

ity
19. electricity
20. activity

"Everybody talks about the weather, but nobody does anything about it."
—Mark Twain

118 Lesson 29 ▪ Suffixes **ion, ation, ition, ance, ence, ive,** and **ity**

Missing Words

Write the List Word that belongs in each sentence.

1. Soccer is a recreational _____activity_____.
2. The ____destructive____ storm caused heavy damage.
3. Anya's ____experience____ as a tutor will help her to be a teacher.
4. The heart controls the ____circulation____ of blood.
5. The title of his ____composition____ was "Sources of Energy."
6. The telephone is a ____communication____ tool.
7. Winnie received an award for ____excellence____ in science.
8. Many people do not believe in the ____existence____ of UFOs.
9. I memorized the ____combination____ to the lock for my locker.
10. Our long-distance phone ____conversation____ lasted an hour!
11. We needed a more detailed ____explanation____ to fully understand how the machine worked.
12. That group was asked to leave because they were causing a ____disturbance____.
13. We take ____electricity____ for granted until the power goes out.
14. I'm going to cite this famous ____quotation____ by Albert Einstein in my report.

Antonyms

Write the List Word that has the opposite meaning of the word given.

1. active ____passive____
2. acceptance ____resistance____
3. subtraction ____addition____
4. similarity ____difference____
5. insufficiency ____abundance____
6. unimaginative ____creative____

Flex Your Spelling Muscles

Writing
Tornadoes, hurricanes, and floods can all turn into a disaster for people who live in areas where they strike. What do you think people should do to prepare for a big storm? Write your advice in one or two paragraphs.

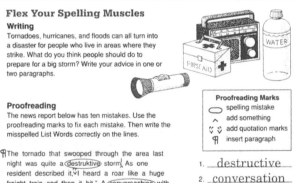

Proofreading
The news report below has ten mistakes. Use the proofreading marks to fix each mistake. Then write the misspelled List Words correctly on the lines.

Proofreading Marks
⟋ spelling mistake
∧ add something
⌄⌄ add quotation marks
¶ insert paragraph

¶The tornado that swooped through the area last night was quite a destruktive storm. As one resident described it, I heard a roar like a huge freight train and then it hit." A conversashion with another witness resulted in this quoetasion "My daughter Anna and I ran for the cellar as the electrisity flickered. The tornado tore off the roof. It was a very frightening experience for many residents. Camunication systems were knocked out for several hours until the disturbence passed.

1. ____destructive____
2. ____conversation____
3. ____quotation____
4. ____electricity____
5. Communication
6. ____disturbance____

Now proofread your storm advice. Fix any mistakes.

Go for the Goal

Take your Final Test. Then fill in your Scoreboard. Send your mistakes to the Word Locker.

SCOREBOARD
number correct | number wrong

★ ★ ★ ★ ★ ★ ★ ★ **All-Star Words** ★ ★ ★ ★ ★ ★ ★ ★

legislation   inspection   correspondence   radiance   originality

Write a sentence for each All-Star Word. Then trade papers with a partner. Take turns saying what the entire word means, and then what the suffix means.

⊙ **Spelling Strategy**   Write roots or root words contained in the List Words on the board. Then ask students which ending (*ion, ation, ition, ance, ence, ive, or ity*) goes with each root to spell a List Word. Call on a volunteer to come to the board and write the entire word, giving its meaning. Discuss roots that had spelling changes before the suffixes were added.

Flex Your Spelling Muscles   *Page 120*

As students complete the **Writing** activity, encourage them to brainstorm ideas, write a first draft, revise, and proofread their work. The **Proofreading** exercise will help them prepare to proofread their advice. To publish their writing, students may want to
• trade paragraphs with a partner and discuss each other's ideas
• read their paragraphs to the class.

✎ Writer's Corner

Students may be interested in reading about weather patterns and clouds in *The Weather Sky* by Bruce McMillan, or a similar book. Encourage groups of students to make charts showing the different kinds of clouds and the type of weather each is associated with.

Go for the Goal/Final Test

1. Write a **composition** for homework tonight.
2. Alaska has an **abundance** of natural resources.
3. Many people believe in the **existence** of UFOs.
4. The telegraph is a system of **communication.**
5. Are **addition** problems easy for you?
6. An elderly man wrote this **creative** story.
7. What does **passive** smoking mean?
8. Tight clothes may cut off blood **circulation.**
9. What a **disturbance** the barking dog caused!
10. Stainless steel has strong **resistance** to rust.
11. What is the **difference** between tin and steel?
12. My alarm clock is powered by **electricity.**
13. I'd like to have a **conversation** with that artist.
14. Swimming is my favorite summertime **activity.**
15. The movie won several awards for **excellence.**
16. Fire and wind are a dangerous **combination.**
17. Will you accept my **explanation** for being late?
18. Connie read a **quotation** by William Shakespeare.
19. The most **destructive** flood happened last year.
20. Hiking up the mountain was a great **experience.**

Remind students to complete the Scoreboard and write any misspelled words in their Word Locker.

★★ **All-Star Words**   You may want to point out that the All-Star Words follow the spelling rule. With a volunteer, complete the activity using a List Word.

91

Lesson 30 • Instant Replay

Objective

To review spelling words with the prefixes *anti*, *counter*, *super*, *sub*, *ultra*, *trans*, and *semi*; and with the suffixes *or*, *er*, *ist*, *logy*, *ology*, *est*, *ness*, *able*, *ible*, *ful*, *hood*, *ship*, *ment*, *ion*, *ation*, *ition*, *ance*, *ence*, *ive*, and *ity*

Time Out   *Pages 121–124*

Check Your Word Locker Based on your observations, note which words are giving students the most difficulty and offer assistance for spelling them correctly. Here are some frequently misspelled words to watch for: *antiseptic, subscription, experience, manufacturer, likable, changeable,* and *existence.*

To give students extra help and practice in taking standardized tests, you may want to have them take the Review Test for this lesson on pages 94–95. After scoring the tests, return them to students so that they can record their misspelled words in their Word Locker.

After practicing their troublesome words, students can work through the exercises for **Lessons 25–29.** Before they begin each exercise, you may want to go over the spelling rule.

Take It Home Invite students to listen for the List Words in **Lessons 25–29** in television shows, movies, and music videos. For a complete list of the words, encourage them to take their *Spelling Workout* books home. Students can also use Take It Home Master 5 on pages 96–97 to help them do the activity. Invite students to bring their lists to class and to compare them with other students' lists.

Time Out

Look again at the prefixes and suffixes added to words. Think about how they change the meanings and the spelling of some root words.

Check Your Word Locker

Look at the words in your Word Locker. Write your most troublesome words from Lessons 25 through 29.

_____

_____

Practice writing your troublesome words with a partner. Write sentences for each word. Trade papers, circle the prefixes, and tell the meaning of each prefix.

Lesson 25

Prefixes and Their Meanings

anti = against   counter = against   super = above, over
ultra = beyond   semi = half   sub = below   trans = across, through

List Words

antiseptic
supersonic
antifreeze
semifinal
semicolon
counteract
submarine
transparent
subscription
counterfeit

Write a List Word to complete each sentence.

1. Our team will play in the semifinal match.
2. The bill was fake; it was counterfeit
3. We put antifreeze in the car in the winter.
4. Use this ointment to counteract the sting.
5. A submarine travels underwater.
6. Use a semicolon to separate those clauses.
7. The nurse uses an antiseptic to kill germs.
8. Our subscription to that magazine is for one year.
9. That window is transparent ; you can see through it.
10. Supersonic aircraft exceeds the speed of sound.

121

Lesson 26

Suffixes and Their Meanings

or, er, ist = one who or something that   counter = against   logy, ology = the study of

List Words

consumer
biology
jeweler
aviator
spectator
typist
journalist
technology
manufacturer
investigator

Write a List Word that means the same or almost the same as the word or phrase given.

1. maker manufacturer
2. goldsmith jeweler
3. detective investigator
4. reporter journalist
5. pilot aviator
6. onlooker spectator
7. industrial science technology
8. buyer or user consumer
9. keyboarder typist
10. life science biology

Lesson 27

Suffixes and Their Meanings

er = more, as in *healthier*   est = most, as in *simplest*   ness changes an adjective into a noun

List Words

tighter
noisiest
dampness
brightest
thickest
emptiness
tinier
cleverness
simplest
cleanliness

Write the List Word that belongs in each group.

1. small, little, tinier
2. loud, ear-splitting, noisiest
3. broad, wide, thickest
4. easy, plain, simplest
5. firm, snug, tighter
6. abandoned, vacant, emptiness
7. wet, moist, dampness
8. intelligence, wit, cleverness
9. dust-free, sanitary, cleanliness
10. brilliant, shining, brightest

122 Lesson 30 ■ Instant Replay

Lesson 28

Suffixes and Their Meanings

able, ible = can, able to be   **ful** = full of   **hood** = state or condition of being
ship = having the qualities of   **ment** = what is

List Words

likable
changeable
adulthood
enrollment
successful
assignment
argument
reversible
convertible
bountiful

Write the List Word that has the same root as the word given.

1. exchange   changeable
2. arguing   argument
3. bounteous   bountiful
4. irreversibly   reversible
5. unlikely   likable
6. adultness   adulthood
7. succeeding   successful
8. reassign   assignment
9. enrolled   enrollment
10. converter   convertible

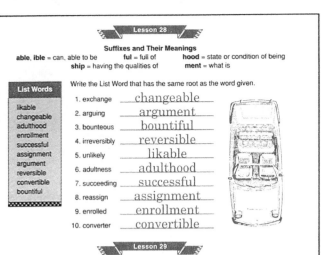

Lesson 29

Suffixes and Their Meanings

ion, ation, ition = the act of or the condition of being   **ance, ence, ity** = quality, fact of being
ive = likely to or having to do with

List Words

composition
destructive
conversation
communication
explanation
abundance
activity
excellence
addition
creative

Write a List Word to match each clue.

1. could describe an artist   creative
2. involves action   activity
3. something you might write   composition
4. describes a fire or storm   destructive
5. a phone call or a letter   communication
6. tells why it happened   explanation
7. more than enough   abundance
8. 2 plus 2   addition
9. talking between people   conversation
10. the best something can be   excellence

Lesson 30 ■ Instant Replay   123

Lessons 25–29

List Words

semicolon
technology
manufacturer
cleanliness
transparent
composition
typist
assignment
submarine
conversation
biology
tinier

Complete each sentence with a List Word.

1. Medical   technology   has enabled us to cure many diseases.
2. Some windows in buildings are not   transparent   .
3. My dad is concerned with   cleanliness   ; he's always straightening up things.
4. The pianist wrote the musical   composition   for that piece.
5. One type of   submarine   can dive to a depth of over 30 meters in one minute.
6. In our field   biology   class, we studied many native birds.
7. Some calculators are   tinier   than the palm of your hand.
8. The   manufacturer   of that product had to close down the factory.
9. He is a very fast   typist   ; he can type over 100 words a minute.
10. That particular   assignment   involved a lot of research.
11. We try to keep each long-distance phone   conversation   brief.
12. A   semicolon   is a cross between a period and a comma.

Go for the Goal

Take your Final Replay Test. Then fill in your Scoreboard. Send any misspelled words to your Word Locker.

SCOREBOARD

number correct	number wrong

Clean Out Your Word Locker
Look in your Word Locker. Cross out each word you spelled correctly on your Final Replay Test. Circle the words you're still having trouble with. Add the words you circled to your Spelling Notebook. What do you notice about the words? Watch for those words as you write.

1. We put *antifreeze* in the car before winter.
2. She easily won the *semifinal* tennis match.
3. Use an *antiseptic* to kill any germs.
4. Here is a *transparent* cover for your drawing.
5. The *submarine* stayed underwater for days.
6. These features will improve *consumer* safety.
7. In *biology* we studied the digestive system.
8. Any *jeweler* can fix that ring for you.
9. What kind of plane does that *aviator* fly?
10. Will you be a *spectator* today instead of a player?
11. Laughter echoed in the *emptiness* of the house.
12. Some dollhouses are even *tinier* than this one.
13. My dog's *cleverness* surprised the trainer.
14. This route is the *simplest,* but not the shortest.
15. In a hospital, *cleanliness* is vital.
16. Your parents are certainly *likable* people.
17. The weather in New England is very *changeable.*
18. My aunt spent most of her *adulthood* traveling.
19. Our class *enrollment* increases every year.
20. Good planning resulted in a *successful* vacation.
21. Our principal spoke of striving for *excellence.*
22. I can do simple *addition* without a calculator.
23. What a *creative* performer Julie is!
24. The citizens wanted an *explanation* of the tax.
25. The storm was *destructive,* but no one was hurt.
26. A magazine *subscription* is a thoughtful present.
27. This lotion will *counteract* that itching.
28. You should use a period instead of a *semicolon.*
29. What time will the *supersonic* plane arrive?
30. These jewels must be *counterfeit!*
31. The *typist* quickly entered the new data.
32. Each *journalist* wrote a separate story.
33. Computer *technology* changes so rapidly!
34. Return the defective radio to the *manufacturer.*
35. The *investigator* found the cause of the fire.
36. Can you tie that knot a little *tighter?*
37. This is the *noisiest* classroom in the building.
38. *Dampness* bothers me more than the cold does.
39. Which star in the sky is the *brightest?*
40. My history book is the *thickest* one in the pile.
41. Tonight's *assignment* is to read two chapters.
42. The problem was resolved without an *argument.*
43. This is a *reversible* coat, so I wear it often.
44. Who owns that new *convertible* in the lot?
45. What a *bountiful* harvest we had this year!
46. My teacher liked my last *composition.*
47. Our tree has an *abundance* of fruit on it.
48. Alex and Mom had a long *conversation.*
49. I like any *activity* that involves the ocean.
50. The climbers sent one *communication* a day.

Clean Out Your Word Locker   Before writing each word, students can say the word and identify its prefix or suffix.

Instant Replay Test

Side A

Read each set of phrases. Fill in the circle next to the phrase
with an underlined word that is spelled wrong.

1. ⓐ a <u>bountyful</u> harvest   ⓒ the <u>creative</u> artist
   ⓑ the chief <u>investigator</u>   ⓓ her <u>likeable</u> manager

2. ⓐ a <u>successful</u> career   ⓒ one appliance <u>mannufacturer</u>
   ⓑ this humid <u>dampness</u>   ⓓ the <u>brightest</u> colors

3. ⓐ an accurate <u>typeist</u>   ⓒ a newspaper <u>journalist</u>
   ⓑ <u>passive</u> behavior   ⓓ this unnecessary <u>semicolon</u>

4. ⓐ the power of <u>electricity</u>   ⓒ academic <u>excellence</u>
   ⓑ the <u>distructive</u> tornado   ⓓ car's <u>antifreeze</u>

5. ⓐ <u>cleverness</u> and ambition   ⓒ the <u>counterfit</u> bills
   ⓑ his renewed <u>subscription</u>   ⓓ a disinterested <u>spectator</u>

6. ⓐ a slight <u>adjustment</u>   ⓒ their homework <u>assignment</u>
   ⓑ a <u>semifinal</u> match   ⓓ a reasonable <u>explaination</u>

7. ⓐ the assistant <u>jeweler</u>   ⓒ <u>byology</u> class
   ⓑ our recent <u>conversation</u>   ⓓ this <u>breakable</u> vase

8. ⓐ this <u>antiseptic</u> cream   ⓒ the <u>tighter</u> pants
   ⓑ the cottage's <u>emptiness</u>   ⓓ her <u>comunication</u> skills

9. ⓐ <u>counterract</u> the disease   ⓒ the youngest <u>investigator</u>
   ⓑ a <u>fanciful</u> tale   ⓓ unexpected <u>sharpness</u>

10. ⓐ her concise <u>composition</u>   ⓒ a child's <u>happiness</u>
    ⓑ a dental <u>appointment</u>   ⓓ importance of <u>clenliness</u>

11. ⓐ his <u>likeable</u> parents   ⓒ her writing <u>activity</u>
    ⓑ the <u>thickkest</u> piece   ⓓ a political <u>argument</u>

12. ⓐ a surfacing <u>submarene</u>   ⓒ his <u>successful</u> attempts
    ⓑ athletic <u>excellence</u>   ⓓ the <u>creative</u> sculptor

13. ⓐ her <u>likeable</u> personality   ⓒ quality of <u>cleverness</u>
    ⓑ an elderly <u>jeweler</u>   ⓓ the <u>noisyest</u> siren

Instant Replay Test

Side B

ead each set of phrases. Fill in the circle next to the phrase
th an underlined word that is spelled wrong.

4.   ⓐ pride and <u>excellence</u>   ⓒ this <u>subscription</u> price
     ⓑ the tunnel's <u>dampness</u>   ⓓ these <u>enrolement</u> procedures

5.   ⓐ this <u>transparant</u> material   ⓒ her permanent <u>assignment</u>
     ⓑ the thorough <u>investigator</u>   ⓓ to fit <u>tighter</u>

6.   ⓐ an <u>antiseptic</u> ointment   ⓒ the <u>simpelest</u> solution
     ⓑ this exhausting <u>activity</u>   ⓓ a frantic <u>spectator</u>

7.   ⓐ those <u>successful</u> teachers   ⓒ his <u>reversable</u> jacket
     ⓑ this important <u>appointment</u>   ⓓ for the <u>semifinal</u>

8.   ⓐ <u>tinyer</u> than yours   ⓒ a <u>creative</u> project
     ⓑ the building's <u>emptiness</u>   ⓓ the <u>brightest</u> idea

9.   ⓐ a heated <u>argument</u>   ⓒ his eventful <u>adulthood</u>
     ⓑ <u>abundance</u> of resources   ⓓ these <u>consumer</u> tendencies

10.   ⓐ this misplaced <u>semicolon</u>   ⓒ the <u>supersonick</u> jet
     ⓑ their friendly <u>conversation</u>   ⓓ a courtroom <u>journalist</u>

11.   ⓐ a sporty <u>convertable</u>   ⓒ a <u>noticeable</u> change
     ⓑ her teacher's <u>explanation</u>   ⓓ check the <u>antifreeze</u>

12.   ⓐ her magazine <u>subscription</u>   ⓒ her lengthy <u>composition</u>
     ⓑ computer <u>tecknology</u>   ⓓ award for <u>excellence</u>

13.   ⓐ the undecided <u>juror</u>   ⓒ an inventor's <u>cleverness</u>
     ⓑ an experienced <u>aviater</u>   ⓓ the observant <u>investigator</u>

14.   ⓐ a red <u>semicircle</u>   ⓒ the cave's <u>dampness</u>
     ⓑ the <u>cruelest</u> punishment   ⓓ this <u>changable</u> weather

15.   ⓐ <u>addision</u> and subtraction   ⓒ a temporary <u>assignment</u>
     ⓑ <u>tighter</u> than those   ⓓ the clown's <u>happiness</u>

TAKE IT HOME

Your child has learned to spell many new words and would enjoy sharing them with you and your family. The following activities will help your child review the words in Lessons 25–29 and provide some family fun, too.

Spelling Star

Your child can "star" in a TV show or music video! Here's how. Encourage your child to write down spelling words as you watch television programs, movies, and music videos. Invite your child to become a "spelling star" by spelling aloud the words he or she listed.

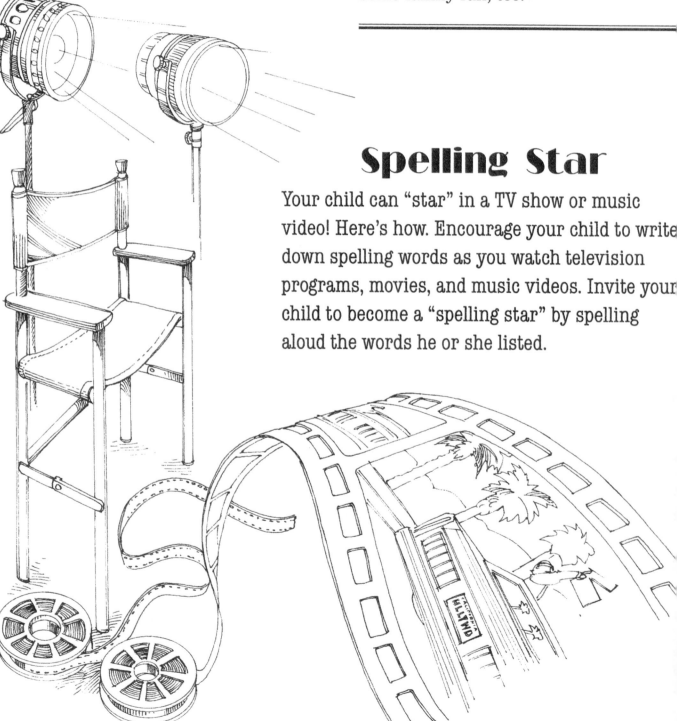

What's My Line?

How many occupations can you and your child guess? Write the spelling word that best answers each play on words. Use the underlined words to help you.

manufacturer	machinist	typist	jeweler	florist
spectator	investigator	aviator	geologist	juror

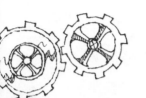 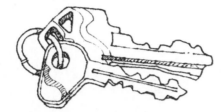

1. Who's turning over a new <u>leaf</u>? _____

2. Who's a <u>cog in a wheel</u>? _____

3. Who has a <u>fly</u> in his or her soup? _____

4. Who's <u>standing watch</u>? _____

5. Who looks on the <u>bright side</u>? _____

6. Who's a <u>rock hound</u>? _____

7. Who's all <u>keyed up</u>? _____

8. Who doesn't <u>have a clue</u>? _____

9. Who's got the <u>goods</u>? _____

10. Who <u>takes sides</u>? _____

Lesson 31

Objective

To spell words in which the final consonant was doubled or the final *e* dropped before adding the suffix

Correlated Phonics Lessons

MCP Phonics, Level F, Lessons 63–64

Warm Up   *Page 125*

In this selection, students read about a unique museum that helps visitors understand their feelings toward other people. Afterward, ask students why they would or would not like to visit the museum.

Call on volunteers to say each boldfaced word, identify the root word, and explain how the spelling of the root word changed when the suffix was added.

On Your Mark/Warm Up Test

1. How quickly the puddles **evaporated** in the heat!
2. When **combining** the ingredients, use a mixer.
3. Juan's sister **graduated** from high school today.
4. How long will that road remain **unpaved?**
5. My teacher **approved** the topic for my report.
6. The cashier **referred** me to the store manager.
7. Ted found homes for the puppies by **advertising.**
8. Lionel's suitcase was **crammed** with clothes.
9. Each class **produced** its own yearbook.
10. Her new bicycle comes **equipped** with a canteen.
11. The class election **occurred** yesterday.
12. Who **memorized** the longest poem?
13. The lion tamer easily **controlled** ten big cats.
14. That new adventure movie is **exciting!**
15. Many of the words in this note are **abbreviated.**
16. By my **calculation,** there should be rain soon.
17. With no **hesitation,** she dived into the pool.
18. Vina is busy **organizing** her photo collection.
19. The wig and glasses **disguised** Sandy's identity.
20. He **realized** that his coat was still on the bus.

Pep Talk/Game Plan   *Pages 126–127*

Introduce the spelling rule and have students read the List Words aloud. Encourage students to look back at their Warm Up Tests and apply the spelling rule to any misspelled words.

As students work through the **Spelling Lineup, Word Parts,** and **Missing Words** exercises, remind them to look back at their List Words or in their dictionaries if they need help. For the **Spelling Lineup,** explain that the spelling rules also apply to the List Words that have the suffix *ion (calculation, hesitation).*

 See **Comparing/Contrasting,** page 15

Warm Up

What kind of displays do you think you would find in the Museum of Tolerance?

A Museum Built on Tolerance

There is an **exciting** new museum in Los Angeles, California, unlike any other in the world. It is not the kind of museum where you'll find display cases **crammed** with artifacts from bygone days. In fact, there are very few glass cases. The Museum of Tolerance is an unusual museum, **equipped** with special effects. It contains displays that will cause you to consider how you feel about others who are different than you. This museum will move you to think about prejudice, and its effect on your life.

During a 2 1/2 hour tour, **combining** audio-visual special effects and a learning center, you get a chance to witness the tragedies that intolerance can cause. For example, in the "Whisper Gallery," visitors are bombarded with recordings of slurs and lies people can say about each other. The effect is chilling. Later in the tour, you hear firsthand accounts of people who have suffered because of prejudice and intolerance. The idea is to show what can happen when lies and ethnic slurs go unchallenged.

As one of the museum's creators said about the visitors to the museum, "We're calling on people to take responsibility for their words and actions."

| ADMIT ONE | Look back at the boldfaced words in the selection. Find the root word in each word. What happened to the spelling of the root word when the suffixes were added? |

On Your Mark

Take your Warm Up Test. Then check your spelling with the List Words on the next page.

Pep Talk

When a short-vowel word or syllable ends in a single consonant, usually double the consonant before adding a suffix that begins with a vowel, as in **equip** + **ed** = equipped.

When you add a suffix that begins with a vowel to a word that ends with **e**, drop the **e** before adding the suffix, as in **unpave** + **ed** = unpaved and **combine** + **ing** = combining.

LIST WORDS

1. evaporated
2. combining
3. graduated
4. unpaved
5. approved
6. referred
7. advertising
8. crammed
9. produced
10. occurred
11. occurred
12. memorized
13. controlled
14. exciting
15. abbreviated
16. calculation
17. hesitation
18. organizing
19. disguised
20. realized

Game Plan
Spelling Lineup

Write the List Words in which the final consonant was doubled before the suffix was added.

1. referred
2. crammed
3. equipped
4. occurred
5. controlled

Write the List Words in which the final *e* was dropped before the suffix was added.

6. evaporated
7. combining
8. graduated
9. unpaved
10. approved
11. advertising
12. produced
13. memorized
14. exciting
15. abbreviated
16. calculation
17. hesitation
18. organizing
19. disguised
20. realized

126   Lesson 31 ■ Doubling Final Consonants; Adding Suffixes to Words Ending in e

Word Parts

Add a suffix to each root word to form a List Word. Write the word on the line.

1. realize	realized	11. approve	approved
2. occur	occurred	12. refer	referred
3. graduate	graduated	13. memorize	memorized
4. combine	combining	14. hesitate	hesitation
5. calculate	calculation	15. cram	crammed
6. excite	exciting	16. disguise	disguised
7. control	controlled	17. abbreviate	abbreviated
8. unpave	unpaved	18. equip	equipped
9. produce	produced	19. advertise	advertising
10. organize	organizing	20. evaporate	evaporated

Missing Words

Write a List Word to complete each sentence.

1. Tony __memorized__ the poem so he would not need notes.

2. The chef is __combining__ all the ingredients in a large bowl.

3. Without any __hesitation__, the firefighter rushed into the burning building.

4. He __controlled__ his emotions well during the moving speech.

5. She __referred__ us to an excellent dentist.

6. We bounced up and down in the back seat as the car traveled down the __unpaved__ country road.

7. The audience laughed and cheered when they saw how many clowns had been __crammed__ into the tiny automobile.

8. Consuelo will be __organizing__ a new file system for the office files.

Flex Your Spelling Muscles

Writing

Write a paragraph telling what you think should be done about prejudice and intolerance and why your ideas would work.

Proofreading

The article below has eleven mistakes. Use the proofreading marks to fix each mistake. Write the misspelled List Words on the lines.

Proofreading Marks	
⬯	spelling mistake
⁄	make small letter
⌃	add something
⌄	add apostrophe

One of the worlds longest borders along which conflict has rarely occured is in North America. The lasting peace between Canada and the United States has prodused a beautiful place that is refared to as the International Peace Garden, which sits on the border in the Turtle Mountain Valley. Aproved and built in 1932, the garden is a symbol of peace. Its the only one of its kind in the world, combineing beauty with a message. What kinds of things will you see there? Youll see an exciteing stone tower made of rocks from both countries.

1.	occurred	4.	Approved
2.	produced	5.	combining
3.	referred	6.	exciting

Now proofread your paragraph. Fix any mistakes.

Go for the Goal

Take your Final Test. Then fill in your Scoreboard. Send your mistakes to the Word Locker.

SCOREBOARD

number correct   number wrong

★ ★ ★ ★ ★ ★ ★ ★ All-Star Words ★ ★ ★ ★ ★ ★ ★ ★

challenged   relating   patrolling   tolerated   admitted

With your partner, write a story using the All-Star Words. Then erase and put the All-Star Words in the wrong places. Trade papers with another team and rewrite their paragraph, using the All-Star Words correctly.

Spelling Strategy

⊙ **Spelling Strategy**   Write *calculate, combine, produce, occur, graduate, control, cram,* and *organize* on the board and ask volunteers to add *ed, ing,* or *ion* to form a List Word. For each word, have the volunteer explain how the spelling of the root word was changed in order to add the suffix. Point out that *controlled* is an exception to the spelling rule about doubling final consonants because the second syllable contains a long vowel, not a short vowel.

Flex Your Spelling Muscles   *Page 128*

As students complete the **Writing** activity, encourage them to brainstorm ideas, write a first draft, revise, and proofread their work. The **Proofreading** exercise will help them prepare to proofread their paragraphs. To publish their writing, students may want to
• submit their paragraphs to a local newspaper
• use their ideas to give a persuasive speech.

✍ Writer's Corner

Students might enjoy requesting a pen pal from the Student Letter Exchange, 630 3rd Avenue, New York, NY 10017. This group arranges correspondence in English between young people in the United States and fifty other countries.

Go for the Goal/Final Test

1. *Combining* ideas helped them solve the problem.
2. The *unpaved* road is rough and bumpy.
3. The librarian *referred* us to the nonfiction section.
4. We *crammed* all our luggage into the car's trunk.
5. The campers were *equipped* with sleeping bags.
6. The actors *memorized* their lines in the play.
7. What an *exciting* roller coaster ride that was!
8. How long will it take to do the *calculation?*
9. Is Carlos *organizing* teams for a baseball game?
10. No one *realized* how far we'd have to walk.
11. I *disguised* myself as an alien from outer space.
12. Being nervous, he spoke with *hesitation.*
13. Mai *abbreviated* many words in her letter.
14. She expertly *controlled* the horses.
15. The accident *occurred* on the first of June.
16. The factory *produced* men's clothing.
17. Is the grocery store *advertising* for cashiers?
18. Dad *approved* our plans to go to the beach.
19. Heather *graduated* from college last year.
20. The water *evaporated,* forming clouds.

Remind students to complete the Scoreboard and write any misspelled words in their Word Locker.

★★ **All-Star Words**   You may want to point out that the All-Star Words follow the spelling rule and help students brainstorm ideas for their stories.

Lesson 32

Objective

To spell words in which suffixes have been added to root words ending in *y*

Correlated Phonics Lesson

MCP Phonics, Level F, Lesson 66

Warm Up   Page 129

In "Ibimi," students learn not only about the history of cranberries, but also about how they are grown. After reading, invite students to describe dishes they like that contain cranberries or other fruit.

Encourage students to look back at the boldfaced words. Ask volunteers to say the words and identify any changes that occurred in the root words when the suffixes were added.

On Your Mark/Warm Up Test

1. Many ***companies*** make donations to charity.
2. We picked strawberries to make jams and ***jellies.***
3. He poured the soup ***sloppily,*** so it spilled.
4. Are the engineers ***surveying*** the vacant lot?
5. The astronomer wrote ***theories*** about quasars.
6. Denise ran ***steadily,*** maintaining an even pace.
7. The Nile River is one of the longest ***waterways.***
8. We ***identified*** several birds on our walk.
9. Which seats in this row are ***occupied?***
10. The dog ***disobeyed*** and followed me to school.
11. Some folk ***remedies*** may be effective.
12. After jogging, I drank the juice ***thirstily.***
13. Let's cut the ***decaying*** branches off the tree.
14. The teacher ***modified*** our regular daily schedule.
15. The universe has several ***galaxies.***
16. What are the major ***industries*** in Turkey?
17. Our ***attorneys*** met with us to discuss the case.
18. How ***dismayed*** we were when our team lost!
19. The microscope ***magnified*** the bacteria.
20. The actor has ***portrayed*** several famous people.

Pep Talk/Game Plan   Pages 130–131

Introduce the spelling rule and have students read the List Words aloud. Encourage students to look back at their Warm Up Tests and apply the spelling rule to any misspelled words.

As students work through the **Spelling Lineup, Vocabulary, Missing Words,** and **Antonyms** exercises, remind them to look back at their List Words or in their dictionaries if they need help.

 See **Charades/Pantomime,** page 15

100

Adding Suffixes to Words Ending in y

Warm Up

How are cranberries grown?

Ibimi

The word *ibimi* means "bitter berry." Ibimi is the name the Pequot Indians gave to a small red fruit that grew in Cape Cod.

When the Pilgrims reached Massachusetts, they, too, found the pink berries that bore pink blossoms. These flowers looked like the small delicate heads of cranes. The Pilgrims **identified** the berries that grew on these vines as crane-berries, which later became known as cranberries.

If you eat a cranberry right after it's been picked, you probably will be **dismayed** by its taste and spit it out. Its waxy coating and sour taste make this berry undelectable in its natural form. Nevertheless, more than half the households in America regularly consume cranberries produced by **companies.**

Cranberries are grown in bogs and marshy wetlands in the U.S. Northeast and Pacific Northwest. In mid-September growers flood the bogs and cover the berries with water. When the water is stirred, the berries come loose from their vines. The cranberries then float to the surface where they are harvested by a machine called an "egg beater." Next, they are transported to processing plants in refrigerated trucks that keep them from **decaying.** Then, cranberries are turned into juice, jams, and **jellies.**

 Look back at the boldfaced words in the selection. Each of these words ends in a suffix. What happens to the root words that end in y when the suffixes are added?

On Your Mark

Take your Warm Up Test. Then check your spelling with the List Words on the next page.

129

Pep Talk

If a word ends in:
- a **vowel** and **y,** add **ed** or **s** without changing the base word, as in disobeyed.
- a **consonant** and **y,** change the **y** to **i** before adding **ed** or **es,** as in occupied.
- a **consonant** and **y,** change the **y** to **i** before adding **ly,** as in sloppily.
- **y,** add **ing** without changing the base word, as in decaying.

LIST WORDS

1. companies
2. jellies
3. sloppily
4. surveying
5. theories
6. steadily
7. waterways
8. identified
9. occupied
10. disobeyed
11. remedies
12. thirstily
13. decaying
14. modified
15. galaxies
16. industries
17. attorneys
18. dismayed
19. magnified
20. portrayed

Game Plan

Spelling Lineup

Add a suffix to each word to form a List Word. Write the List Word on the line.

1. attorney <u>attorneys</u>
2. modify <u>modified</u>
3. company <u>companies</u>
4. magnify <u>magnified</u>
5. waterway <u>waterways</u>
6. identify <u>identified</u>
7. industry <u>industries</u>
8. occupy <u>occupied</u>
9. survey <u>surveying</u>
10. galaxy <u>galaxies</u>
11. steady <u>steadily</u>
12. theory <u>theories</u>
13. portray <u>portrayed</u>
14. dismay <u>dismayed</u>
15. jelly <u>jellies</u>
16. decay <u>decaying</u>
17. thirsty <u>thirstily</u>
18. sloppy <u>sloppily</u>
19. remedy <u>remedies</u>
20. disobey <u>disobeyed</u>

Vocabulary

Write a List Word to complete each sentence.

1. Things are __magnified__ with these: telescopes, microscopes, binoculars.

2. These are used to make __jellies__ : grapes, strawberries, raspberries.

3. __Attorneys__ work with these people: judges, juries, defendants.

4. These are __remedies__ for a cold: fruit juice, warm clothes, bed rest.

5. These are __waterways__ : rivers, creeks, brooks.

6. You might see these through a telescope: planets, __galaxies__ , asteroids.

7. These are words that mean changed: altered, adjusted, __modified__ .

8. These are words that mean anxious: __dismayed__ , saddened, worried.

9. These are different ways to be pictured: photographed, painted, __portrayed__ .

10. These are businesses: industries, shops, __companies__ .

Missing Words

Write a List Word to complete each sentence.

1. The surveyors are __surveying__ the lot for a new building.

2. There are many __theories__ about where UFOs come from.

3. Place all the __decaying__ leaves and twigs in the compost heap.

4. Many __industries__ are following strict guidelines regarding air pollution.

Antonyms

Write the List Word that means the opposite of the word or phrase given.

1. neatly	__sloppily__	4. empty, vacant	__occupied__
2. periodically	__steadily__	5. behaved	__disobeyed__
3. without thirst	__thirstily__	6. left unnamed	__identified__

Lesson 32 ▪ Adding Suffixes to Words Ending in y   131

Flex Your Spelling Muscles

Writing

Harvesting cranberries is a job not many people do. Write a notice for cranberry bog workers. Be sure to include what the job requires. Try to use as many List Words as you can.

Proofreading

This article has eleven mistakes. Use the proofreading marks to fix the mistakes. Write the misspelled List Words correctly on the lines.

Proofreading Marks	
◯	spelling mistake
/	make small letter
∧	add something
ℯ	take something out

Along the waterwayes of the Great Lakes region a special harvest takes place in the summer. The Ojibway people begin suraying the wild rice beds to plan their their harvest. Two people ride ride in each canoe, and one steedily pushes it through the water with a long pole. The Ojibway have occupyed this area and gathered wild rice for about 400 years. Their methods have not been modifyed very much over the years. They pull the stalks over, knock the tops and send the grains into the bottom of the canoe. Nothing is done slaupily.

1. __waterways__		4. __occupied__	
2. __surveying__		5. __modified__	
3. __steadily__		6. __sloppily__	

Now proofread your notice. Fix any mistakes.

Go for the Goal

Take your Final Test. Then fill in your Scoreboard. Send your mistakes to the Word Locker.

SCOREBOARD

number correct	number wrong

★ ★ ★ ★ ★ ★ ★ All-Star Words ★ ★ ★ ★ ★ ★ ★

jockeys   dictionaries   conveyed   glorified   greedily

Write a sentence with the root word for each All-Star Word. Trade papers with your partner. Add the suffixes to make the All-Star Words, and write new sentences.

132   Lesson 32 ▪ Adding Suffixes to Words Ending in y

◎ **Spelling Strategy**   Write *consonant-y* on one side of the board and *vowel-y* on the other. Say the root word in each List Word and have students

• point to the side of the board that applies to the last two letters in the root word
• add a suffix to the root word to form a List Word
• spell the List Word aloud.

After each word is spelled, ask a volunteer to explain the rule that applies to adding the suffix.

Flex Your Spelling Muscles   *Page 132*

As students complete the **Writing** activity, encourage them to brainstorm ideas, write a first draft, revise, and proofread their work. The **Proofreading** exercise will help them prepare to proofread their notices. To publish their writing, students may want to

• combine their notices into a newspaper want-ads section
• use their notices to role-play job interviews.

✍ Writer's Corner

Encourage students to read an encyclopedia entry for your state to find out what its major crops are. Suggest that they make a map to show what crops are grown in different regions of the state.

Go for the Goal/Final Test

1. The train compartment is fully *occupied.*
2. Are geologists *surveying* the field?
3. Have you *modified* your travel plans yet?
4. The flea in the photo is *magnified* many times.
5. The dog *disobeyed* and turned left, not right.
6. Scientists try to test their *theories.*
7. Who *portrayed* Queen Victoria in the movie?
8. How exciting it would be to explore *galaxies!*
9. *Attorneys* attend law school for many years.
10. The farm horse drank from the pail *thirstily.*
11. I'd like to explore America's *waterways.*
12. Janet sells homemade *jellies* at a roadside stand.
13. Water poured *steadily* from the broken pipe.
14. Several *companies* manufacture dishwashers.
15. Are there any new *remedies* for poison ivy?
16. Many people are employed by steel *industries.*
17. I cook *sloppily* when I'm rushed.
18. I *identified* Grandpa in his old school photo.
19. The *decaying* leaves will make rich garden soil.
20. We were *dismayed* to miss your birthday party.

Remind students to complete the Scoreboard and write any misspelled words in their Word Locker.

★★ **All-Star Words**   You may wish to point out that the All-Star Words follow the spelling rule and model the activity using a List Word.

101

Lesson 33

Objective
To spell the plurals of nouns ending in *f, fe,* and *o;* and nouns whose singular and plural forms are the same

Correlated Phonics Lessons
MCP Phonics, Level F, Lessons 69–71

Warm Up   Page 133
In this selection, students read about the word histories of several names, such as *daisy* and *tomato.* Invite the class to brainstorm additional English words that have come from other languages.

Ask volunteers to say each boldfaced word, identify the singular form, and tell whether or not the spelling of the plural form is different.

On Your Mark/Warm Up Test
1. Many western towns hold *rodeos* in the summer.
2. *Kangaroos* are such fascinating animals!
3. The band members were all wearing *tuxedos.*
4. The hotel's *patios* are cool places to sit.
5. Does this store sell car *stereos?*
6. Nina bought two *avocados* at the store.
7. We enjoy discussing our different *beliefs.*
8. The tale of forty *thieves* is one of my favorites.
9. Do importers of jewelry pay high *tariffs?*
10. Some plant *species* have become extinct.
11. The waiters in the Mexican cafe wore *ponchos.*
12. We played a game of *dominoes* after school.
13. These shells are *mementos* from our vacation.
14. *Embargoes* were put on goods from that country.
15. I prefer my *broccoli* with lemon.
16. Aunt Mary made tomato sauce for the *spaghetti.*
17. Let's look for a store that sells *jackknives.*
18. Jill's aunt gave her several *handkerchiefs.*
19. The *Eskimos* trimmed their jackets with fur.
20. The *mosquitoes* are so annoying!

Pep Talk/Game Plan   Pages 134–135
Introduce the spelling rule and have students read the List Words aloud. Encourage students to look back at their Warm Up Tests and apply the spelling rule to any misspelled words.

As students work through the **Spelling Lineup, Word Games,** and **Puzzle** exercises, remind them to look back at their List Words or in their dictionaries if they need help. After students complete the **Spelling Lineup,** you may want to explain that another name for *Eskimo* is *Inuit.*

 See **Picture Clues,** page 15

Plurals

LESSON
33

Warm Up
Why do we call things by a certain name?

What's in a Name?
Did you ever wonder why we call a daisy a daisy? The names of many different **species** of flowers and plants that grow around our **patios** and yards come from other languages. For example, dandelion comes from the French, *dent de lion,* which means lion's tooth. You may well ask why the dandelion doesn't look like a lion's tooth. The name actually refers to the leaves of the plant itself. They are long and deeply indented, like a lion's tooth. Gladioli comes from the Latin word *gladiolus,* which means little sword, and a gladioli is long and slender like a sword. Chrysanthemum is the golden flower. It gets its name from the Greek word for gold, *crysos.*

Many of our foods get their names from other languages as well. We get a few food names from the Nahuatl peoples of Mexico and Central America. Tomato comes from its original Nahuatl name *tomatl.* The singular of **avocados,** avocado, can be traced back to the Nahuatl word *ahuacatl,* which means delicacy. **Broccoli** comes from the Italian word *broccolo,* which means cabbage sprout. And **spaghetti,** which certainly isn't a vegetable, is based on the Italian word *spago,* meaning string!

As for the daisy, its white petals open with the rays of sunshine that mark the beginning of a new day. Then in the evening, when the sun disappears, the daisy closes its petals. Its name comes from the Latin *daeges eage,* or "day's eye."

 Look back at the boldfaced words in the selection. Say the singular form of each plural word. What do you notice about the spelling of some plural forms of words?

On Your Mark
Take your Warm Up Test. Then check your spelling with the List Words on the next page.

Pep Talk
Some words remain the same in singular and plural form, as in species →species.

For most words that end in **f** or **fe**, change the **f** or **fe** to **v** and add **es** to form the plural. Sometimes, just add **s**, as in knife →knives and belief →beliefs.

When a word ends in **o**, sometimes form the plural by adding **es**. Other times just add **s**, as in mosquito →mosquitoes and stereo →stereos.

LIST WORDS

1. rodeos
2. kangaroos
3. tuxedos
4. patios
5. stereos
6. avocados
7. beliefs
8. thieves
9. tariffs
10. species
11. ponchos
12. dominoes
13. mementos
14. embargoes
15. broccoli
16. spaghetti
17. jackknives
18. handkerchiefs
19. Eskimos
20. mosquitoes

Game Plan
Spelling Lineup
Write the List Words under the correct headings.

words that do not change to form the plural
1. ___species___
2. ___broccoli___
3. ___spaghetti___

words that change f or fe to v and add **es** to form the plural
4. ___thieves___
5. ___jackknives___

words that end in **o** and add **es** to form the plural
6. ___dominoes___
7. ___embargoes___
8. ___mosquitoes___

words that end in f or o and just add **s** to form the plural
9. ___rodeos___
10. ___kangaroos___
11. ___tuxedos___
12. ___patios___
13. ___stereos___
14. ___avocados___
15. ___beliefs___
16. ___tariffs___
17. ___ponchos___
18. ___mementos___
19. ___handkerchiefs___
20. ___Eskimos___

Word Games

Write a List Word to match each definition clue.

1. suits worn by bridegrooms — tuxedos
2. cloths often used by people with a cold — handkerchiefs
3. areas where barbecues may be held — patios
4. contests for cowboys — rodeos
5. take what isn't theirs — thieves
6. bugs that won't quit biting — mosquitoes
7. long strands of pasta — spaghetti

Puzzle

Fill in the crossword puzzle by writing a List Word that is the plural form of the word given.

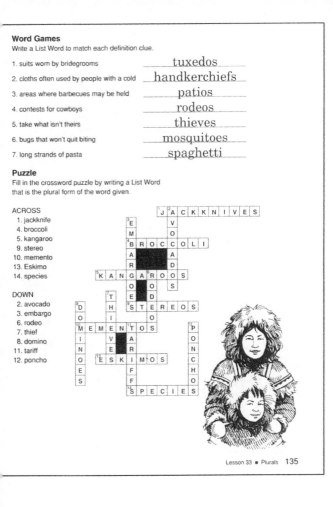

ACROSS
1. jackknife
4. broccoli
5. kangaroo
9. stereo
10. memento
13. Eskimo
14. species

DOWN
2. avocado
3. embargo
6. rodeo
7. thief
8. domino
11. tariff
12. poncho

Lesson 33 ■ Plurals   135

Flex Your Spelling Muscles

Writing

Flowers have many different names. Think of a flower that you know of or like, or use one of the following: mosquito trap, Queen Anne's lace, buttercup, tiger lily, Johnny-jump-up, or snapdragon. Write a poem about its color, name, or shape.

Proofreading

The article below has ten mistakes. Use the proofreading marks to fix each mistake. Then write the misspelled List Words on the lines.

Proofreading Marks
- ⌒ spelling mistake
- / make small letter
- ⌄ add apostrophe

Some spesies of plants are named after people. For Example, the bougainvillea flower comes from Louis Antonine de Bougainville, who was the first European to explore parts of the Pacific Ocean in 1766. He saw the Great Barrier Reef in Australia, but he missed seeing any kangarus The red poinsettia is named for Joel Poinsett, a U.S. politician. When he became the country's minister to Mexico, he'd left behind tarifs and embargos but not his political belefs. Mexico's government resented his interfering in their affairs. Poinsett was also a botanist. One of the memeintoes he brought back from Mexico was the bright, red flower that was named for him.

1. species
2. kangaroos
3. tariffs
4. embargoes
5. beliefs
6. mementos

Now proofread your flower poem. Fix any mistakes.

Go for the Goal

Take your Final Test. Then fill in your Scoreboard. Send your mistakes to the Word Locker.

SCOREBOARD

number correct	number wrong

★ ★ ★ ★ ★ ★ ★ ★ **All-Star Words** ★ ★ ★ ★ ★ ★ ★ ★

heroes   confetti   videos   sheaves   soprano

Write a sentence for each All-Star word. Compare sentences with your partner. Then work with your partner to write a spelling rule for each type of plural represented.

◉ **Spelling Strategy**   Write *singular* and *plural* at the top of two columns on the board. Write each List Word in the *plural* column and call on a volunteer to
• write the singular form in the other column
• explain the rule that applies to forming the plural
• suggest another word that forms its plural according to the same rule.

Flex Your Spelling Muscles   *Page 136*

As students complete the **Writing** activity, encourage them to brainstorm ideas, write a first draft, revise, and proofread their work. The **Proofreading** exercise will help them prepare to proofread their writing. To publish their poems, students may want to send them to *Wombat,* Journal of Young People's Writing and Art, 365 Ashton Drive, Athens, GA 30606.

✍ **Writer's Corner**

Students may enjoy looking through a book such as *Webster's New World Dictionary of Eponyms* by Auriel Douglas. Explain that an eponym is a person for whom something is named, such as *Saturday* for the Roman god Saturn. Encourage students to write entries for an eponym dictionary using words derived from their own names.

Go for the Goal/Final Test

1. Many **Eskimos** live in Alaska.
2. All the campers carried **jackknives.**
3. Raw **broccoli** is a good vegetable snack.
4. Danielle has many **mementos** of her school days.
5. Does this store sell authentic Mexican **ponchos?**
6. **Tariffs** were placed on the imported goods.
7. We get along because we share many **beliefs.**
8. I looked at a lot of **stereos** before buying one.
9. The ushers at the wedding all wore **tuxedos.**
10. The cowboys participated in **rodeos.**
11. **Kangaroos** carry their babies in pouches.
12. All the houses in our neighborhood have **patios.**
13. Guacamole is made with ripe **avocados.**
14. How quickly the police arrested the **thieves!**
15. Dinosaurs are an extinct **species.**
16. All the **dominoes** in the row fell.
17. **Embargoes** are placed on every ship leaving port.
18. The chef boiled the **spaghetti.**
19. People waved **handkerchiefs** as the king passed.
20. We moved inside because of the **mosquitoes.**

Remind students to complete the Scoreboard and write any misspelled words in their Word Locker.

★★ **All-Star Words**   Point out that the All-Star Words follow the spelling rule and review the information in the Pep Talk box with students.

Lesson 34

Objective

To spell words that are homonyms or other words that are often confused, referred to here as "hurdle words"

Warm Up
Page 137

In "One of a Kind Imprints," students read about a form of identification that is uniquely theirs—their fingerprints. Ask students whether they have ever had their fingerprints taken and to suggest other types of personal identification.

Call on volunteers to say each boldfaced word and name another word that sounds the same, but that has a different spelling and meaning.

On Your Mark/Warm Up Test

1. He was so tired that he slept *through* the movie.
2. Seth *threw* the empty can into the recycling bin.
3. We will have to *wait* an hour for the next bus.
4. The man will guess your *weight* for a penny.
5. She refused on *principle* to pay the high price.
6. The *principal* praised the graduating class.
7. Mike can easily jump up and touch the *ceiling.*
8. Mrs. Chang is *sealing* the package with tape.
9. The *weather* is so beautiful today!
10. We haven't heard *whether* or not Julie is coming.
11. Shall I use *coarse* sandpaper on this wood?
12. The university offers a *course* on the Civil War.
13. Several *patients* are waiting to see the doctor.
14. Having *patience* is not easy for young children.
15. Everyone arrived on time *except* Ji-Li.
16. Will you please *accept* my apology?
17. Patty ate yogurt for *dessert.*
18. The sun beat down on the white *desert* sand.
19. That question is too *personal* for me to answer.
20. To apply for a job, go to the *personnel* office.

Pep Talk/Game Plan
Pages 138–139

Introduce the spelling rule and have students read the List Words aloud. Encourage students to look back at their Warm Up Tests and apply the spelling rule to any misspelled words.

As students work through the **Spelling Lineup,** **Missing Words,** and **Definitions** exercises, remind them to look back at their List Words or in their dictionaries if they need help. For the **Spelling Lineup,** make sure students understand that they should first write the List Word that goes with the clue. Beside it, they should write its homonym or a word with a similar sound and spelling.

 See **Rhymes and Songs,** page 14

104

Missing Words

Complete each sentence with a List Word that is a homonym for or sounds similar to the underlined word.

1. The <u>principal</u> discussed the _____principle_____ of honesty.

2. We are ____sealing____ the cracks in the <u>ceiling</u>.

3. I had to <u>wait</u> for the nurse to check my ____weight____

4. The doctor showed ____patience____ with his young <u>patients</u>.

5. ___Whether___ or not we go will depend on the <u>weather</u> forecast.

6. <u>Except</u> for two people, they all arrived to ____accept____ their awards.

7. The boy <u>threw</u> the ball ____through____ the open window.

8. The <u>personnel</u> manager asked him some very ____personal____ questions.

Definitions

On the spaces at the right, write a List Word to solve each definition clue. Then write the letters in the shaded box to solve the riddle.

1. served at the end of a meal   D E S S E R T

2. a school subject   C O U R S E

3. not fine or delicate; harsh   C O A R S E

4. head of a school   P R I N C I P A L

5. remain until something happens   W A I T

6. top part of a room   C E I L I N G

7. people who need a doctor's care   P A T I E N T S

8. employed persons   P E R S O N N E L

9. other than; but   E X C E P T

Riddle: What's the best way to communicate with a fish?

Answer: DROP A LINE

Flex Your Spelling Muscles

Writing

In the future, people might also use their eyes or their voices as identification to unlock doors. Write a letter to a company in which you describe a security device that you have invented for use in the future.

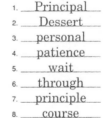

Proofreading

The book review below has fifteen mistakes. Use the proofreading marks to fix each mistake. Circle the misused List Words. Then write the List Words correctly on the lines.

Proofreading Marks
ᭉ ᭒ add quotation marks
∧ add something

The (Principle) Ate (Desert) is such an exciting story. There is nonstop action in this (personnel) story about a clever detective who has the (patients) to (weight) for the criminal to make a mistake. One reviewer says, ˇI read (threw) just the first ten pages, and I knew it was a book of (principal) The author says, ˇOf (coarse) (weather) or not readers like it remains to be seen."

1. _____Principal_____
2. _____Dessert_____
3. _____personal_____
4. _____patience_____
5. _____wait_____
6. _____through_____
7. _____principle_____
8. _____course_____
9. _____whether_____

Now proofread your letter. Fix any mistakes.

Go for the Goal

Take your Final Test. Then fill in your Scoreboard. Send your mistakes to the Word Locker.

SCOREBOARD
number correct	number wrong

★ ★ ★ ★ ★ ★ ★ ★ **All-Star Words** ★ ★ ★ ★ ★ ★ ★ ★

capitol   chute   stationary   reign   martial

Make a list of the All-Star Words. Write a homonym for each word. Work with a partner. One of you write sentences for the first words, and the other write sentences for the homonym pairs. Then compare sentences.

◉ Spelling Strategy You may want to write one half of each List Word pair on the board. Ask students to spell the second word aloud, and write it on the board as they do so. Then call on volunteers to use each word in the pair in a sentence.

Flex Your Spelling Muscles   *Page 140*

As students complete the **Writing** activity, encourage them to brainstorm ideas, write a first draft, revise, and proofread their work. The **Proofreading** exercise will help them prepare to proofread their letters. To publish their writing, students may want to illustrate their inventions, then use their letters and drawings or diagrams to make a bulletin-board display.

✎ Writer's Corner

Students may enjoy turning their thumbprints into drawings by following the directions in *Ed Emberley's Great Thumbprint Drawing Book*. Encourage students to write a story for younger children, using their thumbprint artwork as the illustrations.

Go for the Goal/Final Test

1. The juggler **threw** five balls into the air.
2. I gain **weight** more easily than my sister.
3. Mrs. Hundert is the **principal** of the school.
4. The judges are **sealing** their votes in envelopes.
5. Will you tell me **whether** or not I am right?
6. Lynda is taking an auto repair **course.**
7. You must try to have more **patience!**
8. The candidate will **accept** the nomination.
9. Cactus plants grow well in the **desert.**
10. Your application is in the **personnel** office.
11. Liz looked at the eagle **through** binoculars.
12. We will **wait** ten more minutes for Teresita.
13. He makes it a **principle** never to tell a lie.
14. Water leaked through the crack in the **ceiling.**
15. What time is the **weather** forecast shown on TV?
16. The burlap material is stiff and **coarse.**
17. The doctor has time to see four more **patients.**
18. The store is open every day **except** Sunday.
19. The waiter asked if we had room for **dessert.**
20. Can we discuss the **personal** matter in private?

Remind students to complete the Scoreboard and write any misspelled words in their Word Locker.

★★ **All-Star Words** You may want to point out that the All-Star Words follow the spelling rule. Model completing the activity with a List Word homonym pair.

Lesson 35

Objective
To spell abbreviations of words

Warm Up   *Page 141*
Students might enjoy deciphering Joe Quick's letter in "Short and Sweet." After reading, invite students to read the sentences they liked the best, saying the words that the abbreviations represent.

Ask volunteers to identify the words that the boldfaced abbreviations stand for.

On Your Mark/Warm Up Test
1. The *government* collects taxes. *(govt.)*
2. Linda was elected class *president.* *(pres.)*
3. Pat works in a big *department* store. *(dept.)*
4. Did you interview with that *company?* *(co.)*
5. Mom's business recently *incorporated.* *(inc.)*
6. A pronoun is the *subject* of the sentence. *(subj.)*
7. Is there a new *edition* of that dictionary? *(ed.)*
8. *Volume* 8 of the encyclopedia is missing. *(vol.)*
9. Sue read a *biography* of Lincoln. *(biog.)*
10. They live at *number* 26 Hale Street. *(no.)*
11. My report, for *example,* is about Alaska. *(ex.)*
12. It's the Suns *versus* the Jets tonight. *(vs.)*
13. Does the small pitcher hold a *pint* of milk? *(pt.)*
14. A *quart* is one-fourth of a gallon. *(qt.)*
15. The recipe calls for an *ounce* of butter. *(oz.)*
16. We need a *pound* of meat for the stew. *(lb.)*
17. John is the *manager* of a bank. *(mgr.)*
18. Ed was promoted to *assistant* supervisor. *(asst.)*
19. I can't wait to open the *package!* *(pkg.)*
20. The clerk stacked the *merchandise.* *(mdse.)*

Pep Talk/Game Plan   *Pages 142–143*
Introduce the spelling rule and help students identify the words that the abbreviations in the List Words box represent, emphasizing those spelled with letters not found in the complete words (*oz., lb.,* and *no.*). Then encourage students to look back at their Warm Up Tests and apply the spelling rule to any misspelled words.

As students work through the **Spelling Lineup, Misspelled Words,** and **Abbreviations** exercises, remind them to look back at their List Words or in their dictionaries if they need help. For the **Spelling Lineup,** you may want to do the first few items with students, checking that they write a period at the end of each abbreviation.

 See **Words in Context,** page 14

106

Warm Up
Can you figure out Joe Quick's message to Mrs. X?

Short and Sweet
Here's the letter that Mrs. X received from Joe Quick.

> **SPEEDY CO., INC.**
> 1001 Fast Blvd.   Velocity, NY 00240
>
> Dear Mrs. X,
>
>   As **Pres.** of Speedy Co., Inc., I have read your **biog.** along with those of a **no.** of other applicants. I am pleased that you have applied for a position with us **vs.** one with the **govt.**; however, I believe that an **oz.** of experience is worth more than a **lb.** of ability. Because the **vol.** of your experience is extremely limited, the only position I could possibly offer is an **asst.** to our **mdse. mgr.** in the shipping **dept.** As an **ex.** of what the job entails, you might be asked to ship a two oz. **pkg.** to Taiwan, or a three **lb.** pkg. to Timbuktu. Let me know what you think.
>
>   Sorry to change the **subj.** and cut this letter short, but I'm a very busy guy.
>
> Sincerely,
>
> Joe Quick, Pres.
> Speedy Co., Inc.

Did Mrs. X get the job? What exactly was the job?

SPEEDY CO., INC.	Look back at all the boldfaced abbreviations in the selection. Try to say all the words that the abbreviations stand for.

On Your Mark
Take your Warm Up Test. Then check your spelling with the List Words on the next page.

Pep Talk
An abbreviation is the shortened form of a word that ends with a period. Most are spelled with the first letters of the word, as in company → co. Some are spelled with a combination of letters from the word, as in package → pkg. Others are spelled with letters not found in the original word, as in ounce → oz. and pound → lb.

LIST WORDS

1. govt.
2. pres.
3. dept.
4. co.
5. inc.
6. subj.
7. ed.
8. vol.
9. biog.
10. no.
11. ex.
12. vs.
13. pt.
14. qt.
15. oz.
16. lb.
17. mgr.
18. asst.
19. pkg.
20. mdse.

Game Plan
Spelling Lineup
Write a List Word that is an abbreviation for the word given.

1. manager	mgr.		11. number	no.
2. incorporated	inc.		12. biography	biog.
3. merchandise	mdse.		13. pound	lb.
4. versus	vs.		14. company	co.
5. assistant	asst.		15. government	govt.
6. department	dept.		16. example	ex.
7. ounce	oz.		17. package	pkg.
8. volume	vol.		18. pint	pt.
9. subject	subj.		19. edition	ed.
10. quart	qt.		20. president	pres.

Misspelled Words

In each set of words, circle the correct spelling of the List Word. Then write the correct spelling on the line.

1. depa.   dep.   (dept)   dept.
2. mang.   (mgr.)   mnr.   mgr.
3. (biog.)   bio.   bphy.   biog.
4. (pres.)   prsd.   pdnt.   pres.
5. ver.   (vs.)   vrs.   vs.
6. (no.)   nu.   numb.   no.
7. sub.   sbjt.   (subj.)   subj.
8. qut.   (qt.)   qrt.   qt.
9. (mdse.)   merc.   mrse.   mdse.
10. pnd.   lnd.   (lb.)   lb.
11. (inc.)   in.   inct.   inc.
12. ou.   onc.   (oz.)   oz.

Abbreviations

Write a List Word that is the abbreviation for the underlined word in each sentence.

1. The tour guide showed us an example of a fossil. ex.
2. We found information about England in volume 6 of the encyclopedia. vol.
3. The first edition of a classic would be priceless. ed.
4. Martin wants to work for the government when he graduates. govt.
5. Dr. Tripp introduced us to her young assistant. asst.
6. The delivery service left the package on our doorstep. pkg.
7. The quiche recipe calls for a pint of heavy cream. pt.
8. Carlos applied for a job at my aunt's company. co.

Flex Your Spelling Muscles

Writing

Why do you think people use abbreviations? Write your ideas in a paragraph. Be sure to explain why they are useful or why they create problems. Try to use as many List Words as you can.

Proofreading

The following recipe has nine mistakes. Use the proofreading marks to fix each mistake. Then write the misspelled List Words on the lines.

Proofreading Marks	
◯	spelling mistake
∧	add something
ℐ	take out something

Golden Rich Bread

1 lb. butter   1 (pakg.) yeast
1 (qrt.) milk   6 cups flour
3 (os.) shredded coconut

Mix ingredients together and cover. Set the bowl bowl aside and allow the dough to to rise. Then punch, knead, and push the dough. Put it in a loaf pan and bake for 1 hour. (Recipe from Cooks vs. Kitchens, Second (edi.) New Day Co., King Books, (Ink.) Rochester, New York.)

1. qt.
2. oz.
3. pkg.
4. ed.
5. Inc.

Now proofread your paragraph about abbreviations. Fix any mistakes.

Go for the Goal

Take your Final Test. Then fill in your Scoreboard. Send your mistakes to the Word Locker.

SCOREBOARD

number correct	number wrong

★ ★ ★ ★ ★ ★ ★ **All-Star Words** ★ ★ ★ ★ ★ ★ ★

blvd.   mo.   tsp.   hwy.   etc.

Use your dictionary to find out what the abbreviations mean. Spell out each abbreviation as a complete word in a sentence. Trade papers with your partner. Replace the complete words in the sentences with the All-Star Words.

◉ **Spelling Strategy**   With a partner, students can take turns telling each other the words that the List Word abbreviations stand for. The partner who is listening

• repeats the word
• spells its abbreviation, saying the word *period* at the end.

Flex Your Spelling Muscles   *Page 144*

As students complete the **Writing** activity, encourage them to brainstorm ideas, write a first draft, revise, and proofread their work. The **Proofreading** exercise will help them prepare to proofread their paragraphs. To publish their writing, students may want to use their paragraphs to conduct a class debate on the pros and cons of using abbreviations.

✍ **Writer's Corner**

Students might enjoy looking at *Webster's New World Dictionary of Acronyms and Abbreviations* by Auriel Douglas and Michael Strumpf, or a similar book. Afterward, invite them to write a message using some of their favorite entries and to share it with a classmate.

Go for the Goal/Final Test

1. Give an ***example*** of a compound sentence. (*ex.*)
2. Write a ***biography*** of your best friend. (*biog.*)
3. Where is the morning ***edition*** of the paper? (*ed.*)
4. I work at a recently ***incorporated*** company. (*inc.*)
5. The sales ***department*** gave its report. (*dept.*)
6. The FBI is a ***government*** agency. (*govt.*)
7. A ***pint*** of liquid spilled on the table. (*pt.*)
8. There is an ***ounce*** of gold in that nugget. (*oz.*)
9. The ***manager*** of the organization resigned. (*mgr.*)
10. That ***package*** is wrapped beautifully! (*pkg.*)
11. All the ***merchandise*** is on sale. (*mdse.*)
12. The magician's ***assistant*** laughed. (*asst.*)
13. I'd like one ***pound*** of seedless grapes. (*lb.*)
14. There is a ***quart*** of milk on the counter. (*qt.*)
15. It was Kim ***versus*** José in the finals. (*vs.*)
16. She wore ***number*** 425 in the bicycle race. (*no.*)
17. Who has ***volume*** 3 of the encyclopedia? (*vol.*)
18. Find the simple ***subject*** of the sentence. (*subj.*)
19. Jim's ***company*** makes computer parts. (*co.*)
20. The ***president*** greeted the diplomats. (*pres.*)

Remind students to complete the Scoreboard and write any misspelled words in their Word Locker.

★★ **All-Star Words**   You may want to point out that the All-Star Words follow the spelling rule. Explain to students that they can look up an abbreviation in a dictionary just as they would a complete word.

Lesson 36 • Instant Replay

Objective
To review spelling words with suffixes, plurals of words, homonyms and hurdle words, and abbreviations

Time Out   *Pages 145–148*
Check Your Word Locker Based on your observations, note which words are giving students the most difficulty and offer assistance for spelling them correctly. Here are some frequently misspelled words to watch for: *equipped, occurred, attorneys, portrayed, mosquitoes, personnel,* and *whether.*

To give students extra help and practice in taking standardized tests, you may want to have them take the Review Test for this lesson on pages 110–111. After scoring the tests, return them to students so that they can record their misspelled words in their Word Locker.

After practicing their troublesome words, students can work through the exercises for **Lessons 31–35.** Before they begin each exercise, you may want to go over the spelling rule.

🏠 **Take It Home** Invite students to write down List Words from **Lessons 31–35** and to locate the words on signs and labels at the grocery store. For a complete list of the words, encourage students to take their *Spelling Workout* books home. Students can also use Take It Home Master 6 on pages 112–113 to help them do the activity. In class, they can share their lists and discuss the words they found.

Name_____

Time Out
Look again at how words are spelled when suffixes are added to words that end in **e** or **y**, how plurals are formed, homonyms, hurdle words, and abbreviations.

Check Your Word Locker
Look at the words in your Word Locker. Write your most troublesome words from Lessons 31 through 35.

_____

_____

Practice writing your troublesome words with a partner. Take turns saying the root words for words with suffixes, the singular form for plural words, homonyms, and the complete words for abbreviations.

Lesson 31

Before adding a suffix to a word, sometimes you need to double the final consonant, as in <u>referred</u>, or drop the final **e**, as in <u>organizing</u>.

List Words
combining
approved
referred
crammed
produced
occurred
controlled
exciting
hesitation
realized

Write a List Word that means the same or almost the same as the word given.

1. happened occurred
2. blending combining
3. understood realized
4. thrilling exciting
5. accepted approved
6. crowded crammed
7. created produced
8. uncertainty hesitation
9. mentioned referred
10. managed controlled

145

Lesson 32

Before adding a suffix to a word that ends in **y**, sometimes you need to change the **y** to **i**, as in <u>jellies</u> and <u>magnified</u>.

List Words
jellies
theories
steadily
waterways
remedies
decaying
modified
industries
attorneys
magnified

Circle the correctly spelled List Word. Write the word on the line.

1. (jellies) jellys _jellies_
2. decaing (decaying) _decaying_
3. magnifyed (magnified) _magnified_
4. (attorneys) attornies _attorneys_
5. (waterways) waterwaies _waterways_
6. theorys (theories) _theories_
7. (modified) modifyed _modified_
8. steadly (steadily) _steadily_
9. industryes (industries) _industries_
10. (remedies) remedyes _remedies_

Lesson 33

Some words are the same in both the singular and plural form. To form the plural of most words that end in **f** or **fe**, change the **f** or **fe** to **v** and add **es.** Sometimes just add **s**. Some words that end in o take **es**, others just an **s**.

List Words
tuxedos
patios
stereos
thieves
tariffs
species
ponchos
mementos
spaghetti
mosquitoes

Write the List Words in alphabetical order.

1. mementos
2. mosquitoes
3. patios
4. ponchos
5. spaghetti
6. species
7. stereos
8. tariffs
9. thieves
10. tuxedos

Lesson 34

Words that sound the same, but are spelled differently and have different meanings, are homonyms. Some words have similar spellings and pronunciations, but different meanings.

List Words

through
weight
principal
ceiling
weather
coarse
patients
accept
desert
personnel

Study the relationship between the first two underlined words. Then write a List Word that has the same relationship with the third underlined word.

1. <u>Tall</u> is to <u>short</u> as <u>smooth</u> is to __coarse__
2. <u>Feet</u> is to <u>height</u> as <u>pounds</u> is to __weight__
3. <u>Stairs</u> is to <u>up</u> as <u>tunnel</u> is to __through__
4. <u>Ship</u> is to <u>crew</u> as <u>office</u> is to __personnel__
5. <u>Sell</u> is to <u>buy</u> as <u>give</u> is to __accept__
6. <u>Side</u> is to <u>top</u> as <u>wall</u> is to __ceiling__
7. <u>Wet</u> is to <u>lake</u> as <u>dry</u> is to __desert__
8. <u>Team</u> is to <u>captain</u> as <u>school</u> is to __principal__
9. <u>Population</u> is to <u>people</u> as <u>climate</u> is to __weather__
10. <u>Lawyer</u> is to <u>clients</u> as <u>doctor</u> is to __patients__

Lesson 35

Abbreviations are shortened forms of words formed with the first letters of the word or with a combination of letters in the word. Others are formed with letters that are not in the original word.

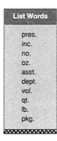

List Words

pres.
inc.
no.
oz.
asst.
dept.
vol.
qt.
lb.
pkg.

Write the List Word or List Words to complete each sentence.

1. Please give me a 1 __lb.__ , 1 __oz.__ __pkg.__ of beef.
2. Make an appointment to see the __pres.__ with her __asst.__
3. Please buy one __qt.__ of skim milk.
4. She works in the manufacturing __dept.__ of Speedy Co., __Inc.__
5. What __no.__ is __vol.__ S of the encyclopedia?

Lessons 31–35

List Words

controlled
decaying
weather
personnel
inc.
exciting
industries
asst.
stereos
magnified
theories
spaghetti
modified
patients
tuxedos

Write a List Word to solve each definition clue.

1. thrilling — __exciting__
2. made larger — __magnified__
3. big businesses — __industries__
4. kind of pasta — __spaghetti__
5. unproven ideas — __theories__
6. dressy kinds of suits — __tuxedos__
7. under a doctor's care — __patients__
8. incorporated (abbreviation) — __inc.__
9. sleet, snow, rain — __weather__
10. changed in some way — __modified__
11. regulated or operated — __controlled__
12. staff of people — __personnel__
13. assistant (abbreviation) — __asst.__
14. sound systems — __stereos__
15. spoiling — __decaying__

Go for the Goal

Take your Final Replay Test. Then fill in your Scoreboard. Send any misspelled words to your Word Locker.

SCOREBOARD

number correct	number wrong

Clean Out Your Word Locker
Look in your Word Locker. Cross out each word you spelled correctly on your Final Replay Test. Circle the words you're still having trouble with. Add the words you circled to your Spelling Notebook. What do you notice about the words? Watch for those words as you write.

Go for the Goal/Final Replay Test   Page 148

1. Suddenly the same idea **occurred** to both of us.
2. A series of gates **controlled** the flow of water.
3. Our last game was the most **exciting** one of all.
4. After a moment's **hesitation,** I started speaking.
5. No one **realized** how late it had gotten.
6. Can you use the grapes to make **jellies?**
7. What unbelievable **theories** those are!
8. Rain fell **steadily** for three days.
9. Some inland **waterways** are used by large boats.
10. Those **remedies** for hiccups sound quite odd.
11. Several **species** of birds are yellow.
12. The riders brought **ponchos** in case of rain.
13. A scrapbook can help you keep **mementos.**
14. My neighbor always makes his own **spaghetti.**
15. One bat can eat thousands of **mosquitoes.**
16. Push those letters **through** the slot in the door.
17. The doctor wrote down my height and **weight.**
18. Our school **principal** spoke at the assembly.
19. Did Arlene decide to paint the **ceiling?**
20. The **weather** report begins at nine o'clock.
21. Meet the **president** of our organization. (*pres.*)
22. Where is the sports **department?** (*dept.*)
23. Our company was **incorporated** in 1990. (*inc.*)
24. This set is missing **volume** 2. (*vol.*)
25. We are looking for shipment **number** 17. (*no.*)
26. Be careful when **combining** chemicals!
27. The mayor **approved** the new design for City Hall.
28. The footnote **referred** to a book about animals.
29. We **crammed** our uniforms into one bag.
30. A small generator **produced** electricity.
31. The **decaying** wood provided shelter for insects.
32. Each owner **modified** the building in some way.
33. Our state tries to attract various **industries.**
34. Several **attorneys** volunteered their time.
35. The tin roof **magnified** the sound of the rain.
36. All the men wore **tuxedos** to the formal dance.
37. These bricks are used to build decks and **patios.**
38. Today there are many different kinds of **stereos.**
39. Were the **thieves** caught quickly?
40. The government recently changed its **tariffs.**
41. Her jacket was made from some **coarse** material.
42. Most of the **patients** look forward to visitors.
43. John was pleased to **accept** our offer of help.
44. Most **desert** animals survive with little water.
45. My job is to interview all new **personnel.**
46. The recipe calls for one **quart** of milk. (*qt.*)
47. This packet holds an **ounce** of yeast. (*oz.*)
48. That is a fifty-**pound** bag of sand. (*lb.*)
49. Ms. Fujimura is the **assistant** manager. (*asst.*)
50. I took the **package** to the post office. (*pkg.*)

Clean Out Your Word Locker   Before writing each word, students can say the word and identify its suffix or tell whether it is an abbreviation or part of a homonym/hurdle pair.

Instant Replay Test

Side A

Read each set of words. Fill in the circle next to the word or abbreviation that is spelled wrong.

1.   ⓐ theories   ⓒ crammed
   ⓑ spagetti   ⓓ mementos

2.   ⓐ industries   ⓒ pckg.
   ⓑ waterways   ⓓ approved

3.   ⓐ stereos   ⓒ controled
   ⓑ exciting   ⓓ principal

4.   ⓐ wieght   ⓒ oz.
   ⓑ ponchos   ⓓ produced

5.   ⓐ patios   ⓒ combining
   ⓑ accept   ⓓ tarrifs

6.   ⓐ personell   ⓒ desert
   ⓑ avocados   ⓓ pres.

7.   ⓐ relized   ⓒ advertising
   ⓑ no.   ⓓ patients

8.   ⓐ jellies   ⓒ corse
   ⓑ ceiling   ⓓ lb.

9.   ⓐ crammed   ⓒ species
   ⓑ decaiing   ⓓ vol.

10.   ⓐ dominoes   ⓒ mementos
   ⓑ organizing   ⓓ attornies

11.   ⓐ except   ⓒ industries
   ⓑ exciting   ⓓ thrugh

12.   ⓐ remedies   ⓒ waterways
   ⓑ hesitasion   ⓓ approved

13.   ⓐ desert   ⓒ species
   ⓑ disguised   ⓓ astt.

Instant Replay Test

Side B

Read each set of words. Fill in the circle next to the word or abbreviation that is spelled wrong.

14. 　(a) principal 　　(c) waterways
　　 (b) magnifyed 　　(d) no.

15. 　(a) produced 　　(c) theives
　　 (b) galaxies 　　(d) patients

16. 　(a) pres. 　　　(c) refered
　　 (b) stereos 　　(d) ceiling

17. 　(a) wether 　　(c) approved
　　 (b) accept 　　(d) exciting

18. 　(a) theories 　　(c) oz.
　　 (b) surveying 　　(d) modefied

19. 　(a) depmt. 　　(c) equipped
　　 (b) ponchos 　　(d) principle

20. 　(a) stedily 　　(c) memorized
　　 (b) patience 　　(d) companies

21. 　(a) crammed 　　(c) patios
　　 (b) incp. 　　　(d) jellies

22. 　(a) sealing 　　(c) masquitos
　　 (b) mementos 　　(d) lb.

23. 　(a) remedies 　　(c) except
　　 (b) vol. 　　　(d) ocurred

24. 　(a) species 　　(c) abbreviated
　　 (b) qrt. 　　　(d) industries

25. 　(a) exciting 　　(c) stereos
　　 (b) tuxidoes 　　(d) rodeos

6

TAKE IT HOME

Your child has learned to spell many new words in Lessons 31–35 and would enjoy sharing them with you and your family. The activity ideas below can make reviewing those words fun for the whole family.

Shop-N-Spell

On what kind of shopping list will you find kangaroos, mosquitoes, and galaxies? A spelling-word list! The next time you make out a grocery list for broccoli, spaghetti, and avocados, for example, ask your child to prepare a list of spelling words that might be found at a store. Then you and your child can "shop" for the words on signs and labels.

Word Clues

Can you and your child complete each mini-puzzle with a spelling word? The words that are already given are clues.

Writing and Proofreading Guide

1. Choose a topic to write about.
2. Write your ideas. Don't worry about mistakes.
3. Now organize your writing so that it makes sense.
4. Proofread your work.

    Use these proofreading marks to check your work.

Proofreading Marks

⬭	spelling mistake
☰	capital letter
⊙	add period
∧	add something
⌄	add apostrophe
ℒ	take out something
¶	indent paragraph
/	make small letter
⌄ ⌄	add quotation marks

the electronic keyboard is a (remarkible) musical instrument that can can produce the sounds of drums, pianos, or violins ⊙

5. Write your final copy.

    The electronic keyboard is a remarkable musical instrument that can produce the sounds of drums, pianos, or violins.

6. Share your writing.

Using Your Dictionary

The Spelling Workout Dictionary shows you
many things about your spelling words.

The **entry word** listed in
alphabetical order is the
word you are looking up.

The sound-spelling or **respelling** tells how
to pronounce the word.

The **part of speech** is
given as an abbreviation.

im·prove (im pr$\overline{oo}$v′) **v.** I to make or become better
[Business has *improved*.] **2** to make good use of [She
improved her spare time by reading.] — **im·proved′,
im·prov′ing**

Sample sentences or phrases
show how to use the work.

Other **forms** of the
word are given.

The **definition** tells what the
word means. There may be
more than one definition.

Pronunciation Key

SYMBOL	KEY WORDS	SYMBOL	KEY WORDS	SYMBOL	KEY WORDS	SYMBOL	KEY WORDS
a	ask, fat	oo	look, pull	b	bed, dub	t	top, hat
ā	ape, date	ōō	ooze, tool	d	did, had	v	vat, have
ä	car, lot	ou	out, crowd	f	fall, off	w	will, always
				g	get, dog	y	yet, yard
e	elf, ten	u	up, cut	h	he, ahead	z	zebra, haze
ē	even, meet	ʉ	fur, fern	j	joy, jump		
				k	kill, bake	ch	chin, arch
i	is, hit	ə	a in ago	l	let, ball	ŋ	ring, singer
i	ice, fire		e in agent	m	met, trim	sh	she, dash
			e in father	n	not, ton	th	thin, truth
ō	open, go		i in unity	p	put, tap	*th*	then, father
ô	law, horn		o in collect	r	red, dear	zh	s in pleasure
oi	oil, point		u in focus	s	sell, pass		

Aa

ab·bre·vi·ate (ə brē′vē āt) *v.* to make shorter by cutting out part [The word "Street" is often *abbreviated* to "St."] —**ab·bre′vi·at·ed, ab·bre′vi·at·ing**

ab·stract (ab strakt′ *or* ab′strakt) *adj.* **1** thought of apart from a particular act or thing [A just trial is a fair one, but justice itself is an *abstract* idea.] **2** formed with designs taken from real things, but not actually like any real object or being [an *abstract* painting].

a·bun·dance (ə bun′dəns) *n.* a great supply; an amount more than enough [Where there is an *abundance* of goods, prices are supposed to go down.]

ac·cel·er·a·tor (ak sel′ər āt′ər) *n.* a thing that accelerates an action; especially, the foot pedal that can make an automobile go faster by feeding the engine more gasoline.

ac·cept (ak sept′) *v.* **1** to take what is offered or given [Will you *accept* $20 for that old bicycle?] **2** to answer "yes" to [We *accept* your invitation.] **3** to believe to be true [to *accept* a theory.]

ac·cess (ak′ses) *n.* **1** a way of approach [The *access* to the park is by this road.] **2** the right or ability to approach, enter, or use [Do the students have *access* to a good library?]

ac·com·plish (ə käm′plish) *v.* to do; carry out [The task was *accomplished* in one day.]

ac·cor·di·on (ə kôr′dē ən) *n.* a musical instrument with keys, metal reeds, and a bellows. It is played by pulling out and pressing together the bellows to force air through the reeds, which are opened by fingering the keys.

ac·count (ə kount′) *v.* **1** to give a detailed record of money handled [Our treasurer can *account* for every penny spent.] **2** to give a satisfactory reason; explain [How do you *account* for your absence from school?] ◆*n.* **1** *often* **accounts**, *pl.* a statement of money received, paid, or owed; record of business dealings. **2** a report or story [The book is an *account* of their travels.]

a·chieve·ment (ə chēv′mənt) *n.* **1** the act of achieving something [his *achievement* of a lifelong dream]. **2** something achieved by skill, work, courage, etc. [The landing of spacecraft on the moon was a remarkable *achievement*.]

ac·knowl·edge (ak näl′ij) *v.* **1** to admit to be true [I *acknowledge* that you are right.] **2** to recognize the authority of [They *acknowledged* him as their king.] **3** to recognize and answer or express one's thanks for [She *acknowledged* my greeting by smiling. Have you written to your uncle to *acknowledge* his gift?] —**ac·knowl′edged, ac·knowl′edg·ing**

ac·quaint·ance (ə kwānt′ns) *n.* **1** knowledge of a thing or person got from one's own experience [She has some *acquaintance* with modern art.] **2** a person one knows but not as a close friend.

ac·tiv·i·ty (ak tiv′ə tē) *n.* **1** the condition of being active; action; motion [There was not much *activity* in the shopping mall today.] **2** normal power of mind or body; liveliness; alertness [His mental *activity* at age eighty was remarkable.] **3** something that one does besides one's regular work [We take part in many *activities* after school.] —*pl.* **ac·tiv′i·ties**

ad·di·tion (ə dish′ən) *n.* **1** an adding of numbers to get a sum or total. **2** a joining of one thing to another thing [The lemonade was improved by the *addition* of sugar.] **3** a thing or part added [The gymnasium is a new *addition* to our school.]

ad·just·ment (ə just′mənt) *n.* **1** a changing or settling of things to bring them into proper order or relation [She made a quick *adjustment* to her new job.] **2** a way or device by which parts are adjusted [An *adjustment* on our television set can make the picture brighter.]

ad·mit (ad mit′) *v.* **1** to permit or give the right to enter [One ticket *admits* two persons.] **2** to accept as being true; confess [Lucy will not *admit* her mistake.] —**ad·mit′ted, ad·mit′ting**

ad·o·les·cent (ad′ə les′ənt) *adj.* growing up; developing from a child to an adult. ◆*n.* a boy or girl between childhood and adulthood; teen-age person.

a·dult (ə dult′ *or* ad′ult) *adj.* grown up; having reached full size and strength [an *adult* person or plant]. ◆*n.* **1** a man or woman who is fully grown up; mature person. **2** an animal or plant that is fully developed. —**a·dult′hood** *n.*

ad·van·tage (ad van′tij) *n.* **1** a more favorable position; better chance [My speed gave me an *advantage* over them.] **2** a thing, condition, or event that can help one; benefit [What are the *advantages* of a smaller school?]

ad·ver·tise (ad′vər tīz) *v.* **1** to tell about a product in public and in such a way as to make people want to buy it [to *advertise* cars on television]. **2** to announce or ask for publicly, as in a newspaper [to *advertise* a house for rent; to *advertise* for a cook]. —**ad′ver·tised, ad′ver·tis·ing** —**ad′ver·tis′er** *n.*

accordion

alligator

ad·ver·tis·ing (ad'vər tīz' iŋ) *n.* **1** an advertisement or advertisements. **2** the work of preparing advertisements and getting them printed or on radio and TV [*Advertising* is a major industry in this country.]

ad·vise (ad vīz') *v.* **1** to give advice or an opinion to [The doctor *advised* me to have an operation.] **2** to notify; inform [The letter *advised* us of the time of the meeting.] —**ad·vised', ad·vis'ing**

af·fec·tion (ə fek'shən) *n.* fond or tender feeling; warm liking.

af·ford (ə fôrd') *v.* **1** to have money enough to spare for: *usually used with* can *or* be able [Can we *afford* a new car?] **2** to be able to do something without taking great risks [I can *afford* to speak frankly.]

ag·ri·cul·tur·al (ag'ri kul'chər əl) *adj.* of agriculture; of growing crops and raising livestock; farming.

ail·ment (āl'mənt) *n.* an illness; sickness.

al·li·ga·tor (al'ə gāt'ər) *n.* a large lizard like the crocodile, found in warm rivers and marshes of the U.S. and China.

al·might·y (ôl mīt'ē) *adj.* having power with no limit; all-powerful.

al·though (ôl thō') *conj.* in spite of the fact that; even if; though [*Although* the sun is shining, it may rain later.]

an·a·lyze (an'ə līz) *v.* to separate or break up any thing or idea into its parts so as to examine them and see how they fit together [to *analyze* the causes of war]. —**an'a·lyz'er** *n.*

an·cient (ān'chənt *or* ān'shənt) *adj.* **1** of times long past; belonging to the early history of people, before about 500 A.D. **2** having lasted a long time; very old [their *ancient* quarrel.]

an·gle (aŋ'gəl) *n.* **1** the shape made by two straight lines meeting in a point, or by two surfaces meeting along a line. **2** the way one looks at something; point of view [Consider the problem from all *angles*.] ◆*v.* to move or bend at an angle. —**an'gled, an'gling**

an·nounce (ə nouns') *v.* **1** to tell the public about; proclaim [to *announce* the opening of a new store.] **2** to say; tell [Mother *announced* she wasn't going with us.] —**an·nounced', an·nounc'ing**

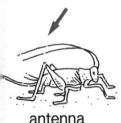
antenna

an·ten·na (an ten'ə) *n.* **1** either of a pair of slender feelers on the head of an insect, crab, lobster, etc. —*pl.* **an·ten·nae** (an ten'ē) *or* **an·ten'nas** **2** a wire or set of wires used in radio and television to send and receive signals; aerial. —*pl.* **an·ten'nas**

an·ti·bod·y (an'ti bäd'e) *n.* a specialized protein that is formed in the body to neutralize a particular foreign substance that is harmful, making the body immune to it. —*pl.* **an'ti·bod'ies**

an·tic·i·pate (an tis'ə pāt') *v.* to look forward to; expect [We *anticipate* a pleasant trip.] —**an·tic'i·pat·ed, an·tic'i·pat·ing** —**an·tic'i·pa'tion** *n.*

an·ti·dote (an'ti dōt) *n.* **1** a substance that is taken to work against the effect of a poison. **2** anything that works against an evil or unwanted condition [The party was a good *antidote* to the sadness we felt.]

☆**an·ti·freeze** (an'ti frēz') *n.* a liquid with a low freezing point, such as alcohol, put in the water of automobile radiators to prevent freezing.

an·tique (an tēk') *adj.* very old; of former times; made or used a long time ago. ◆*n.* a piece of furniture or silverware, a tool, etc. made many years ago [They sell *antiques* of colonial America.]

an·ti·sep·tic (an'ti sep'tik) *adj.* **1** preventing infection by killing germs. **2** free from living germs; sterile [an *antiseptic* room]. ◆*n.* any substance used to kill germs or stop their growth, as alcohol or iodine.

an·ti·so·cial (an'ti sō'shəl) *adj.* not liking to be with other people [Are you so *antisocial* that you never have visitors?]

ap·par·el (ə per'əl) *n.* clothing; garments; dress [They sell only children's *apparel*.] ◆*v.* to dress; clothe [The king was *appareled* in purple robes.] —**ap·par'eled** *or* **ap·par'elled, ap·par'el·ing** *or* **ap·par'el·ling**

ap·pear (ə pir') *v.* **1** to come into sight or into being [A ship *appeared* on the horizon. Leaves *appear* on the tree every spring.] **2** to seem; look [He *appears* to be in good health.] **3** to come before the public [The actor will *appear* on television. The magazine *appears* monthly.]

ap·plause (ə plôz' *or* ə pläz') *n.* the act of showing that one enjoys or approves of something, especially by clapping one's hands.

ap·point·ment (ə point'mənt) *n.* **1** the act of appointing or the fact of being appointed [the *appointment* of Jones as supervisor]. **2** an arrangement to meet someone or be somewhere at a certain time [an *appointment* for lunch].

ap·pre·ci·ate (ə prē'shē āt') *v.* **1** to think well of; understand and enjoy [I now *appreciate* modern art.] **2** to recognize and be grateful for [We *appreciate* all you have done for us.] —**ap·pre'ci·at·ed, ap·pre'ci·at·ing** —**ap·pre'ci·a'tion** *n.*

ap·proach (ə prōch') *v.* to come closer or draw nearer [We saw three riders *approaching*. Vacation time *approaches*.] —**ap·proach'a·ble** *adj.*

ap·prove (ə prōōv') *v.* **1** to think or say to be good, worthwhile, etc.; be pleased with: *often used with* of [She doesn't *approve* of smoking.] **2** to give one's consent to [Has the mayor *approved* the plans?] —**ap·proved', ap·prov'ing**

ar·gu·ment (är'gyoō mənt) *n.* **1** the act of arguing; discussion in which people disagree; dispute. **2** a reason given for or against something [What are your *arguments* for wanting to study mathematics?]

ar·range·ment (ə rānj′mənt) *n.* **1** the act of arranging or putting in order. **2** the way in which something is arranged [a new *arrangement* of pictures on the wall]. **3** a preparation; plan: *usually used in pl.*, **arrangements** [*Arrangements* have been made for the party.]

as·cend (ə send′) *v.* to go up; move upward; rise; climb [The procession *ascended* the hill.]

a·shamed (ə shāmd′) *adj.* feeling shame because something bad, wrong, or foolish was done [They were *ashamed* of having broken the window.]

as·sign·ment (ə sīn′mənt) *n.* **1** the act of assigning. **2** something assigned, as a lesson.

asst. *abbreviation for* **assistant.**

as·sure (ə shoor′) *v.* **1** to make a person sure of something; convince [What can we do to *assure* you of our friendship?] **2** to tell or promise positively [I *assure* you I'll be there.] **3** to make a doubtful thing certain; guarantee [Their gift of money *assured* the success of our campaign.] —**as·sured′, as·sur′ing**

as·ter·isk (as′tər isk) *n.* a sign in the shape of a star (*) used in printing and writing to call attention to a footnote or other explanation or to show that something has been left out.

as·ter·oid (as′tər oid) *n.* any of the many small planets that move in orbits around the sun between the orbits of Mars and Jupiter.

as·tro·naut (as′trə nôt *or* as′trə nät) *n.* a person trained to make rocket flights in outer space.

ath·lete (ath′lēt) *n.* a person who is skilled at games, sports, or exercises in which one needs strength, skill, and speed.

at·tain (ə tān′) *v.* to get by working hard; gain; achieve [to *attain* success].

at·tor·ney (ə tur′nē) *n.* a lawyer. —*pl.* **at·tor′neys**

auc·tion (ôk′shən *or* äk′shən) *n.* a public sale at which each thing is sold to the person offering to pay the highest price. ◆ *v.* to sell at an auction [They *auctioned* their furniture instead of taking it with them.]

Aus·tral·ia (ô strāl′yə *or* ä strāl′yə) **1** an island continent in the Southern Hemisphere, southeast of Asia. **2** a country made up of this continent and Tasmania.— **Aus·tral′ian** *adj., n.*

au·then·tic (ô then′tik *or* ä *th*en′tik) *adj.* **1** that can be believed; reliable; true [an *authentic* news report]. **2** that is genuine; real [an *authentic* antique]. —**au·then′ti·cal·ly** *adv.*

au·to·mat·ic (ôt′ə mat′ik *or* ät′ə mat′ik) *adj.* **1** done without thinking about it, as though by a machine; unconscious [Breathing is usually *automatic*.] **2** moving or working by itself [*automatic* machinery].—**au′to·mat′i·cal·ly** *adv.*

au·tumn (ôt′əm *or* ät′əm) *n.* the season of the year that comes between summer and winter; fall. ◆*adj.* of or like autumn. —**au·tum·nal** (ô tum′n'l) *adj.*

a·vi·a·tor (ā′vē āt′ər) *n.* a person who flies airplanes; pilot.

☆**av·o·ca·do** (av′ə kä′dō *or* äv′ə kä′dō) *n.* a tropical fruit that is shaped like a pear and has a thick, green or purplish skin and a single large seed. Its yellow, buttery flesh is used in salads, sauces, dips, etc. —*pl.* **av′o·ca′dos**

a·void (ə void′) *v.* **1** to keep away from; get out of the way of; shun [to *avoid* crowds]. **2** to keep from happening [Try to *avoid* spilling the milk.] —**a·void′a·ble** *adj.* —**a·void′ance** *n.*

awe·some (ô′səm *or* ä′səm) *adj.* **1** causing one to feel awe [The burning building was an *awesome* sight.] **2** showing awe [He had an *awesome* look on his face.]

awn·ing (ôn′iŋ *or* än′iŋ) *n.* a covering made of canvas, metal, or wood fixed to a frame over a window, door, etc. to keep off the sun and rain.

a·wry (ə rī′) *adv., adj.* **1** twisted to one side; askew [The curtains were blown *awry* by the wind.] **2** wrong; amiss [Our plans went *awry*.]

ax·le (ak′səl) *n.* **1** a rod on which a wheel turns, or one connected to a wheel so that they turn together. **2** the bar joining two opposite wheels, as of an automobile.

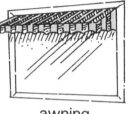

awning

back·gam·mon (bak′gam ən) *n.* a game played on a special board by two people. The players have fifteen pieces each, which they move after throwing dice to get a number.

bad·min·ton (bad′mint'n *or* bad′mit'n) *n.* a game like tennis, in which a cork with feathers in one end is batted back and forth across a high net by players using light rackets.

bail (bāl) *n.* money left with a law court as a guarantee that an arrested person will appear for trial. u *v.* to have an arrested person set free by giving bail.

bail·iff (bāl′if) *n.* **1** a sheriff's assistant. **2** an officer who has charge of prisoners and jurors in a court.

bank·rupt (baŋk′rupt) *adj.* not able to pay one's debts and freed by law from the need for doing so [Any property a *bankrupt* person may still have is usually divided among those to whom the person owes money.]

ban·quet (baŋ′kwət) *n.* a formal dinner or feast for many people. Banquets, during which speeches are made, are often held to celebrate something or to raise money.

a	ask, fat
ā	ape, date
ä	car, lot
e	elf, ten
ē	even, meet
i	is, hit
ī	ice, fire
ō	open, go
ô	law, horn
oi	oil, point
oo	look, pull
ōo	ooze, tool
ou	out, crowd
u	up, cut
u	fur, fern
ə	a in ago
	e in agent
	e in father
	i in unity
	o in collect
	u in focus
ch	chin, arch
ŋ	ring, singer
sh	she, dash
th	thin, truth
th	then, father
zh	s in pleasure

bare·ly (ber′lē) *adv.* **1** only just; no more than; scarcely [It is *barely* a year old.] **2** in a bare way; meagerly [a *barely* furnished room, with only a bed in it].

be·lief (bē lēf′) *n.* **1** a believing or feeling that certain things are true or real; faith [You cannot destroy my *belief* in the honesty of most people.] **2** trust or confidence [I have *belief* in Pat's ability.] **3** anything believed or accepted as true; opinion [What are your religious *beliefs*?]

be·lieve (bē lēv′) *v.* **1** to accept as true or real [Can we *believe* that story?] **2** to have trust or confidence [I know you will win; I *believe* in you.] —**be·lieved′, be·liev′ing** —**be·liev′a·ble** *adj.* —**be·liev′er** *n.*

bi·an·nu·al (bī an′yōō əl) *adj.* coming twice a year. —**bi·an′nu·al·ly** *adv.*

bi·fo·cals (bī′fō kəlz) *pl.n.* eyeglassses in which each lens has two parts, one for reading and seeing nearby objects and the other for seeing things far away.

bil·lion (bil′yən) *n., adj.* a thousand millions (1,000,000,000).

bin·oc·u·lars (bi näk′yə lərz) *n.pl.* a pair of small telescopes fastened together for use with both eyes [Field glasses are a kind of *binoculars*.]

biog. *abbreviation for* **biographical** *or* **biography.**

bi·ol·o·gy (bī äl′ə jē) *n.* the science of plants and animals; the study of living things and the way they live and grow. —**bi·ol′o·gist** *n.*

bi·plane (bī′plān) *n.* the earlier type of airplane with two main wings, one above the other.

bis·cuit (bis′kit) *n.* ☆a small bread roll made of dough quickly raised with baking powder.

bi·sect (bī sekt′ *or* bī′sekt) *v.* **1** to cut into two parts [Budapest is *bisected* by the Danube River.] **2** to divide into two equal parts [A circle is *bisected* by its diameter.]

bit·ter (bit′ər) *adj.* **1** having a strong, often unpleasant taste [The seed in a peach pit is *bitter*.] **2** full of sorrow, pain, or discomfort [Poor people often suffer *bitter* hardships.] —**bit′ter·ness** *n.*

bi·week·ly (bī wēk′lē) *adj., adv.* once every two weeks.

bleak (blēk) *adj.* **1** open to wind and cold; not sheltered; bare [the *bleak* plains]. **2** cold and cutting; harsh [a *bleak* wind]. **3** not cheerful; gloomy [a *bleak* story]. **4** not hopeful or promising [a *bleak* future].

Blvd. *abbreviation for* **Boulevard.**

boil (boil) *v.* **1** to bubble up and become steam or vapor by being heated [Water *boils* at 100°C.] **2** to heat a liquid until it bubbles up in this way [to *boil* water]. **3** to cook in a boiling liquid [to *boil* potatoes].

bor·ough (bur′ō) *n.* **1** in some States, a town that has a charter to govern itself. **2** one of the five main divisions of New York City.

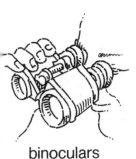

binoculars

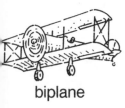

biplane

bor·row (bär′ō *or* bôr′ō) *v.* **1** to get to use something for a while by agreeing to return it later [You can *borrow* that book from the library.] **2** to take another's word, idea, etc. and use it as one's own [The Romans *borrowed* many Greek myths.] —**bor′row·er** *n.*

bough (bou) *n.* a large branch of a tree.

boul·der (bōl′dər) *n.* any large rock made round and smooth by weather and water.

boun·ti·ful (boun′tə fəl) *adj.* **1** giving much gladly; generous [a *bountiful* patron]. **2** more than enough; plentiful [a *bountiful* harvest]. —**boun′ti·ful·ly** *adv.*

bowl·ing (bōl′iŋ) *n.* a game in which each player rolls a heavy ball along a wooden lane (**bowling alley**), trying to knock down ten wooden pins at the far end.

brave (brāv) *adj.* willing to face danger, pain, or trouble; not afraid; full of courage. —**brav′er, brav′est** ◆*n.* a Native American warrior. ◆*v.* to face without fear; defy [We *braved* the storm.] —**braved, brav′ing** —**brave′ly** *adv.* —**brave′ness** *n.*

brawn·y (brôn′ē *or* brän′ē) *adj.* strong and muscular. —**brawn′i·er, brawn′i·est** —**brawn′i·ness** *n.*

break·a·ble (brāk′ə bəl) *adj.* that can be broken or that is likely to break.

brief (brēf) *adj.* **1** not lasting very long; short in time [a *brief* visit]. **2** using just a few words; not wordy; concise [a *brief* news report]. —**brief′ly** *adv.* —**brief′ness** *n.*

bright (brīt) *adj.* **1** shining; giving light; full of light [a *bright* star; a *bright* day]. **2** very strong or brilliant in color or sound [a *bright* red; the *bright* tones of a cornet]. **3** lively; cheerful [a *bright* smile]. **4** having a quick mind; clever [a *bright* child]. ◆*adv.* in a bright manner [stars shining *bright*]. —**bright′ly** *adv.* —**bright′ness** *n.*

broc·co·li (bräk′ə lē) *n.* a vegetable whose tender shoots and loose heads of tiny green buds are cooked for eating.

bro·chure (brō shoor′) *n.* a pamphlet, now especially one that advertises something.

bronze (bränz) *n.* **1** a metal that is an alloy of copper and tin. **2** a reddish-brown color like that of bronze. —**bronzed, bronz′ing** *v.*

bruise (brōōz) *v.* **1** to hurt a part of the body, as by a blow, without breaking the skin [Her *bruised* knee turned black-and-blue.] **2** to hurt the outside of [Some peaches fell and were *bruised*.] —**bruised, bruis′ing** ◆*n.* an injury to the outer part or flesh that does not break the skin but darkens it in color.

budg·et (buj′ət) *n.* a careful plan for spending the money that is received in a certain period. ◆*v.* **1** to plan the spending of money; make a budget. **2** to plan in detail how to spend [I *budget* my time as well as my money.]

buf·fet (bə fā′ *or* bʊo fā′) *n.* platters of food on a buffet or table from which people serve themselves.

build·ing (bil′diŋ) *n.* **1** anything that is built with walls and a roof; a structure, as a house, factory, or school. **2** the act or work of one who builds.

bun·ga·low (buŋ′gə lō) *n.* a small house with one story and an attic.

Cc

cal·ci·um (kal′sē əm) *n.* a chemical element that is a soft, silver-white metal. It is found combined with other elements in the bones and teeth of animals and in limestone, marble, chalk, etc.

cal·cu·late (kal′kyoo lāt′) *v.* **1** to find out by using arithmetic; compute [*Calculate* the amount of cloth you will need for the skirt.] **2** to find out by reasoning; estimate [Try to *calculate* the effect of your decision.] —**cal′cu·lat·ed, cal′cu·lat·ing**

cal·cu·la·tion (kal′kyoo lā′shən) *n.* **1** the act of calculating. **2** the answer found by calculating. **3** careful or shrewd thought or planning.

cam·er·a (kam′ər ə) *n.* **1** a closed box for taking pictures. The light that enters when a lens or hole at one end is opened by a shutter forms an image on the film or plate at the other end. **2** that part of a TV transmitter which picks up the picture to be sent and changes it to electrical signals.

cam·paign (kam pān′) *n.* a series of planned actions for getting something done [a *campaign* to get someone elected]. ◆*v.* to take part in a campaign. —**cam·paign′er** *n.*

Ca·na·di·an (kə nā′dē ən) *adj.* of Canada or its people. ◆*n.* a person born or living in Canada.

can·ta·loupe *or* **can·ta·loup** (kan′tə lōp) *n.* a muskmelon, especially a kind that has a hard, rough skin and sweet, juicy, orange-colored flesh.

can·vas (kan′vəs) *n.* **1** a strong, heavy cloth of hemp, cotton, or linen, used for tents, sails, oil paintings, etc. **2** an oil painting on canvas.

ca·pac·i·ty (kə pas′i tē) *n.* **1** the amount of space that can be filled; room for holding [a jar with a *capacity* of 2 quarts]. **2** the ability to be, learn, or become; skill or fitness [the *capacity* to be an actor]. —*pl.* —**ca·pac′i·ties**

cap·i·tal (kap′it'l) *adj.* where the government is located [a *capital* city]. *See also* **capital letter.** ◆*n.* **1** *same as* **capital letter.** **2** a city or town where the government of a state or nation is located.

capital letter the form of a letter that is used to begin a sentence or a name [THIS IS PRINTED IN CAPITAL LETTERS.]

Cap·i·tol (kap′it'l) the building in which the U.S. Congress meets, in Washington, D.C. ◆*n. usually* **capitol** the building in which a State legislature meets.

car·bo·hy·drate (kär′bō hī′drāt) *n.* any of a group of substances made up of carbon, hydrogen, and oxygen, including the sugars and starches. Carbohydrates are an important part of our diet.

car·bon (kär′bən) *n.* a chemical element that is not a metal, found in all plant and animal matter. Diamonds and graphite are pure carbon, while coal and charcoal are forms of impure carbon.

car·bu·ret·or (kär′bə rāt′ər) *n.* the part of a gasoline engine that mixes air with gasoline spray to make the mixture that explodes in the cylinders.

care·ful (ker′fəl) *adj.* **1** taking care so as not to have mistakes or accidents; cautious [Be *careful* in crossing streets.] **2** done or made with care [*careful* work]. —**care′ful·ly** *adv.* —**care′ful·ness** *n.*

car·i·ca·ture (kar′i kə chər) *n.* a picture or imitation of a person or thing in which certain features or parts are exaggerated in a joking or mocking way. ◆*v.* to make or be a caricature of [Cartoonists often *caricature* the President.] —**car′i·ca·tured, car′i·ca·tur·ing** —**car′i·ca·tur·ist** *n.*

car·ni·val (kär′ni vəl) *n.* an entertainment that travels from place to place, with sideshows, amusement rides, refreshments, etc.

car·tridge (kär′trij) *n.* **1** the metal or cardboard tube that holds the gunpowder and the bullet or shot for use in a firearm. **2** a small container used in a larger device, as one holding ink for a pen. **3** a roll of camera film in a case. **4** a unit holding the needle for a phonograph.

cas·tle (kas′əl) *n.* a large building or group of buildings that was the home of a king or noble in the Middle Ages. Castles had thick walls, moats, etc. to protect them against attack.

cas·u·al (kazh′oo əl) *adj.* **1** happening by chance; not planned [a *casual* visit]. **2** not having any particular purpose [a *casual* glance; a *casual* remark]. **3** for wear at times when dressy clothes are not needed [*casual* sports clothes]. —**cas′u·al·ly** *adv.* —**cas′u·al·ness** *n.*

ca·ter (kā′tər) *v.* to provide food and service [Smith's business is *catering* for large parties.] —**ca′ter·er** *n.*

cau·li·flow·er (kôl′ə flou ər *or* käl′ə flou ər) *n.* a kind of cabbage with a head of white, fleshy flower clusters growing tightly together.

ceil·ing (sēl′iŋ) *n.* the inside top part of a room, opposite the floor.

bungalow

a	ask, fat
ā	ape, date
ä	car, lot
e	elf, ten
ē	even, meet
i	is, hit
ī	ice, fire
ō	open, go
ô	law, horn
oi	oil, point
oo	look, pull
ōō	ooze, tool
ou	out, crowd
u	up, cut
u	fur, fern
ə	a in ago
	e in agent
	e in father
	i in unity
	o in collect
	u in focus
ch	chin, arch
ŋ	ring, singer
sh	she, dash
th	thin, truth
th	then, father
zh	s in pleasure

120

cel·e·brate (sel′ə brāt) *v.* **1** to honor a victory, the memory of something, etc. in some special way [to *celebrate* a birthday with a party; to *celebrate* the Fourth of July with fireworks]. **2** to have a good time: *used only in everyday talk* [Let's *celebrate* when we finish painting the garage.] —**cel′e·brat·ed, cel′e·brat·ing** —**cel′e·bra′tion** *n.*

cel·lo (chel′ō) *n.* a musical instrument like a violin but larger and having a deeper tone. *Its full name is* **violoncello.** —*pl.* **cel′los** or **cel·li** (chel′ē)

cello

cha·grin (shə grin′) *n.* a feeling of being embarrassed and annoyed because one has failed or has been disappointed. ◆ *v.* to embarrass and annoy [Our hostess was *chagrined* when the guest to be honored failed to appear.]

chal·lenge (chal′ənj) *v.* **1** to question the right or rightness of; refuse to believe unless proof is given [to *challenge* a claim; to *challenge* something said or the person who says it]. **2** to call to take part in a fight or contest; dare [He *challenged* her to a game of chess.] **3** to call for skill, effort, or imagination [That puzzle will really *challenge* you.] —**chal′lenged, chal′leng·ing** ◆ *n.* **1** the act of challenging [I accepted his *challenge* to a race.] **2** something that calls for much effort; hard task [Climbing Mt. Everest was a real *challenge*.]

change·a·ble (chān′jə bəl) *adj.* changing often or likely to change [*changeable* weather].

check·ers (chek′ərz) *n.pl.* a game played on a checkerboard by two players, each of whom tries to capture all 12 pieces of the other player: *used with a singular verb.*

chem·is·try (kem′is trē) *n.* the science in which substances are examined to find out what they are made of, how they act under different conditions, and how they are combined or separated to form other substances.

chess (ches) *n.* a game played on a chessboard by two players. Each has 16 pieces (called **chess′men**) which are moved in trying to capture the other's pieces and checkmate the other's king.

chis·el (chiz′əl) *n.* a tool having a strong blade with a sharp edge for cutting or shaping wood, stone, or metal. ◆ *v.* to cut or shape with a chisel. —**chis′eled** or **chis′elled, chis′el·ing** or **chis′el·ling** —**chis′el·er** or **chis′el·ler** *n.*

chisel

chives (chīvz) *n.pl.* a plant related to the onion, having slender, hollow leaves that are chopped up and used for flavoring.

cho·les·ter·ol (kə les′tər ôl) *n.* a waxy substance found in the body and in certain foods. When there is much of it in the blood, it is thought to cause hardening of the arteries.

chor·us (kôr′əs) *n.* **1** a group of people trained to speak or sing together [Ancient Greek plays usually had a *chorus* which explained what the actors were doing.] **2** singers and dancers who work together as a group and not as soloists, as in a musical show. **3** the part of a song that is repeated after each verse; refrain [The *chorus* of "The Battle Hymn of the Republic" begins "Glory, glory, hallelujah!"] ◆ *v.* to speak or sing together or at the same time [The Senators *chorused* their approval.]

chrome (krōm) *n.* chromium, especially when it is used to plate steel or other metal

chute (shoot) *n.* **1** a part of a river where the water moves swiftly. **2** a waterfall. **3** a long tube or slide in which things are dropped or slid down to a lower place [a laundry *chute*].

cir·cuit (sur′kət) *n.* **1** the act of going around something; course or journey in a circle [The moon's *circuit* of the earth takes about 28 days.] **2** the complete path of an electric current; also, any hookup, wiring, etc. that is connected into this path.

cir·cu·la·tion (sur′kyə lā′shən) *n.* **1** free movement around from place to place [The fan kept the air in *circulation*.] **2** the movement of blood through the veins and arteries. **3** the average number of copies of a magazine or newspaper sent out or sold in a certain period [Our school paper has a weekly *circulation* of 630.]

cir·cum·fer·ence (sər kum′fər əns) *n.* **1** the line that bounds a circle or other rounded figure or area. **2** the length of such a line [The *circumference* of the pool is 70 feet.]

clause (klôz *or* kläz) *n.* a group of words that includes a subject and a verb, but that forms only part of a sentence: in the sentence "She will visit us if she can," "She will visit us" is a clause that could be a complete sentence, and "if she can" is a clause that depends on the first clause.

clean·ly (klen′lē) *adj.* always keeping clean or kept clean. —**clean′li·ness** *n.*

clev·er (klev′ər) *adj.* **1** quick in thinking or learning; smart; intelligent. **2** showing skill or fine thinking [a *clever* move in chess]. —**clev′er·ly** *adv.* —**clev′er·ness** *n.*

close (klōz) *v.* **1** to make no longer open; shut [*Close* the door.] **2** to bring or come to a finish; end [to *close* a speech]. —**closed, clos′ing** ◆ *n.* an end; finish.

clothes (klōz *or* klō*th*z) *n.pl.* cloth or other material made up in different shapes and styles to wear on the body; dresses, suits, hats, underwear, etc.; garments.

Co. or **co.** *abbreviation for* **company, county.**

coarse (kôrs) *adj.* **1** made up of rather large particles; not fine [*coarse* sand]. **2** rough or harsh to the touch [*coarse* cloth]. **3** not polite or refined; vulgar; crude [a *coarse* joke]. —**coarse′ly** *adv.* —**coarse′ness** *n.*

121

co·coa (kō′kō) *n.* **1** a powder made from roasted cacao seeds, used in making chocolate. **2** a drink made from this powder by adding sugar and hot water or milk.

cof·fee (kôf′ē *or* käf′ē) *n.* a dark-brown drink made by brewing the roasted and ground seeds of a tropical plant in boiling water.

co·logne (kə lōn′) *n.* a sweet-smelling liquid like perfume, but not so strong.

col·umn (käl′əm) *n.* **1** a long, generally round, upright support; pillar. Columns usually stand in groups to hold up a roof or other part of a building, but they are sometimes used just for decoration. **2** any long, upright thing like a column [a *column* of water; the spinal *column*]. **3** any of the long sections of print lying side by side on a page and separated by a line or blank space [Each page of this book has two *columns*.]

com·bi·na·tion (käm′bi nā′shən) *n.* **1** the act of combining or joining [He succeeded by a *combination* of hard work and luck.] **2** the series of numbers or letters that must be turned to in the right order to open a kind of lock called a ☆**combination lock** [Most safes have a *combination lock*.]

com·bine (kəm bīn′) *v.* to come or bring together; join; unite [to *combine* work with pleasure; to *combine* chemical elements]. —**com·bined′, com·bin′ing**

com·ment (käm′ent) *n.* a remark or note that explains or gives an opinion [The teacher's *comments* on the poem helped us to understand it.] ◆*v.* to make comments or remarks [Doctors should not *comment* on their patients to others.]

com·mo·tion (kə mō′shən) *n.* a noisy rushing about; confusion [There was a great *commotion* as the ship began to sink.]

com·mu·ni·cate (kə myōō′nə kāt′) *v.* to make known; give or exchange information [to *communicate* by telephone; to *communicate* ideas by the written word]. —**com·mu′ni·cat·ed, com·mu′ni·cat·ing**

com·mu·ni·ca·tion (kə myōō′ni kā′shən) *n.* **1** the act of communicating [the *communication* of disease; the *communication* of news]. **2** a way or means of communicating [The hurricane broke down all *communication* between the two cities.] **3** information, message, letter, etc. [They received the news in a *communication* from their lawyer.]

com·pact (kəm pakt′ *or* käm′pakt) *adj.* closely and firmly packed together [Tie the clothes in a neat, *compact* bundle.] ◆*n.* (käm′pakt) ☆a model of automobile smaller and cheaper than the standard model.

com·pa·ny (kum′pə nē) *n.* a group of people; especially, a group joined together in some work or activity [a *company* of actors; a business *company*]. —*pl.* **com′pa·nies**

com·pare (kəm per′) *v.* **1** to describe as being the same; liken [The sound of thunder can be *compared* to the roll of drums.] **2** to examine certain things in order to find out how they are alike or different [How do the two cars *compare* in size and price?] —**com·pared′, com·par·ing**

com·pel (kəm pel′) *v.* to make do something; force [Many men were *compelled* by the draft to serve in the armed forces.] —**com·pelled′, com·pel·ling**

com·pet·i·tor (kəm pet′i tər) *n.* a person who competes; rival [business *competitors*].

com·plaint (kəm plānt′) *n.* **1** the act of complaining or finding fault. **2** something to complain about [The tenants gave a list of their *complaints* to the landlord.]

com·plete (kəm plēt′) *adj.* **1** having no parts missing; full; whole [a *complete* deck of cards]. **2** finished; ended [No one's education is ever really *complete*.] **3** thorough; perfect [I have *complete* confidence in my doctor.] ◆*v.* to make complete; finish or make whole, full, perfect, etc. [When will the new road be *completed*?] —**com·plet′ed, com·plet′ing** —**com·plete′ly** *adv.*

com·po·si·tion (käm′pə zish′ən) *n.* **1** the act, work, or style of composing something. **2** something composed, as a piece of writing or a musical work. **3** the parts or materials of a thing and the way they are put together [We shall study the *composition* of this gas.]

com·po·sure (kəm pō′zhər) *n.* calmness of mind; self-control; serenity.

com·pound (käm′pound) *n.* anything made up of two or more parts or materials; mixture. ◆*adj.* made up of two or more parts ["Handbag" is a *compound* word.]

con·ceal (kən sēl′) *v.* to hide or keep secret; put or keep out of sight [I *concealed* my amusement. The thief *concealed* the stolen jewelry in a pocket.]

con·ceit (kən sēt′) *n.* too high an opinion of oneself; vanity [His *conceit* shows when he talks about how bright he is.] —**con·ceit′ed** *adj.*

con·ces·sion·aire (kən sesh ə ner′) *n.* the owner or operator of a business, such as a refreshment stand.

con·demn (kən dem′) *v.* **1** to say that a person or thing is wrong or bad [We *condemn* cruelty to animals.] **2** to declare to be guilty; convict [A jury tried and *condemned* them.] —**con·dem·na·tion** (kän′dem nā′shən) *n.*

con·fer·ence (kän′fər əns) *n.* a meeting of people to discuss something [A *conference* on education was held in Washington.]

con·fet·ti (kən fet′ē) *pl.n.* [*used with a singular verb*] bits of colored paper thrown about at carnivals and parades [*Confetti* was all over the street.]

column

con·fir·ma·tion (kän fər mā′shən) *n.* **1** the act of confirming, or making sure. **2** something that confirms or proves.

con·fuse (kən fyo͞oz′) *v.* **1** to mix up, especially in the mind; put into disorder; bewilder [You will *confuse* us with so many questions.] **2** to fail to see or remember the difference between; mistake [You are *confusing* me with my twin.] —**con·fused′, con·fus′ing** —**con·fus·ed·ly** (kən fyo͞oz′id lē) *adv.*

con·ju·gate (kän′jə gāt) *v.* to list the different forms of a verb in person, number, and tense [*Conjugate* "to be," beginning "I am, you are, he is."] —**con′ju·gat·ed, con′ju·gat·ing** —**con′ju·ga′tion** *n.*

con·science (kän′shəns) *n.* a sense of right and wrong; feeling that keeps one from doing bad things [My *conscience* bothers me after I tell a lie.]

con·scious (kän′shəs) *adj.* aware of one's own feelings or of things around one [*conscious* of a slight noise].

con·sum·er (kən so͞om′ər) *n.* a person or thing that consumes; especially, a person who buys goods for his own needs and not to sell to others or to use in making other goods for sale.

con·tain·er (kən tān′ər) *n.* a thing for holding something; box, can, bottle, pot, etc.

con·trol (kən trōl′) *v.* **1** to have the power of ruling, guiding, or managing [A thermostat *controls* the heat.] **2** to hold back; curb [*Control* your temper!] —**con·trolled′, con·trol′ling** ◆*n.* **1** power to direct or manage [He's a poor coach, with little *control* over the team.] **2** a part or thing that controls a machine [the *controls* of an airplane]. —**con·trol′la·ble** *adj.*

con·ven·tion (kən ven′shən) *n.* a meeting of members or delegates from various places, held every year or every few years [a political *convention*; a national *convention* of English teachers].

con·ver·sa·tion (kän′vər sā′shən) *n.* a talk or a talking together.

con·vert·i·ble (kən vurt′ə bəl) *adj.* that can be converted [Matter is *convertible* into energy.] ◆*n.* ☆an automobile with a top that can be folded back.

con·vey (kən vā′) *v.* **1** to take from one place to another; carry or transport [The cattle were *conveyed* in trucks to the market.] **2** to make known; give [Please *convey* my best wishes to them.]

corps (kôr) *n.* **1** a section or a special branch of the armed forces [the Marine *Corps*]. **2** a group of people who are joined together in some work or organization [a press *corps*].

cor·re·spond·ence (kôr ə spän′dens) *n.* **1** the writing and receiving of letters [to engage in *correspondence*]. **2** the letters written or received [The *correspondence* concerning the new contract is in the file.]

coun·sel (koun′səl) *n.* **1** the act of talking together in order to exchange ideas or opinions; discussion [They took *counsel* before making the decision.] **2** the lawyer or lawyers who are handling a case. ◆ *v.* to give advice to; advise [a person who *counsels* students]. —**coun′seled** or **coun′selled, coun′sel·ing** or **coun′sel·ling**

coun·se·lor or **coun·sel·lor** (koun′sə lər) *n.* **1** a person who advises; advisor. **2** a lawyer. **3** a person in charge of children at a camp.

coun·ter·act (koun tər akt′) *v.* to act against; to stop or undo the effect of [The rains will help *counteract* the dry spell.]

coun·ter·at·tack (koun′tər ə tak) *n.* an attack made in return for another attack. ◆*v.* to attack so as to answer the enemy's attack.

coun·ter·bal·ance (koun′tər bal əns) *n.* a weight, power, or force that balances or acts against another.

coun·ter·feit (koun′tər fit) *adj.* made in imitation of the real thing so as to fool or cheat people [*counterfeit* money]. ◆*n.* a thing that is counterfeit. ◆*v.* to make an imitation of in order to cheat [to *counterfeit* money]. —**coun′ter·feit·er** *n.*

coun·ter·part (koun′tər pärt) *n.* **1** a person or thing that is very much like another [He is his father's *counterpart*.] **2** a thing that goes with another thing to form a set [This cup is the *counterpart* to that saucer.]

course (kôrs) *n.* **1** a going on from one point to the next; progress in space or time [the *course* of history; the *course* of a journey]. **2** a way or path along which something moves; channel, track, etc. [a golf *course*; race*course*]. **3** a part of a meal served at one time [The main *course* was roast beef.] **4** a complete series of studies [I took a business *course* in high school.] **5** any of these studies [a mathematics *course*]. —**coursed, cours′ing**

cow·ard (kou′ərd) *n.* a person who is unable to control his fear and so shrinks from danger or trouble.

cram (kram) *v.* **1** to pack full or too full [Her suitcase is *crammed* with clothes.] **2** to stuff or force [He *crammed* the papers into a drawer.] **3** to study many facts in a hurry, as for a test. —**crammed, cram′ming**

cray·on (krā′ən *or* krā′än) *n.* a small stick of chalk, charcoal, or colored wax, used for drawing or writing. ◆*v.* to draw with crayons.

cra·zy (krā′zē) *adj.* **1** mentally ill; insane. **2** very foolish or mad [a *crazy* idea]. **3** very eager or enthusiastic: *used only in everyday talk* [I'm *crazy* about the movies.] —**cra′zi·er, cra′zi·est** —**cra′zi·ly** *adv.* —**cra′zi·ness** *n.*

cre·a·tion (krē ā′shən) *n.* 1 the act of creating. 2 the whole world and everything in it; universe. 3 anything created or brought into being.

cre·a·tive (krē ā′tiv) *adj.* creating or able to create; inventive; having imagination and ability. —**cre·a·tiv·i·ty** (krē′ā tiv′ə tē) *n.*

crepe or **crêpe** (krāp) *n.* 1 a thin, crinkled cloth. 2 (krāp *or* krep) a very thin pancake, rolled up or folded with a filling: *usually* **crêpe.**

cres·cent (kres′ənt) *n.* 1 the shape of the moon in its first or last quarter. 2 anything shaped like this, as a curved bun or roll. ◆*adj.* shaped like a crescent.

croc·o·dile (kräk′ə dīl) *n.* a large lizard like the alligator, that lives in and near tropical rivers. It has a thick, tough skin, a long tail, large jaws, and pointed teeth.

crois·sant (krə sänt′) *n.* a rich, flaky bread roll made in the form of a crescent.

cro·quet (krō kā′) *n.* an outdoor game in which the players use mallets to drive a wooden ball through hoops in the ground.

cru·el (krōō′əl) *adj.* 1 liking to make others suffer; having no mercy or pity [The *cruel* Pharaoh made slaves of the Israelites.] 2 causing pain and suffering [*cruel* insults; a *cruel* winter]. —**cru′el·ly** *adv.*

cruise (krōōz) *v.* 1 to sail or drive about from place to place, as for pleasure or in searching for something. 2 to move smoothly at a speed that is not strained [The airplane *cruised* at 300 miles per hour.] —**cruised, cruis′ing** ◆*n.* a ship voyage from place to place for pleasure.

crumb (krum) *n.* a tiny piece broken off, as of bread or cake.

crutch (kruch) *n.* a support used under the arm by a lame person to help in walking. — *pl.* **crutch′es**

crys·tal (kris′təl) *n.* 1 a clear, transparent quartz that looks like glass. 2 a very clear, sparkling glass. 3 something made of such glass, as a goblet or bowl. 4 any of the regularly shaped pieces into which many substances are formed when they become solids. A crystal has a number of flat surfaces in an orderly arrangement [Salt, sugar, and snow are made up of *crystals.*] ◆*adj.* made of crystal.

cul·ture (kul′chər) *n.* 1 improvement by study or training, especially of the mind, manners, and taste; refinement. 2 the ideas, skills, arts, tools, and way of life of a certain people in a certain time; civilization [the *culture* of the Aztecs]. —**cul′tur·al** *adj.* —**cul′tur·al·ly** *adv.*

cur·few (kur′fyōō) *n.* a time in the evening beyond which certain persons or all people must not be on the streets [Our town has a nine o'clock *curfew* for children.]

cur·ren·cy (kur′ən sē) *n.* ☆ the money in common use in any country; often, paper money. —*pl.* **cur′ren·cies**

cus·tom (kus′təm) *n.* 1 a usual thing to do; habit [It is my *custom* to have tea after dinner.] 2 something that has been done for a long time and so has become the common or regular thing to do [the *custom* of eating turkey on Thanksgiving]. 3 **customs,** *pl.* taxes collected by a government on goods brought in from other countries; also, the government agency that collects these taxes. ◆*adj.* made or done to order [*custom* shoes].

cym·bal (sim′bəl) *n.* a round brass plate, used in orchestras and bands, that makes a sharp, ringing sound when it is hit. Cymbals can be used in pairs that are struck together.

cy·press (sī′prəs) *n.* an evergreen tree with cones and dark leaves.

crocodile

Dd

damp (damp) *adj.* slightly wet; moist [*damp* clothes; *damp* weather]. ◆*n.* a slight wetness; moisture [Rains caused *damp* in the basement.] —**damp′ly** *adv.* —**damp′ness** *n.*

dare (der) *v.* 1 to face bravely or boldly; defy [The hunter *dared* the dangers of the jungle.] 2 to call on someone to do a certain thing in order to show courage; challenge [She *dared* me to swim across the lake.] —**dared, dar′ing** ◆*n.* a challenge to prove that one is not afraid [I accepted her *dare* to swim across the lake.]

dar·ing (der′iŋ) *adj.* bold enough to take risks; fearless. ◆*n.* bold courage.

de·bate (dē bāt′) *v.* 1 to give reasons for or against; argue about something, especially in a formal contest between two opposite sides [The Senate *debated* the question of foreign treaties.] 2 to consider reasons for and against [I *debated* the problem in my own mind.] —**de·bat′ed, de·bat′ing** ◆*n.* the act of debating something; discussion or formal argument. —**de·bat′er** *n.*

de·brief (dē brēf′) *v.* to question someone who has ended a mission, to get information [The astronaut was *debriefed* after the space flight.]

debt (det) *n.* 1 something that one owes to another [a *debt* of $25; a *debt* of gratitude]. 2 the condition of owing [I am greatly in *debt* to you.]

de·cay (dē kā′) *v.* 1 to become rotten by the action of bacteria [The fallen apples *decayed* on the ground.] 2 to fall into ruins; become no longer sound, powerful, rich, beautiful, etc. [Spain's power *decayed* after its fleet was destroyed.] ◆*n.* a rotting or falling into ruin.

a	ask, fat
ā	ape, date
ä	car, lot
e	elf, ten
ē	even, meet
i	is, hit
ī	ice, fire
ō	open, go
ô	law, horn
oi	oil, point
͞oo	look, pull
͞oo	ooze, tool
ou	out, crowd
u	up, cut
ʉ	fur, fern
ə	a in ago
	e in agent
	e in father
	i in unity
	o in collect
	u in focus
ch	chin, arch
ŋ	ring, singer
sh	she, dash
th	thin, truth
th	then, father
zh	s in pleasure

de·cent (dē′sənt) *adj.* **1** proper and fitting; not to be ashamed of; respectable [*decent* manners; *decent* language]. **2** fairly good; satisfactory [a *decent* wage]. **3** kind; generous; fair [It was *decent* of you to lend me your car.] —**de′cent·ly** *adv.*

de·cep·tive (dē sep′tiv) *adj.* deceiving; not what it seems to be. —**de·cep′tive·ly** *adv.*

dec·i·bel (des′ə bəl) *n.* a unit for measuring the relative loudness of sound.

de·cline (dē klīn′) *v.* **1** to bend or slope downward [The lawn *declines* to the sidewalk.] **2** to become less in health, power, or value; decay [A person's strength usually *declines* in old age.] **3** to refuse something, especially in a polite way [I am sorry I must *decline* your invitation.] ◆ *n.* **1** the process or result of becoming less, smaller, or weaker; decay [a *decline* in prices]. **2** the last part [the *decline* of life] **3** a downward slope [We slid down the *decline*.]

dec·o·ra·tion (dek′ə rā′shən) *n.* **1** anything used for decorating; ornament [*decorations* for the Christmas tree]. **2** a medal, ribbon, etc. given as a sign of honor.

decoration

de·crease (dē krēs′ *or* dē′krēs) *v.* to make or become gradually less or smaller [She has *decreased* her weight by dieting. The pain is *decreasing*.] —**de·creased′, de·creas′ing** ◆ *n.* a decreasing or growing less [a *decrease* in profits].

ded·i·cate (ded′i kāt) *v.* **1** to set aside for a special purpose [The church was *dedicated* to the worship of God. The doctor has *dedicated* her life to cancer research.] **2** to say at the beginning of a book, etc. that it was written in honor of, or out of affection for, a certain person [He *dedicated* his novel to his wife.] —**ded′i·cat·ed, ded′i·cat·ing** —**ded′i·ca′tion** *n.*

de·fi·cien·cy (dē fish′ən sē) *n.* an amount short of what is needed; shortage [A *deficiency* of vitamin C causes scurvy.] —*pl.* **de·fi′cien·cies**

de·lete (dē lēt′) *v.* to take out or cross out something printed or written [Her name has been *deleted* from the list of members.] —**de·let′ed, de·let′ing** —**de·le·tion** (di lē′shən) *n.*

de·liv·er·y (dē liv′ər ē) *n.* the act of delivering; a transferring or distributing [daily *deliveries* to customers; the *delivery* of a prisoner into custody]. —*pl.* **de·liv′er·ies**

den·im (den′im) *n.* a coarse cotton cloth that will take hard wear and is used for work clothes or play clothes.

de·pend (dē pend′) *v.* **1** to be controlled or decided by [The attendance at the game *depends* on the weather.] **2** to put one's trust in; be sure of [You can't *depend* on the weather.] **3** to rely for help or support [They *depend* on their parents for money.]

de·pos·it (dē päz′it) *v.* **1** to place for safekeeping, as money in a bank. **2** to give as part payment or as a pledge [They *deposited* $500 on a new car.] **3** to lay down [I *deposited* my books on the chair. The river *deposits* tons of mud at its mouth.] ◆ *n.* **1** something placed for safekeeping, as money in a bank. **2** something left lying, as sand, clay, or minerals deposited by the action of wind, water, or other forces of nature.

dept. *abbreviation for* **department**.

depth (depth) *n.* **1** the fact of being deep, or how deep a thing is; deepness [the *depth* of the ocean; a closet five feet in *depth*; the *depth* of a color; the great *depth* of their love]. **2** the middle part [the *depth* of winter].

de·scend (dē send′) *v.* **1** to move down to a lower place [to *descend* from a hilltop; to *descend* a staircase]. **2** to become lesser or smaller [Prices have *descended* during the past month.] **3** to come from a certain source [They are *descended* from pioneers.]

des·ert (dez′ərt) *n.* a dry sandy region with little or no plant life. ◆ *adj.* **1** of or like a desert. **2** wild and not lived in [a *desert* island].

de·serve (də zurv′) *v.* to have a right to; be one that ought to get [This matter *deserves* thought. You *deserve* a scolding.] —**de·served′, de·serv′ing** —**de·serv′ed·ly** *adv.*

de·serv·ing (də zur′viŋ) *adj.* that ought to get help or a reward [a *deserving* student].

de·sign·er (də zī′nər) *n.* a person who designs or makes original plans [a dress *designer*].

de·sir·a·ble (də zīr′ə bəl) *adj.* worth wanting or having; pleasing, excellent, beautiful, etc. —**de·sir·a·bil′i·ty** *n.* —**de·sir′a·bly** *adv.*

de·spair (də sper′) *n.* a giving up or loss of hope [Sam is in *despair* of ever getting a vacation.] ◆ *v.* to lose or give up hope [The prisoner *despaired* of ever being free again.]

des·sert (də zurt′) *n.* ☆something sweet served at the end of a meal, as fruit, pie, or cake.

de·struc·tive (dē struk′tiv) *adj.* destroying or likely to destroy [a *destructive* windstorm].

de·vel·op (dē vel′əp) *v.* **1** to make or become larger, fuller, better, etc.; grow or expand [The seedling *developed* into a tree. Reading *develops* one's knowledge.] **2** to bring or come into being and work out gradually; evolve [Dr. Salk *developed* a vaccine for polio. Mold *developed* on the cheese.] **3** to treat an exposed photographic film or plate with chemicals, so as to show the picture.

di·ag·o·nal (dī ag′ə nəl) *adj.* **1** slanting from one corner to the opposite corner, as of a square. **2** going in a slanting direction [a tie with *diagonal* stripes]. ◆*n.* a diagonal line, plane, course, or part. —**di·ag′o·nal·ly** *adv.*

dic·tion·ar·y (dik′shə ner′ē) *n.* a book in which the words of a language, or of some special field, are listed in alphabetical order with their meanings, pronunciations, and other information [a school *dictionary*]. —*pl.* —**dic·tion·ar′ies**

die·sel (dē′zəl *or* dē′səl) *n. often* **Diesel 1** a kind of internal-combustion engine that burns fuel oil by using heat produced by compressing air: *also called* **diesel engine** **or diesel motor**. **2** a locomotive or motor vehicle with such an engine.

dif′fer·ence (dif′ər əns *or* dif′rəns) *n.* **1** the state of being different or unlike [the *difference* between right and wrong]. **2** a way in which people or things are unlike [a *difference* in size]. **3** the amount by which one quantity is greater or less than another [The *difference* between 11 and 7 is 4.]

dif·fuse (di fyōos′) *adj.* **1** spread out; not centered in one place [This lamp gives *diffuse* light.] **2** using more words than are needed; wordy [a *diffuse* style of writing]. ◆ *v.* (di fyōoz′)**1** to spread out in every direction; scatter widely [to *diffuse* light]. **2** to mix together [to *diffuse* gases or liquids].

di·gest (di jest′ *or* dī jest′) *v.* to change food in the stomach and intestines into a form that can be used by the body [Small babies cannot *digest* solid food.] —**di·gest′i·ble** *adj.*

di·no·saur (dī′nə sôr) *n.* any of a group of reptiles that lived millions of years ago. Dinosaurs had four legs and a long, tapering tail, and some were almost 100 feet long.

dis·ap·point (dis ə point′) *v.* to fail to give or do what is wanted, expected, or promised; leave unsatisfied [I am *disappointed* in the weather. You promised to come, but *disappointed* us.]

dis·ap·point·ment (dis′ə point′mənt) *n.* **1** a disappointing or being disappointed [one's *disappointment* over not winning]. **2** a person or thing that disappoints [The team is a *disappointment* to us.]

dis·ci·pline (dis′ə plin) *n.* **1** training that teaches one to obey rules and control one's behavior [the strict *discipline* of army life]. **2** the result of such training; self-control; orderliness [The pupils showed perfect *discipline*.] ◆*v.* **1** to train in discipline [Regular chores help to *discipline* children.] **2** to punish. —**dis′ci·plined, dis′ci·plin·ing**

dis·count (dis′kount) *n.* an amount taken off a price, bill, or debt [He got a 10% *discount* by paying cash, so the radio cost $90 instead of $100.] ◆*v.* to take off a certain amount as a discount from a price, bill, etc.

dis·ease (di zēz′) *n.* a condition of not being healthy; sickness; illness [Chicken pox is a common childhood *disease*. Some fungi cause *disease* in animals and plants.] —**dis·eased′** *adj.*

dis·guise (dis gīz′) *v.* **1** to make seem so different as not to be recognized [to *disguise* oneself with a false beard; to *disguise* one's voice]. **2** to hide so as to keep from being known [She *disguised* her dislike of him by being very polite.] —**dis·guised′, dis·guis′ing** ◆*n.* any clothes, makeup, way of acting, etc. used to hide who or what one is.

dis·may (dis mā′) *v.* to fill with fear or dread so that one is not sure of what to do [We were *dismayed* at the sight of the destruction.] ◆*n.* loss of courage or confidence when faced with trouble or danger [The doctor's report filled her with *dismay*.]

dis·o·bey (dis′ ō bā′) *v.* to fail to obey or refuse to obey.

dis·tort (di stôrt′) *v.* **1** to twist out of its usual shape or look [The old mirror gave a *distorted* reflection.] **2** to change so as to give a false idea [The facts were *distorted*.] —**dis·tor′tion** *n.*

dis·turb·ance (di stur′bəns) *n.* **1** a disturbing or being disturbed. **2** anything that disturbs. **3** noisy confusion; uproar; disorder.

di·vi·sor (də vī′zər) *n.* the number by which another number is divided [In $6 \div 3 = 2$, the number 3 is the *divisor*.]

dom·i·no (däm′ə nō) *n.* a small, oblong piece of wood, plastic, etc. marked with dots on one side. A set of these pieces is used in playing the game called **dominoes**, in which the halves are matched. —*pl.* **dom′i·noes** or **dom′i·nos**

doubt (dout) *v.* to think that something may not be true or right; be unsure of; question [I *doubt* that those are the correct facts. Never *doubt* my love.] ◆*n.* a doubting; being unsure of something [I have no *doubt* that you will win.] —**doubt′er** *n.*

dough·nut (dō′nut) *n.* a small, sweet cake fried in deep fat, usually shaped like a ring.

down·stream (doun′strēm) *adv., adj.* in the direction in which a stream is flowing.

draw·back (drô′bak *or* drä′bak) *n.* a condition that acts against one; hindrance; disadvantage.

drought (drout) or **drouth** (drouth) *n.* a long period of dry weather, with little or no rain.

drow·sy (drou′zē) *adj.* **1** sleepy or half asleep. **2** making one feel sleepy [*drowsy* music]. —**drow′si·er, drow′si·est** —**drow′si·ly** *adv.* —**drow′si·ness** *n.*

du·ti·ful (dōot′ə fəl *or* dyōot′ə fəl) *adj.* doing or ready to do one's duty; having a proper sense of duty [a *dutiful* parent]. —**du′ti·ful·ly** *adv.*

domino

a	ask, fat
ā	ape, date
ä	car, lot
e	elf, ten
ē	even, meet
i	is, hit
ī	ice, fire
ō	open, go
ô	law, horn
oi	oil, point
oo	look, pull
ōo	ooze, tool
ou	out, crowd
u	up, cut
u	fur, fern
ə	a in ago
	e in agent
	e in father
	i in unity
	o in collect
	u in focus
ch	chin, arch
ŋ	ring, singer
sh	she, dash
th	thin, truth
th	then, father
zh	s in pleasure

Ee

ear·nest (ʉr′nəst) *adj.* not light or joking; serious or sincere [an *earnest* wish].
—**ear′nest·ly** *adv.* —**ear′nest·ness** *n.*

earn (ʉrn) *v.* **1** to get as pay for work done [She *earns* $10 an hour.] **2** to get or deserve because of something done [He *earned* a medal for swimming.] **3** to get as profit [Your savings *earn* 5% interest.] —**earn′ings** *pl. n.*

ear·ring (ir′riŋ) *n.* an ornament worn on or in the lobe of the ear.

earth·en·ware (ʉrth′ən wer) *n.* the coarser sort of dishes, vases, jars, etc. made of baked clay.

ea·sel (ē′zəl) *n.* a standing frame for holding an artist's canvas, a chalkboard, etc.

east·ward (ēst′wərd) *adv., adj.* in the direction of the east [an *eastward* journey; to travel *eastward*].

ech·o (ek′ō) *n.* sound heard again when sound waves bounce back from a surface. —*pl.* **ech′oes** ◆*v.* —**ech′oed, ech′o·ing**

e·clipse (e klips′) *n.* a hiding of all or part of the sun by the moon when it passes between the sun and the earth (called a **solar eclipse**); also, a hiding of the moon by the earth's shadow (called a **lunar eclipse**). ◆*v.* to cause an eclipse of; darken. —**e·clipsed′, e·clips′ing**

e·col·o·gy (ē kä l′ə jē) *n.* the science that deals with the relations between all living things and the conditions that surround them. —**e·col′o·gist** *n.*

ed. *abbreviation for:* **1** edition *or* editor. —*pl.* **eds. 2** education.

ed·u·ca·tion (ej′ə kā′shən) *n.* **1** the act or work of educating or training people; teaching [a career in *education*]. **2** the things a person learns by being taught; schooling or training [a high-school *education*].

ef·fec·tive (ə fek′tiv) *adj.* **1** making a certain thing happen; especially, bringing about the result wanted [an *effective* remedy]. **2** in force or operation; active [The law becomes *effective* Monday.] **3** making a strong impression on the mind; impressive [an *effective* speaker]. —**ef·fec′tive·ly** *adv.*

ef·fi·cient (ə fish′ənt) *adj.* bringing about the result or effect wanted with the least waste of time, effort, or materials [an *efficient* method of production; an *efficient* manager]. —**ef·fi′cien·cy** *n.*

E·gyp·tian (ē jip′shən) *adj.* of Egypt, its people, or their culture. ◆*n.* **1** a person born or living in Egypt. **2** the language of the ancient Egyptians. Modern Egyptians speak Arabic.

earring

easel

e·lec·tric·i·ty (ē lek′tris′i tē) *n.* a form of energy that comes from the movement of electrons and protons. It can be produced by friction (as by rubbing wax with wool), by chemical action (as in a storage battery), or by induction (as in a dynamo or generator). Electricity is used to produce light, heat, power, etc. Electricity moving in a stream, as through a wire, is called **electric current**.

em·bank·ment (im baŋk′mənt) *n.* a long mound or wall of earth, stone, etc. used to keep back water, hold up a roadway, etc.

em·bar·go (em bär′gō) *n.* a government order that forbids certain ships to leave or enter its ports.—*pl.* **em·bar′goes** ◆*v.* to put an embargo upon. —**em·bar′goed, em·bar′go·ing**

em·bat·tle (em bat′l) *v.* to prepare for battle. —**em·bat′tled, em·bat′tling**

em·bel·lish (em bel′ish) *v.* to decorate or improve by adding something [to *embellish* a talk with details]. —**em·bel′lish·ment** *n.*

em·bit·ter (em bit′ər) *v.* to make bitter; make feel angry or hurt [He was *embittered* by her remark.]

em·bla·zon (em blā′zən) *v.* **1** to decorate with bright colors or in a rich, showy way [The bandstand was *emblazoned* with bunting.] **2** to mark with an emblem [The shield was *emblazoned* with a golden lion.]

em·broi·der·y (em broi′dər ē) *n.* **1** the art or work of embroidering. **2** an embroidered decoration. —*pl.* **em·broi′der·ies**

em·pha·size (em′fə sīz) *v.* to give special force or attention to; stress [I want to *emphasize* the importance of honesty.] —**em′pha·sized, em′pha·siz·ing**

em·ploy·ment (e ploi′mənt) *n.* **1** the condition of being employed. **2** one's work, trade, or profession.

em·pow·er (em pou′ər) *v.* to give certain power or rights to; authorize [The warrant *empowered* the police to search the house.]

emp·ty (emp′tē) *adj.* having nothing or no one in it; not occupied; vacant [an *empty* jar; an *empty* house]. —**emp′ti·er, emp′ti·est** ◆*v.* **1** to make or become empty [The auditorium was *emptied* in ten minutes.] **2** to take out or pour out [*Empty* the dirty water in the sink.] **3** to flow out; discharge [The Amazon *empties* into the Atlantic.] —**emp′tied, emp′ty·ing** —*pl.* **emp′ties** —**emp′ti·ly** *adv.* —**emp′ti·ness** *n.*

en·com·pass (en kum′pəs) *v.* **1** to surround on all sides; enclose or encircle [a lake *encompassed* by mountains]. **2** to have in it; contain or include [A dictionary *encompasses* much information.]

en·cour·age (en kʉr′ij) *v.* **1** to give courage or hope to; make feel more confident [Praise *encouraged* her to try harder.] **2** to give help to; aid; promote [Rain *encourages* the growth of plants.] —**en·cour′aged, en·cour′ag·ing** —**en·cour′age·ment** *n.*

en·dan·ger (en dān′jər) *v.* to put in danger or peril [to *endanger* one's life].

en·dow (en dou′) *v.* **1** to provide with some quality or thing [a person *endowed* with musical talent; a land *endowed* with natural resources]. **2** to provide a gift of money to a college, hospital, museum, etc., that will bring a regular income to help support it. —**en·dow′ment** *n.*

en·gage (en gāj′) *v.* **1** to promise to marry [Harry is *engaged* to Grace.] **2** to promise or undertake to do something [She *engaged* to tutor the child after school.] **3** to draw into; involve [She *engaged* him in conversation.] —**en·gaged′, en·gag′ing**

Eng·lish (iŋ′glish) *adj.* of England, its people, language, etc. ◆*n.* **1** the language spoken in England, the U.S., Canada, Australia, New Zealand, Liberia, etc. **2** a course in school for studying the English language or English literature.

en·grave (en grāv′) *v.* **1** to carve or etch letters, designs, etc. on [a date *engraved* on a building]. **2** to cut or etch a picture, lettering, etc. into a metal plate, wooden block, etc. to be used for printing; also, to print from such a plate, block, etc. [an *engraved* invitation]. —**en·graved′, en·grav′ing** —**en·grav′er** *n.*

en·light·en (en līt′n) *v.* to get someone to have knowledge or know the truth; get rid of ignorance or false beliefs; inform. —**en·light′en·ment** *n.*

en·list (en list′) *v.* **1** to join or get someone to join; especially, to join some branch of the armed forces [She *enlisted* in the navy. This office *enlisted* ten new recruits.] **2** to get the support of [Try to *enlist* your parents' help.] —**en·list′ment** *n.*

en·roll or **en·rol** (en rōl′) *v.* **1** to write one's name in a list, as in becoming a member; register [New students must *enroll* on Monday.] **2** to make someone a member [We want to *enroll* you in our swim club.] —**en·rolled′, en·roll′ing**

en·roll·ment or **en·rol·ment** (en rōl′mənt) *n.* **1** the act of enrolling. **2** the number of people enrolled.

en·sure (en shoor′) *v.* **1** to make sure or certain [Good weather will *ensure* a large attendance.] **2** to make safe; protect [Seat belts help to *ensure* you against injury in a car accident.] —**en·sured′, en·sur′ing**

e·qui·lat·er·al (ē′kwi lat′ər əl) *adj.* having all sides equal in length.

e·quip (ē kwip′) *v.* to provide with what is needed; outfit [The soldiers were *equipped* for battle. The car is *equipped* with power brakes.] —**e·quipped′, e·quip′ping**

☆**es·ca·la·tor** (es′kə lāt′ər) *n.* a stairway whose steps are part of an endless moving belt, for carrying people up or down.

es·cape (e skāp′) *v.* **1** to break loose; get free, as from prison. **2** to keep from getting hurt, killed, etc.; keep safe from; avoid [Very few people *escaped* the plague.] —**es·caped′, es·cap′ing** ◆*n.* **1** the act of escaping [The prisoners made their plans for an *escape*.] **2** a way of escaping [The fire closed in and there seemed to be no *escape*.]

Es·ki·mo (es′kə mō) *n.* **1** any member of a group of people who live mainly in the arctic regions of the Western Hemisphere. —*pl.* **Es′ki·mos** or **Es′ki·mo 2** the language of the Eskimos. ◆*adj.* of the Eskimos.

es·say (es′ā) *n.* a short piece of writing on some subject, giving the writer's personal ideas.

es·teem (e stēm′) *v.* to have a good opinion of; regard as valuable; respect [I *esteem* his praise above all other.] ◆*n.* good opinion; high regard; respect [to hold someone in high *esteem*].

etc. *abbreviation for* **et cetera.**

e·vap·o·rate (ē vap′ə rāt) *v.* **1** to change into vapor [Heat *evaporates* water. The perfume in the bottle has *evaporated*.] **2** to disappear like vapor; vanish [Our courage *evaporated* when we saw the lion.] **3** to make thicker by heating so as to take some of the water from [to *evaporate* milk]. —**e·vap′o·rat·ed, e·vap′o·rat·ing** —**e·vap′o·ra′tion** *n.*

☆**ev·er·glade** (ev′ər glād) *n.* a large swamp.

ex. *abbreviation for* **example, extra.**

ex·cel·lence (ek′sə ləns) *n.* the fact of being better or greater; extra goodness [We all praised the *excellence* of their singing.]

ex·cept (ek sept′) *prep.* leaving out; other than; but [Everyone *except* you liked the movie.] ◆*v.* to leave out; omit; exclude [Only a few of the students were *excepted* from her criticism.] ◆*conj.* were it not that; only: *used only in everyday talk* [I'd go with you *except* I'm tired.]

ex·cit·ing (ek sīt′iŋ) *adj.* causing excitement; stirring; thrilling [an *exciting* story].

ex·haust (eg zôst′ *or* eg zäst′) *v.* **1** to use up completely [Our drinking water was soon *exhausted*.] **2** to let out the contents of; make completely empty [The leak soon *exhausted* the gas tank.] **3** to use up the strength of; tire out; weaken [They are *exhausted* from playing tennis.] ◆*n.* the used steam or gas that comes from the cylinders of an engine; especially, the fumes from the gasoline engine in an automobile.

ex·hib·it (eg zib′it) *v.* to show or display to the public [to *exhibit* stamp collections]. ◆*n.* **1** something exhibited to the public [an art *exhibit*]. **2** something shown as evidence in a court of law.

engrave

a	ask, fat
ā	ape, date
ä	car, lot
e	elf, ten
ē	even, meet
i	is, hit
ī	ice, fire
ō	open, go
ô	law, horn
oi	oil, point
ℊ	look, pull
ōō	ooze, tool
ou	out, crowd
u	up, cut
ʉ	fur, fern
ə	a in ago
	e in agent
	e in father
	i in unity
	o in collect
	u in focus
ch	chin, arch
ŋ	ring, singer
sh	she, dash
th	thin, truth
th	then, father
zh	s in pleasure

ex·ist·ence (eg zis′təns) *n.* **1** the condition of being; an existing. **2** life or a way of life [a happy *existence*]. —**ex·ist′ent** *adj.*

ex·pe·ri·ence (ek spir′ē əns) *n.* **1** the fact of living through a happening or happenings [*Experience* teaches us many things.] **2** something that one has done or lived through [This trip was an *experience* that I'll never forget.] **3** skill that one gets by training, practice, and work [a lawyer with much *experience*]. ◆*v.* to have the experience of [to *experience* success]. —**ex·pe′ri·enced, ex·pe′ri·enc·ing**

ex·pla·na·tion (eks′plə nā′shən) *n.* **1** the act of explaining [This plan needs *explanation*.] **2** something that explains [This long nail is the *explanation* for the flat tire.] **3** a meaning given in explaining [different *explanations* of the same event].

ex·ploit (eks′ploit) *n.* a daring act or bold deed [the *exploits* of Robin Hood. ◆*v.* (ek sploit′) to use in a selfish way; take unfair advantage of [Children were *exploited* when they had to work in factories.] —**ex′ploi·ta′tion** *n.*

fabric

ex·plore (ek splôr′) *v.* **1** to travel in a region that is unknown or not well known, in order to find out more about it [to *explore* a wild jungle]. **2** to look into or examine carefully [to *explore* a problem]. —**ex·plored′, ex·plor′ing** —**ex′plo·ra′tion** *n.* —**ex·plor′er** *n.*

ex·po·sure (ek spō′zhər) *n.* **1** the fact of being exposed [tanned by *exposure* to the sun]. **2** the time during which film in a camera is exposed to light; also, a section of film that can be made into one picture [Give this film a short *exposure*. There are twelve *exposures* on this film.]

ex·tra·ter·res·tri·al (eks′trə tər res′trē əl) *adj.* being, happening, or coming from a place not the earth [a science fiction story about *extraterrestrial* beings].

ex·treme (ek strēm′) *adj.* **1** to the greatest degree; very great [*extreme* pain]. **2** far from what is usual; also, very far from the center of opinion [She holds *extreme* political views.] ◆*n.* either of two things that are as different or as far from each other as possible [the *extremes* of laughter and tears]. —**ex·treme′ly** *adv.*

eye·sight (ī′sīt) *n.* **1** the ability to see; sight; vision [keen *eyesight*]. **2** the distance a person can see [Keep within *eyesight*!]

fab·ric (fab′rik) *n.* a material made from fibers or threads by weaving, knitting, etc., as any cloth, felt, lace, etc.

fa·cial (fā′shəl) *adj.* of or for the face. ◆☆*n.* a treatment intended to make the skin of the face look better, as by massage and putting on creams and lotions.

faith·ful (fāth′fəl) *adj.* **1** remaining loyal; constant [*faithful* friends]. **2** showing a strong sense of duty or responsibility [*faithful* attendance]. —**faith′ful·ly** *adv.* —**faith′ful·ness** *n.*

fal·low (fal′ō) *adj.* plowed but left unplanted during the growing season [Farmers let the land lie *fallow* at times to kill weeds, make the soil richer, etc.] ◆*n.* land that lies fallow.

fan·ci·ful (fan′si fəl) *adj.* **1** full of fancy; having or showing a quick and playful imagination [*fanciful* costumes for the Halloween party]. **2** not real; imaginary [a *fanciful* idea that horseshoes bring luck].

fas·ci·nate (fas′ə nāt) *v.* to hold the attention of by being interesting or delightful; charm [The puppet show *fascinated* the children.] —**fas′ci·nat·ed, fas′ci·nat·ing** —**fas′ci·na′tion** *n.*

fas·ten (fas′ən) *v.* **1** to join or become joined; attach [The collar is *fastened* to the shirt.] **2** to make stay closed or in place, as by locking or shutting [*Fasten* the door.] —**fas′ten·er** *n.*

fel·low·ship (fel′ō ship′) *n.* **1** friendship; companionship. **2** a group of people having the same activities or interests. **3** money given to a student at a university or college to help him or her study for a higher degree.

fen·der (fen′dər) *n.* a metal piece over the wheel of a car, bicycle, etc. that protects against splashing water or mud.

fes·ti·val (fes′tə vəl) *n.* **1** a day or time of feasting or celebrating; happy holiday [The Mardi Gras in New Orleans is a colorful *festival*.] **2** a time of special celebration or entertainment [Our town holds a maple sugar *festival* every spring.] ◆*adj.* of or for a festival [*festival* music].

fetch (fech) *v.* to go after and bring back; get [The dog *fetched* my slippers.]

fierce (firs) *adj.* **1** wild or cruel; violent; raging [a *fierce* dog; a *fierce* wind]. **2** very strong or eager [a *fierce* effort]. —**fierc′er, fierc′est** —**fierce′ly** *adv.* —**fierce′ness** *n.*

fif·teen (fif′tēn′) *n., adj.* five more than ten; the number 15.

filth·y (fil′thē) *adj.* full of filth; disgusting. **filth′i·er, filth′i·est**

firm (furm) *adj.* **1** that does not easily give way when pressed; solid [*firm* muscles]. **2** that cannot be moved easily; fixed; stable [He stood as *firm* as a rock.] **3** that stays the same; not changing; constant [a *firm* friendship]. —**firm′ly** *adv.* —**firm′ness** *n.*

flash·bulb (flash′bulb) *n.* a light bulb that gives a short, bright light for taking photographs.

flo·rist (flôr′ist) *n.* a person whose business is selling flowers, house plants, etc.

flour·ish (flur′ish) *v.* to grow strongly and well; be successful or healthy; prosper [Daisies *flourish* in full sun.]

fo·li·age (fō′lē ij) *n.* the leaves of a tree or plant, or of many trees or plants.

fol·ly (fä′lē) *n.* a lack of good sense; foolishness.

fore·close (fôr klōz′) *v.* to end a mortgage and become the owner of the mortgaged property [A bank can *foreclose* a mortgage if payments on its loan are not made in time.] —**fore·closed′, fore·clos′ing** —**fore·clo′sure** *n.*

fore·ground (fôr′ground) *n.* the part of a scene or picture that is or seems to be nearest to the one looking at it.

for·eign·er (fôr′in ər *or* fär′in ər) *n.* a person from another country, thought of as an outsider.

fore·knowl·edge (fôr′nä′lij) *n.* knowledge of something before it happens.

fore·most (fôr′mōst) *adj.* first in position or importance [the *foremost* writers of their time]. ♦ *adv.* before all else [to be first and *foremost* a dancer].

fore·sight (fôr′sīt) *n.* **1** a foreseeing. **2** the power to foresee. **3** a looking forward. **4** a looking ahead and planning for the future.

fore·warn (fôr wôrn′) *v.* to warn ahead of time [We were *forewarned* we wouldn't get tickets later.] —**fore·warn′ing** *n.*

foun·da·tion (foun dā′shən) *n.* **1** the part at the bottom that supports a wall, house, etc.; base. **2** the basis on which an idea, belief, etc. rests.

found·er (foun′dər) *n.* a person who founds, or establishes [the *founder* of a city].

fra·grant (frā′grənt) *adj.* having a sweet or pleasant smell.

☆**frank·furt·er** *or* **frank·fort·er** (fraŋk′fər tər) *n.* a smoked sausage of beef or beef and pork; wiener.

freight (frāt) *n.* a load of goods shipped by train, truck, ship, or airplane. ♦ *v.* to carry or send by freight [Cars are often *freighted* by trains or trucks to where they are sold.]

fre·quen·cy (frē′kwən sē) *n.* **1** the fact of being frequent, or happening often. **2** the number of times something is repeated in a certain period [a *frequency* of 1,000 vibrations per second]. The frequency of radio waves is measured in hertz. —*pl.* **fre′quen·cies**

fruit·ful (frōōt′fəl) *adj.* **1** bearing much fruit [a *fruitful* tree]. **2** producing a great deal [Mozart was a *fruitful* composer.] —**fruit′ful·ly** *adv.* —**fruit′ful·ness** *n.*

gal·ax·y (gal′ək sē) ♦ *n.* any vast group of stars. —*pl.* **gal′ax·ies**

gal·ler·y (gal′ər ē) *n.* **1** a balcony, especially the highest balcony in a theater, with the cheapest seats. **2** the people who sit in these seats. **3** a place for showing or selling works of art. —*pl.* —**gal′ler·ies**

gawk (gôk *or* gäk) *v.* to stare in a stupid way [The crowd *gawked* at the overturned truck.]

gear (gir) *n.* **1** *often* **gears,** *pl.* a part of a machine consisting of two or more wheels having teeth that fit together so that when one wheel moves the others are made to move [The *gears* pass on the motion of the engine to the wheels of the car.] **2** tools and equipment needed for doing something [My *gear* for fishing consists of a rod, lines, and flies.] ♦ *v.* to adjust or make fit [Our new cafeteria is *geared* to handle more students.]

gen·tle (jent′l) *adj.* **1** mild, soft, or easy; not rough [a *gentle* touch]. **2** tame; easy to handle [a *gentle* horse]. **3** gradual; not sudden [a *gentle* slope]. **4** courteous, kindly, or patient [a *gentle* nature]. — **gen′tler, gen′tlest**

gen·u·ine (jen′yōō in) *adj.* **1** really being what it seems to be; not false; true [a *genuine* diamond]. **2** sincere or honest [*genuine* praise]. —**gen′u·ine·ly** *adv.* —**gen′u·ine·ness** *n.*

ge·ol·o·gy (jē ä′lə jē) *n.* the study of the earth's crust and of the way in which its layers were formed. It includes the study of rocks and fossils. —**ge·ol′o·gist** *n.*

gloom·y (glōōm′ē) *adj.* **1** dark or dim [a *gloomy* dungeon]. **2** having or giving a feeling of deep sadness [a *gloomy* mood; a *gloomy* story]. —**gloom′i·er, gloom′i·est** —**gloom′i·ly** *adv.* —**gloom′i·ness** *n.*

glo·ri·fy (glôr′ə fī) *v.* **1** to give glory to; cause to be famous and respected [Our town *glorified* the hero by building a statue.] **2** to praise in worship [to *glorify* God]. **3** to make seem better than is really so [to *glorify* war]. —**glo′ri·fied, glo′ri·fy·ing**

gnarled (närld) *adj.* full of gnarls or knobs; twisted and knotty [a *gnarled* tree; *gnarled* hands].

gnome (nōm) *n.* a dwarf in folk tales who lives inside the earth and guards the treasures there.

govt. *or* **Govt.** *abbreviation for* **government.**

gear

a	ask, fat
ā	ape, date
ä	car, lot
e	elf, ten
ē	even, meet
i	is, hit
ī	ice, fire
ō	open, go
ô	law, horn
oi	oil, point
ᴏᴏ	look, pull
o̅o̅	ooze, tool
ou	out, crowd
u	up, cut
ʉ	fur, fern
ə	a in ago
	e in agent
	e in father
	i in unity
	o in collect
	u in focus
ch	chin, arch
ŋ	ring, singer
sh	she, dash
th	thin, truth
th	then, father
zh	s in pleasure

130

gra·cious (grā′shəs) *adj.* **1** kind, polite, and charming [a *gracious* host and hostess]. **2** full of grace, comfort, and luxury [*gracious* living].

grad·u·ate (gra′jōō ət) *n.* a person who has finished a course of study at a school or college and has been given a diploma or degree. ◆*v.* (gra′jōō āt′) **1** to make or become a graduate of a school or college. **2** to mark off with small lines for measuring [A thermometer is a tube *graduated* in degrees.] —**grad′u·at·ed, grad′u·at·ing** —**grad′u·a′tion** *n.*

greas·y (grē′sē *or* grē′zē) *adj.* **1** smeared with grease [*greasy* hands]. **2** full of grease [*greasy* food]. **3** like grease; oily [a *greasy* salve]. —**greas′i·er, greas′i·est** —**greas′i·ly** *adv.* —**greas′i·ness** *n.*

greed·y (grēd′ē) *adj.* wanting or taking all that one can get with no thought of what others need [The *greedy* little boy ate all the cookies.] **gredd′i·er, greed′i—est** —**greed′i·ly** *adv.* —**greed′i·ness** *n.*

greet·ing (grēt′iŋ) *n.* **1** the act or words of one who greets. **2** *often* **greetings,** *pl.* a message of regards from someone not present.

growth (grōth) *n.* **1** the act of growing; a becoming larger or a developing. **2** the amount grown; increase [a *growth* of two inches over the summer]. **3** something that grows or has grown [He shaved off the two weeks' *growth* of beard. A tumor is an abnormal *growth* in the body.]

guar·an·tee (ger ən tē′ *or* ger′ən tē) *n.* **1** a promise to replace something sold if it does not work or last as it should [a one-year *guarantee* on the clock]. **2** a promise or assurance that something will be done [You have my *guarantee* that we'll be on time.] ◆ *v.* **1** to give a guarantee or guaranty for. **2** to promise or assure [I cannot *guarantee* that she will be there.] —**guar·an·teed′, guar·an·tee′ing**

guess (ges) *v.* **1** to judge or decide about something without having enough facts to know for certain [Can you *guess* how old he is?] **2** to judge correctly by doing this [She *guessed* the exact number of beans in the jar.] **3** to think or suppose [I *guess* you're right.] ◆*n.* a judgment formed by guessing; surmise [Your *guess* is as good as mine.] —**guess′er** *n.*

guilt·y (gil′tē) *adj.* **1** having done something wrong; being to blame for something [She is often *guilty* of telling lies.] **2** judged in court to be a wrongdoer [The jury found him *guilty* of robbery.] **3** caused by a feeling of guilt [a *guilty* look]. —**guilt′i·er, guilt′i·est** —**guilt′i·ly** *adv.* —**guilt′i·ness** *n.*

gui·tar (gi tär′) *n.* a musical instrument with six strings. It is played by plucking the strings with the fingers or with a plectrum. —**gui·tar′ist** *n.*

gym·na·si·um (jim nā′zē əm) *n.* a building or room with equipment for doing exercises and playing games.

guitar

hand·ker·chief (haŋ′kər chif) *n.* a small piece of cloth for wiping the nose, eyes, or face, or worn as a decoration.

hap·py (hap′ē) *adj.* **1** feeling or showing pleasure or joy; glad; contented [a *happy* child; a *happy* song]. **2** lucky; fortunate [The story has a *happy* ending.] —**hap′pi·er, hap′pi·est** —**hap′pi·ly** *adv.* —**hap′pi·ness** *n.*

hatch·et (hach′ət) *n.* a small ax with a short handle.

haz·ard·ous (haz′ər dəs) *adj.* dangerous; risky.

head·ache (hed′āk) *n.* a pain in the head.

health·y (hel′thē) *adj.* **1** having good health; well [a *healthy* child]. **2** showing good health [a *healthy* appetite]. **3** good for one's health; healthful [a *healthy* climate]. —**health′i·er, health′i·est** —**health′i·ness** *n.*

height (hīt) *n.* **1** the distance from the bottom to the top; tallness [the *height* of a building; a child four feet in *height*]. **2** the highest point or degree [to reach the *height* of fame].

hem·i·sphere (hem′i sfir′) *n.* **1** half of a sphere or globe [The dome of the church was in the shape of a *hemisphere*.] **2** any of the halves into which the earth's surface is divided in geography.

he·ro (hir′ō *or* hē′rō) *n.* **1** a person who is looked up to for having done something brave or noble [Washington was the *hero* of the American Revolution.] **2** the most important person in a novel, play, or movie, especially if the person is good or noble. —*pl.* —**he′roes**

hes·i·ta·tion (hez′i tā′shən) *n.* **1** the act of hesitating, as because of doubt, fear, etc.; unsure or unwilling feeling [I agreed without *hesitation*.] **2** a pausing for a moment [talk filled with *hesitations*].

hex·a·gon (hek′sə gän) *n.* a flat figure with six angles and six sides.

hon·or·a·ble (än′ər ə bəl) *adj.* **1** worthy of being honored [an *honorable* trade]. **2** honest, upright, and sincere [*honorable* intentions]. **3** bringing honor [*honorable* mention]. —**hon′or·a·bly** *adv.*

hor·i·zon·tal (hôr′ə zänt′l) *adj.* parallel to the horizon; not vertical; level; flat [The top of a table is *horizontal*; its legs are vertical.] ◆*n.* a horizontal line, plane, etc. —**hor′i·zon′tal·ly** *adv.*

horse·rad·ish (hôrs′rad′ish) *n.* **1** a plant with a long, white root, that has a sharp, burning taste. **2** a relish made by grating this root.

hexagon

house·hold (hous′hōld) *n.* **1** all the persons who live in one house, especially a family. **2** the home and its affairs [to manage a *household*].

Hud·son (hud′sən) a river in eastern New York. Its mouth is at New York City.

hus·band (huz′bənd) *n.* the man to whom a woman is married.

hwy. *abbreviation for* **highway.**

hymn (him) *n.* **1** a song praising or honoring God. **2** any song of praise.

hy·phen·ate (hī′fənāt) *v.* to join or write with a hyphen. —**hy′phen·at·ed, hy′phen·at·ing** —**hy′phen·a′tion** *n.*

hyp·no·tize (hip′nə tīz) *v.* to put someone into a state of hypnosis or a condition like it. —**hyp′no·tized, hyp′no·tiz·ing** —**hyp′no·tist** *n.*

i·ci·cle (ī′sik əl) *n.* a hanging stick of ice formed by water freezing as it drips down.

I·da·ho (ī′də hō) a State in the northwestern part of the U.S.: abbreviated **Ida., ID**

i·den·ti·fy (ī den′tə fī) *v.* **1** to think of or treat as the same [The Roman god Jupiter is *identified* with the Greek god Zeus.] **2** to show or prove to be a certain person or thing [She was *identified* by a scar on her chin.] —**i·den′ti·fied, i·den′ti·fy·ing**

ig·ni·tion (ig nish′ən) *n.* **1** the act of setting on fire or catching fire. **2** the switch, spark plugs, etc. that set fire to the mixture of gases in the cylinders of a gasoline engine.

il·le·gal (i lē′gəl) *adj.* not legal; not allowed by law; against the law. —**il·le′gal·ly** *adv.*

il·leg·i·ble (il lej′ə bəl) *adj.* hard to read or impossible to read, as because badly written or printed.—**il·leg′i·bly** *adv.*

Il·li·nois (il′ə noi′) a State in the north central part of the U.S.: abbreviated **Ill., IL**

il·lit·er·ate (il lit′ər ət) *adj.* **1** not educated; especially, not knowing how to read or write. **2** showing a lack of education [an *illiterate* letter]. ◆*n.* a person who does not know how to read or write. —**il·lit′er·a·cy** *n.*

il·log·i·cal (il läj′i kəl) *adj.* not logical; showing poor reasoning. —**il·log′i·cal·ly** *adv.*

il·lu·mi·nate (il lōō′mə nāt′) *v.* **1** to give light to; light up [Candles *illuminated* the room.] **2** to make clear; explain [The teacher *illuminated* the meaning of the poem.] —**il·lu′mi·nat′·ed, il·lu′mi·nat′·ing**

im·ma·te·ri·al (im′ə tir′ē əl) *adj.* **1** of no importance [The cost is *immaterial* if the quality is good.] **2** not made of matter; spiritual.

im·ma·ture (im ə toor′ *or* im ə choor′) *adj.* not mature; not fully grown or developed [*immature* fruit; *immature* judgment]. —**im′ma·tu′ri·ty** *n.*

☆**im·mi·grant** (im′ə grənt) *n.* a person who comes into a foreign country to make a new home.

im·mor·tal (im môrt′l) *adj.* **1** never dying; living forever [The Greek gods were thought of as *immortal* beings.] **2** having fame that will last a long time [Shakespeare is an *immortal* poet.] ◆*n.* a being that lasts forever. —**im·mor·tal·i·ty** (i′môr tal′ə tē) *n.* —**im·mor′tal·ly** *adv.*

im·pair (im per′) *v.* to make worse, less, or weaker; damage [The disease *impaired* her hearing.]

im·pa·tient (im pā′shənt) *adj.* **1** not patient; not willing to put up with delay, annoyance, etc. [Some parents become *impatient* when their children cry.] **2** eager to do something or for something to happen [Rita is *impatient* to go swimming.] —**im·pa′tient·ly** *adv.*

im·per·fect (im pur′fikt) *adj.* not perfect; having some fault or flaw [an *imperfect* diamond].

im·po·lite (im pə līt′) *adj.* not polite; rude. —**im·po·lite′ly** *adv.* —**im·po·lite′ness** *n.*

im·prac·ti·cal (im prak′ti kəl) *adj.* not practical; not useful, efficient, etc.

im·print (im print′) *v.* **1** to mark by pressing or stamping [The paper was *imprinted* with the state seal.] **2** to fix firmly [Her face is *imprinted* in my memory.] ◆ *n.* (im′print) a mark made by pressing; print [the *imprint* of a dirty hand on the wall].

im·prop·er (im präp′ər) *adj.* **1** not proper or suitable; unfit [Sandals are *improper* shoes for tennis.] **2** not true; wrong; incorrect [an *improper* street address]. **3** not decent; in bad taste [*improper* jokes]. —**im·prop′er·ly** *adv.*

in·a·bil·i·ty (in′ə bil′ə tē) *n.* the condition of being unable; lack of ability or power.

inc. *abbreviation for* **included, income, incorporated, increase.**

in·ca·pa·ble (in kā′pə bəl) *adj.* **1** not capable; not having the ability or power needed [*incapable* of helping]. **2** not able to undergo; not open to [*incapable* of change]. —**in′ca·pa·bil′i·ty** *n.*

in·cred·i·ble (in kred′ə bəl) *adj.* so great, unusual, etc. that it is hard or impossible to believe [an *incredible* story; *incredible* speed]. —**in·cred′i·bly** *adv.*

Illinois

a	ask, fat
ā	ape, date
ä	car, lot
e	elf, ten
ē	even, meet
i	is, hit
ī	ice, fire
ō	open, go
ô	law, horn
oi	oil, point
ơ	look, pull
ơơ	ooze, tool
ou	out, crowd
u	up, cut
u	fur, fern
ə	a in ago
	e in agent
	e in father
	i in unity
	o in collect
	u in focus
ch	chin, arch
ŋ	ring, singer
sh	she, dash
th	thin, truth
th	then, father
zh	s in pleasure

ivory

in·def·i·nite (in def′ə nit) **adj. 1** having no exact limits [an *indefinite* area]. **2** not clear or exact in meaning; vague [*indefinite* instructions]. **3** not sure or positive; uncertain [*indefinite* plans]. —**in·def′i·nite·ly adv.**

in·di·rect (in′də rekt′) **adj. 1** not direct or straight; by a longer way; roundabout [an *indirect* route]. **2** not straight to the point [an *indirect* reply]. —**in′di·rect′ly adv.**

in·dus·try (in′dəs trē) **n. 1** any branch of business or manufacturing [the steel *industry*; the motion-picture *industry*]. **2** all business and manufacturing [Leaders of *industry* met in Chicago.] —*pl.* **in′dus·tries**

in · flate (in flāt′) **v.** to cause to swell out by putting in air or gas; blow up [to *inflate* a balloon]. —**in · flat′a · ble adj.**

in·for·ma·tion (in′fər mā′shən) **n. 1** an informing or being informed [This is for your *information* only.] **2** something told or facts learned; news or knowledge; data [An encyclopedia gives *information* about many things.] **3** a person or service that answers certain questions [Ask *information* for the location of the shoe department.]

in · spec · tion (in spek′shən) **n. 1** the act or process of looking at carefully. **2** an official examination or review [The *inspection* of the troops was postponed.]

in·struc·tor (in struk′tər) **n. 1** a teacher. ☆**2** a college teacher ranking below an assistant professor.

in·stru·ment (in′strə mənt) **n. 1** a tool or other device for doing very exact work, for scientific purposes, etc. [surgical *instruments*]. **2** a device used in making musical sound, as a flute, violin, piano, etc.

in·su·late (in′sə lāt) **v.** to separate or cover with a material that keeps electricity, heat, or sound from escaping [electric wire *insulated* with rubber; a furnace *insulated* with asbestos]. —**in′su·lat·ed, in′su·lat·ing**

in·su·la·tor (in′sə lāt′ər) **n.** anything that insulates; especially, a device of glass or porcelain, for insulating electric wires.

in·sure (in shoor′) **v.** to get or give insurance on [We *insured* our car against theft. Will your company *insure* my house against storms?] —**in·sured′, in·sur′ing** —**in·sur′a·ble adj.**

in·tel·li·gent (in tel′ə jənt) **adj.** having or showing intelligence, especially high intelligence. —**in·tel′li·gent·ly adv.**

in·tol·er·ant (in tä′lər ənt) **adj.** not tolerant; not willing to put up with ideas or beliefs that are different from one's own, or not willing to put up with people of other races or backgrounds. —**in·tol′er·ance n.**

in · trude (in trood′) **v.** to force oneself or one's thoughts on others without being asked or wanted [I don't like to *intrude* when you are so busy.] —**in · trud′ed, in · trud′ing** —**in · tru′sion n.**

in·ven·tion (in ven′shən) **n. 1** the act of inventing [the *invention* of television]. **2** something invented [the many *inventions* of Edison]. **3** the ability to invent [a novelist who shows great *invention* in telling a story].

in·ves·ti·gate (in ves′tə gāt′) **v.** to search into so as to learn the facts; examine in detail [to *investigate* an accident]. —**in·ves′ti·gat·ed, in·ves′ti·gat·ing** —**in·ves′ti·ga′tion n.** —**in·ves′ti·ga′tor n.**

ir·ra·tion·al (ir rash′ən əl) **adj.** that does not make sense; not rational; absurd [an *irrational* fear of the dark]. —**ir·ra′tion·al·ly adv.**

ir·reg·u·lar (ir reg′yə lər) **adj. 1** not regular; not like the usual rule, way, or custom [an *irregular* diet]. **2** not straight, even, or the same throughout [an *irregular* design]. —**ir·reg′u·lar·ly adv.**

ir · rel · e · vant (ir rel′ə vənt) **adj.** having nothing to do with the subject; not to the point [That remark about the candidate's height was *irrelevant* to the issues of the campaign.]

ir·re·spon·si·ble (ir′rē spän′sə bəl) **adj.** not responsible; not showing a sense of duty; doing as one pleases. —**ir′re·spon′si·bly adv.**

is·sue (ish′ōō *or* ish′yōō) **n. 1** a thing or group of things sent or given out [the July *issue* of a magazine]. **2** a problem to be talked over [The candidates will debate the *issues*.] ◆**v. 1** to put forth or send out [The city *issues* bonds. The general *issued* an order.] **2** to give or deal out; distribute [The teacher *issued* new books.] —**is′sued, is′su·ing**

i·vo·ry (ī′vər ē *or* ī′vrē) **n. 1** the hard, white substance that forms the tusks of the elephant, walrus, etc. **2** any substance like ivory, as the white plastic used on piano keys. **3** the color of ivory; creamy white. —*pl.* **i′vo·ries** ◆**adj. 1** made of or like ivory. **2** having the color of ivory; creamy-white.

☆**jack·knife** (jak′nīf) **n. 1** a large pocketknife. **2** a dive in which the diver touches the feet with the hands while in the air. —*pl.* **jack′knives** ◆**v.** to bend at the middle as in a jackknife dive. —**jack′knifed, jack′knif·ing**

Jef·fer·son (jef′ər sən), **Thomas** 1743-1826; the third president of the United States, from 1801 to 1809.

jel·ly (jel′ē) *n.* **1** a soft, firm food that looks smooth and glassy, and is easily cut, spread, etc. Jelly is made from cooked fruit syrup, meat juice, or gelatin. **2** any substance like this. —*pl.* **jel′lies** ✦*v.* to become, or make into, jelly. —**jel′lied, jel′ly·ing**

jew·el·er or **jew·el·ler** (jōōl′ər) *n.* a person who makes, sells, or repairs jewelry, watches, etc.

jock·ey (jäk′ē) *n.* a person whose work is riding horses in races.

jour·nal·ism (jur′nəl iz əm) *n.* the work of gathering, writing, or editing the news for publication in newspapers or magazines or for broadcasting on radio or television.

jour·nal·ist (jur′nəl ist) *n.* a person whose work is journalism, as a reporter, news editor, etc. —**jour′nal·is′tic** *adj.*

juic·y (jōō′sē) *adj.* full of juice [a *juicy* plum]. —**juic′i·er, juic′i·est**

ju·ror (joor′ər *or* jur′ər) *n.* a member of a jury.

ju·ven·ile (jōō′və nəl *or* jōō′və nīl) *adj.* **1** young or youthful. **2** of, like, or for children or young people [*juvenile* ideas; *juvenile* books]. ✦*n.* a child or young person.

kan·ga·roo (kaŋ gə rōō′) *n.* an animal of Australia with short forelegs and strong, large hind legs, with which it makes long leaps. The female carries her young in a pouch in front.—*pl.* **kan·ga·roos′**

Ken·ne·dy (ken′ə dē) **John F.** 1917–1963; the 35th president of the United States, from 1961 to 1963. He was assassinated.

Ken·tuck·y (kən tuk′ē) a state in the eastern central part of the U.S.: abbreviated **Ky., KY**

key·board (kē′bôrd) *n.* the row or rows of keys of a piano, organ, typewriter, etc.

kin·dling (kind′liŋ) *n.* bits of dry wood or the like, for starting a fire.

kitch·en (kich′ən) *n.* a room or place for preparing and cooking food.

kneel (nēl) *v.* to rest on a knee or knees [Some people *kneel* when they pray.] —**knelt** or **kneeled, kneel′ing**

knelt (nelt) *a past tense and past participle of* **kneel.**

☆**knick·ers** (nik′ərz) *n.pl.* short, loose trousers gathered in just below the knees.

knot·hole (nät′hōl) *n.* a hole in a board or tree trunk where a knot has fallen out.

knowl·edge (nä′lij) *n.* **1** the fact or condition of knowing [*Knowledge* of the murder spread through the town.] **2** what is known or learned, as through study or experience [a scientist of great *knowledge*]. **3** all that is known by all people.

knuck·le (nuk′əl) *n.* a joint of the finger, especially one connecting a finger to the rest of the hand.

Ko·re·a (kô rē′ə) a country in eastern Asia, divided into two republics, North Korea and South Korea. —**Ko·re′an** *adj., n.*

kangaroo

lan·guage (laŋ′gwij) *n.* **1** human speech or writing that stands for speech [People communicate by means of *language.*] **2** the speech of a particular nation, tribe, etc. [the Greek *language*; the Navaho *language*]. **3** any means of passing on one's thoughts or feelings to others [sign *language*].

laugh·a·ble (laf′ə bəl) *adj.* causing laughter; funny; ridiculous [a *laughable* costume].

launch (lônch *or* länch) *v.* **1** to throw, hurl, or send off into space [to *launch* a rocket]. **2** to cause to slide into the water; set afloat [to *launch* a new ship]. ✦*n.* the act of launching a ship, spacecraft, etc.

laun·dry (lôn′drē *or* län′drē) *n.* **1** a place where laundering is done. **2** clothes, linens, etc. that have been, or are about to be, washed and ironed. —*pl.* **laun′dries**

law-a·bid·ing (lô′ə bīd′iŋ *or* lä′ə bīd′iŋ) *adj.* obeying the law [*law-abiding* citizens].

lb. *abbreviation for* **pound.** —*pl.* **lbs.**

lec·ture (lek′chər) *n.* **1** a talk on some subject to an audience or class. **2** a long or tiresome scolding. ✦*v.* **1** to give a lecture. **2** to scold. —**lec′tured, lec′tur·ing** —**lec′tur·er** *n.*

leg·is·la·tion (lej′is lā′shən) *n.* **1** the act or process of making laws. **2** the laws made.

lei·sure·ly (lē′zhər lē *or* lezh′ər lē) *adj.* without hurrying; slow [a *leisurely* walk]. ✦*adv.* in a slow, unhurried way [We talked *leisurely.*]

light·ning (līt′niŋ) *n.* a flash of light in the sky caused by the passing of electricity from one cloud to another or between a cloud and the earth.

lik·a·ble or **like·a·ble** (līk′ə bəl) *adj.* easy to like because pleasing, friendly, etc.

lim·it·ed (lim′it əd) *adj.* **1** having a limit or limits; restricted in some way [This offer is good for a *limited* time only.] ☆**2** making only a few stops [a *limited* bus].

lim·ou·sine (lim ə zēn′ *or* lim′ə zēn) *n.* **1** a large automobile driven by a chauffeur, who is sometimes separated from the passengers by a glass window. ☆**2** a buslike sedan used to carry passengers to or from an airport.

Lin·coln (liŋ′kən) **Abraham** 1809–1865; 16th president of the United States, from 1861 to 1865. He was assassinated.

a	ask, fat
ā	ape, date
ä	car, lot
e	elf, ten
ē	even, meet
i	is, hit
ī	ice, fire
ō	open, go
ô	law, horn
oi	oil, point
ഞ	look, pull
ōō	ooze, tool
ou	out, crowd
u	up, cut
ʉ	fur, fern
ə	a in ago
	e in agent
	e in father
	i in unity
	o in collect
	u in focus
ch	chin, arch
ŋ	ring, singer
sh	she, dash
th	thin, truth
th	then, father
zh	s in pleasure

134

1 69

lis·ten (lis′ən) *v.* to pay attention in order to hear; try to hear [*Listen* to the rain. *Listen* when the counselor speaks.] —**lis′ten·er** *n.*

live·li·hood (līv′lē hood′) *n.* a means of living, or of supporting oneself [She earns her *livelihood* as a teacher.]

lock·smith (läk′smith) *n.* a person whose work is making or repairing locks and keys.

lounge (lounj) *v.* to move, sit, or lie in an easy or lazy way; loll. —**lounged, loung′ing** ✦*n.* a room with comfortable furniture where people can lounge. —**loung′er** *n.*

lunch·eon (lun′chən) *n.* a lunch; especially, a formal lunch with others.

lus·cious (lush′əs) *adj.* 1 having a delicious taste or smell; full of flavor [a *luscious* steak]. 2 very pleasing to see, hear, etc. [the *luscious* sound of violins]. —**lus′cious·ly** *adv.*

lux·u·ry (luk′shər ē *or* lug′zhər ē) *n.* 1 the use and enjoyment of the best and most costly things that give one the most comfort and pleasure [a life of *luxury*]. 2 anything that gives one such comfort, usually something one does not need for life or health [Jewels are *luxuries.*] —*pl.* **lux′u·ries**

Mm

ma·chin·er·y (mə shēn′ər ē) *n.* 1 machines in general [the *machinery* of a factory]. 2 the working parts of a machine [the *machinery* of a printing press]. —*pl.* **ma·chin′er·ies**

ma·chin·ist (mə shēn′ist) *n.* 1 a person who is skilled in working with machine tools. 2 a person who makes, repairs, or runs machinery.

mag·i·cal (maj′i kəl) *adj.* of or like magic. —**mag′i·cal·ly** *adv.*

mag·nif·i·cent (mag nif′ə sənt) *adj.* rich, fine, noble, beautiful, etc. in a grand way; splendid [a *magnificent* castle; a *magnificent* idea].

mag·ni·fy (mag′nə fī) *v.* to make look or seem larger or greater than is really so [This lens *magnifies* an object to ten times its size. He *magnified* the seriousness of his illness.] —**mag′ni·fied, mag′ni·fy·ing**

main·stay (mān′stā) *n.* 1 the line that runs forward from the upper part of the mainmast, helping to hold it in place. 2 the main or chief support [She was the *mainstay* of her family.]

main·te·nance (mānt′n əns) *n.* 1 a maintaining or being maintained; upkeep or support [Taxes pay for the *maintenance* of schools.] 2 a means of support; livelihood [a job that barely provides a *maintenance*].

mallet

mal·let (mal′ət) *n.* 1 a wooden hammer made with a short handle for use as a tool. 2 a wooden hammer made with a long handle for playing croquet or with a long, flexible handle for playing polo.

man·age·a·ble (man′ij ə bəl) *adj.* that can be managed, controlled, or done.

man·u·fac·tur·er (man′yoo fak′chər ər) *n.* a person or company that manufactures; especially, a factory owner.

mar·tial (mär′shəl) *adj.* 1 having to do with war or armies [*martial* music]. 2 showing a readiness or eagerness to fight [*martial* spirit].

mas·ter·piece (mas′tər pēs) *n.* 1 a thing made or done with very great skill; a great work of art. 2 the best thing that a person has ever made or done [*The Divine Comedy* was Dante's *masterpiece.*]

match (mach) *n.* 1 any person or thing equal to or like another in some way [Joan met her *match* in chess when she played Joe.] 2 two or more people or things that go well together [That suit and tie are a good *match.*] 3 a game or contest between two persons or teams [a tennis *match*]. ✦*v.* 1 to go well together [Do your shirt and tie *match*?] 2 to make or get something like or equal to [Can you *match* this cloth?] 3 to be equal to [I could never *match* that lawyer in an argument.]

may·on·naise (mā ə nāz′ *or* mā′ə nāz) *n.* a thick, creamy salad dressing made of egg yolks, olive oil, lemon juice or vinegar, and seasoning.

mdse. *abbreviation for* **merchandise.**

meas·ure (mezh′ər) *v.* 1 to find out the size, amount, or extent of, as by comparing with something else [*Measure* the child's height with a yardstick. How do you *measure* a person's worth?] 2 to set apart or mark off a certain amount or length of [*Measure* out three pounds of sugar.] —**meas′ured, meas′ur·ing** ✦*n.* 1 the size, amount, or extent of something, found out by measuring [The *measure* of the bucket is 15 liters.] 2 a system of measuring [Liquid *measure* is a system of measuring liquids.]

me·chan·ic (mə kan′ik) *n.* a worker skilled in using tools or in making, repairing, and using machinery [an automobile *mechanic*].

med·i·cine (med′ə sən) *n.* 1 any substance used in or on the body to treat disease, lessen pain, heal, etc. 2 the science of treating and preventing disease.

mel·low (mel′ō) *adj.* 1 soft, sweet, and juicy from ripeness [a *mellow* apple]. 2 having a good flavor from being aged; not bitter [a *mellow* wine]. 3 rich, soft, and pure; not harsh [the *mellow* tone of a cello]. 4 made gentle and kind by age or experience [a *mellow* teacher].

me·men·to (mə men′tō) *n.* an object kept to remind one of something; souvenir [This toy is a *memento* of my childhood.] —*pl.* **me·men′tos** or **me·men′toes**

mem·o·rize (mem′ər īz) *v.* ☆to fix in one's memory exactly or word for word; learn by heart. —**mem′o·rized, mem′o·riz·ing** —**mem′o·ri·za′tion** *n.*

Mex·i·can (mek′si kən) *adj.* of Mexico, its people, their dialect of Spanish, or their culture. ◆*n.* a person born or living in Mexico.

mgr. *abbreviation for* **manager**.

mi·cro·phone (mī′krə fōn) *n.* a device for picking up sound that is to be made stronger, as in a theater, or sent over long distances, as in radio. Microphones change sound into electric waves, which go into electron tubes and are changed back into sound by loudspeakers.

midg·et (mij′ət) *n.* **1** a very small person. **2** anything very small of its kind.

mid·point (mid′point) *n.* a point in the middle or at the center.

mid·sum·mer (mid′sum′ər) *n.* **1** the middle of summer. **2** the period around June 21.

Mid·west·ern (mid′wes′tərn) *adj.* of, in, or having to do with the Middle West.

mil·dew (mil′dōō *or* mil′dyōō) *n.* a fungus that appears as a furry, white coating on plants or on damp, warm paper, cloth, etc. ◆*v.* to become coated with mildew.

mil·lion·aire (mil yə ner′) *n.* a person who has at least a million dollars, pounds, etc.

mi·nor·i·ty (mī nôr′ə tē *or* mi nôr′ə tē) *n.* **1** the smaller part or number; less than half [A *minority* of the Senate voted for the law.] **2** a small group of people of a different race, religion, etc. from the main group of which it is a part. —*pl.* **mi·nor′i·ties**

mis·cal·cu·late (mis kal′kyōō lāt′) *v.* to make a mistake in figuring or planning; misjudge [Our manager *miscalculated* the pitcher's strength and we lost the game.]

mis·cel·la·ne·ous (mis′ə lā′nē əs) *adj.* of many different kinds; mixed; varied [A *miscellaneous* collection of objects filled the shelf.]

mis·chief (mis′chif) *n.* **1** harm or damage [Gossip can cause great *mischief*.] **2** action that causes harm, damage, or trouble. **3** a playful trick; prank. **4** playful, harmless spirits [a child full of *mischief*].

mis·chie·vous (mis′chə vəs) *adj.* **1** causing some slight harm or annoyance, often in fun; naughty [a *mischievous* act]. **2** full of playful tricks; teasing [a *mischievous* child]. **3** causing harm or damage; injurious [*mischievous* slander].

mis·pro·nounce (mis prə nouns′) *v.* to pronounce in a wrong way [Some people *mispronounce* "cavalry" as "calvary."] —**mis·pro·nounced′, mis·pro·nounc′ing** —**mis·pro·nun·ci·a·tion** (mis′prə nun′sē ā′shən) *n.*

mis·tle·toe (mis′əl tō) *n.* an evergreen plant with waxy white, poisonous berries, growing as a parasite on certain trees. People kiss under the mistletoe at Christmas.

mis·un·der·stand (mis′un dər stand′) *v.* to understand in a way that is wrong; give a wrong meaning to. —**mis·un·der·stood** (mis′un der stōōd′), **mis′under·stand′ing**

mo. *abbreviation for* **month**.

mo·bile (mō′bəl *or* mō′bīl *or* mō′bēl) *adj.* that can be moved quickly and easily [a *mobile* army]. ◆*n.* (mō′bēl) a kind of sculpture made of flat pieces, rods, etc. that hang balanced from wires so as to move easily in air currents. —**mo·bil·i·ty** (mō bil′ə tē) *n.*

mod·i·fy (mäd′ə fī) *v.* **1** to make a small or partial change in [Exploration has *modified* our maps of Antarctica.] **2** to make less harsh, strong, etc. [to *modify* a jail term]. **3** to limit the meaning of; describe or qualify [In the phrase "old man" the adjective "old" *modifies* the noun "man."] —**mod′i·fied, mod′i·fy·ing** —**mod′i·fi·ca′tion** *n.* —**mod′i·fi′er** *n.*

mois·ten (mois′ən) *v.* to make or become moist.

mon·o·gram (män′ə gram) *n.* initials, especially of a person's name, put together in a design and used on clothing, stationery, and so on.

mon·o·rail (män′ə rāl) *n.* **1** a railway having cars that run on a single rail, or track, and are hung from it or balanced on it. **2** this track.

mon·o·syl·la·ble (män′ō sil′ə bəl) *n.* a word of one syllable, as *he* or *thought*. —**mon·o·syl·lab·ic** (män′ə si lab′ik) *adj.*

mo·not·o·nous (mə nät′n əs) *adj.* **1** going on and on in the same tone [a *monotonous* voice]. **2** having little or no change; boring or tiresome [a *monotonous* trip; *monotonous* work].

mon·soon (män sōōn′) *n.* **1** a wind of the Indian Ocean and southern Asia, blowing from the southwest from April to October, and from the northeast the rest of the year. **2** the rainy season, when this wind blows from the southwest.

mor·al (môr′əl) *adj.* **1** having to do with right and wrong in conduct [Cheating is a *moral* issue.] **2** good or right according to ideas of being decent and respectable [She was a *moral* woman all her life.] ◆*n.* **1** a lesson about what is right and wrong, taught by a story or event [the *moral* of a fable]. **2 morals**, *pl.* standards of behavior having to do with right and wrong; ethics.

mos·qui·to (mə skēt′ō) *n.* a small insect with two wings. The female bites animals to suck their blood. Some mosquitoes spread diseases, as malaria. —*pl.* **mos·qui′toes** *or* **mos·qui′tos**

mouth·ful (mouth′fool) *n.* **1** as much as the mouth can hold. **2** as much as is usually put into the mouth at one time. —*pl.* **mouth′fuls**

microphone

a	ask, fat
ā	ape, date
ä	car, lot
e	elf, ten
ē	even, meet
i	is, hit
ī	ice, fire
ō	open, go
ô	law, horn
oi	oil, point
σσ	look, pull
ōō	ooze, tool
ou	out, crowd
u	up, cut
ʉ	fur, fern
ə	a in ago
	e in agent
	e in father
	i in unity
	o in collect
	u in focus
ch	chin, arch
ŋ	ring, singer
sh	she, dash
th	thin, truth
th	then, father
zh	s in pleasure

136

mud·dy (mud′ē) *adj.* full of mud or smeared with mud [a *muddy* yard; *muddy* boots]. —**mud′di·er, mud′di·est** ◆*v.* to make or become muddy. —**mud′died, mud′dy·ing**

mu·ral (myoor′əl) *n.* a picture or photograph, especially a large one, painted or put on a wall. ◆*adj.* of or on a wall [a *mural* painting].

mus·cle (mus′əl) *n.* **1** the tissue in an animal's body that makes up the fleshy parts. Muscle can be stretched or tightened to move the parts of the body. **2** any single part or band of this tissue [The biceps is a *muscle* in the upper arm.] **3** strength that comes from muscles that are developed; brawn.

oboe

my·thol·o·gy (mi thäl′ə jē) *n.* **1** myths as a group; especially, all the myths of a certain people [Roman *mythology*]. —*pl.* **my·thol′o·gies 2** the study of myths. —**myth·o·log·i·cal** (mith′ə läj′i kəl) *adj.*

Nn

nar·rate (ner′āt) *v.* to give the story of in writing or speech; tell what has happened [Our guest *narrated* her adventures.] —**nar′rat·ed, nar′rat·ing** —**nar′ra·tor** *n.*

na·tion (nā′shən) *n.* **1** a group of people living together in a certain region under the same government; state; country [the Swiss *nation*]. **2** a group of people sharing the same history, language, customs, etc. [the Iroquois *nation*].

nau·se·a (nô′zhə *or* nä′zhə *or* nô′zē ə) *n.* a feeling of sickness in the stomach that makes a person want to vomit.

ne·go·ti·ate (ni gō′shē āt′) *v.* to talk over a problem, business deal, dispute, etc. in the hope of reaching an agreement [to *negotiate* a contract]. —**ne·go′ti·at·ed, ne·go′ti·at·ing** —**ne·go′ti·a′tion** *n.* —**ne·go′ti·a′tor** *n.*

octagon

neigh·bor·ly (nā′bər lē) *adj.* friendly, kind, helpful, etc. [It was very *neighborly* of you to shovel the snow from my walk.] —**neigh′bor·li·ness** *n.*

niece (nēs) *n.* **1** the daughter of one's brother or sister. **2** the daughter of one's brother-in-law or sister-in-law.

No. or **no.** *abbreviation for* **number**.

nois·y (noi′zē) *adj.* **1** making noise [a *noisy* bell]. **2** full of noise [a *noisy* theater]. —**nois′i·er, nois′i·est** —**nois′i·ly** *adv.* —**nois′i·ness** *n.*

no·tice·a·ble (nōt′is ə bəl) *adj.* easily seen; likely to be noticed; remarkable [*noticeable* improvement]. —**no′tice·a·bly** *adv.*

nour·ish (nur′ish) *v.* to feed; provide with the things needed for life and growth [Water and sunlight *nourished* the plants.] —**nour′ish·ing** *adj.*

nui·sance (noo′səns *or* nyoo′səns) *n.* an act, thing, or person that causes trouble or bother [It's such a *nuisance* to put on boots just to go next door.]

numb (num) *adj.* not able to feel, or feeling very little [*numb* with cold]. ◆ *v.* to make numb [The cold *numbed* his toes.]

nu·tri·tion (noo trish′ən *or* nyoo trish′ən) *n.* **1** the process by which an animal or plant takes in food and uses it in living and growing. **2** food; nourishment. **3** the study of the foods people should eat for health and well-being. —**nu·tri′tion·al** *adj.*

Oo

o·boe (ō′bō) *n.* a woodwind instrument whose mouthpiece has a double reed. —**o′bo·ist** *n.*

ob·serv·a·to·ry (äb zurv′ə tôr′ē) *n.* a building with telescopes and other equipment in it for studying the stars, weather conditions, etc. —*pl.* **ob·serv′a·to′ries**

ob·serve (əb zurv′) *v.* **1** to see, watch, or notice [I *observed* that the child was smiling.] **2** to examine and study carefully [to *observe* an experiment]. —**ob·served′, ob·serv′ing** —**ob·serv′er** *n.*

ob·vi·ous (äb′vē əs) *adj.* easy to see or understand; plain; clear [an *obvious* rust stain; an *obvious* danger]. —**ob′vi·ous·ly** *adv.* —**ob′vi·ous·ness** *n.*

oc·ca·sion (ə kā′zhən) *n.* **1** a suitable time; good chance; opportunity [Did you have *occasion* to visit with them?] **2** a particular time [We've met on several *occasions*.] **3** a special time or happening [Independence Day is an *occasion* to celebrate.]

oc·cu·py (äk′yoo pī′) *v.* **1** to live in [to *occupy* a house]. **2** to take up; fill [The store *occupies* the entire building.] **3** to keep busy; employ [Many activities *occupy* his time.] —**oc′cu·pied, oc′cu·py·ing**

oc·cur (ə kur′) *v.* **1** to come into one's mind [The idea never *occurred* to me.] **2** to happen; take place [That event *occurred* years ago.] —**oc·curred′, oc·cur′ring**

oc·ta·gon (äk′tə gän) *n.* a flat figure having eight angles and eight sides.

of·fi·cer (ôf′i sər *or* äf′i sər) *n.* **1** a person holding some office, as in a business, club, or government. **2** a member of a police force. **3** a person who commands others in an army, navy, etc. [Generals and lieutenants are commissioned *officers*.]

of·fi·cial (ə fish′əl) *n.* 1 a person who holds an office, especially in government. ☆2 a person who sees to it that the rules are followed in a game, as a referee or umpire. ◆*adj.* 1 of or having to do with an office [an *official* record; *official* duties]. 2 coming from a person who has authority [an *official* request]. 3 fit for an important officer; formal [an *official* welcome]. —**of·fi′cial·ly** *adv.*

oint·ment (oint′mənt) *n.* an oily cream rubbed on the skin to heal it or make it soft and smooth; salve.

or·gan·ize (ôr′gə nīz) *v.* to arrange or place according to a system [The library books are *organized* according to their subjects.] —**or′gan·ized, or′gan·iz·ing** —**or′gan·iz′er** *n.*

o·rig·i·nal·i·ty (ə rij′ə nal′ə tē) *n.* the quality or condition of being fresh, new, or creative.

or·phan·age (ôr′fən ij) *n.* a home for taking care of a number of orphans

out·ra·geous (out rā′jəs) *adj.* 1 doing great injury or wrong [*outrageous* crimes]. 2 so wrong or bad that it hurts or shocks [an *outrageous* lie]. —**out·ra′geous·ly** *adv.*

o·ver·due (ō vər dōō′ *or* ō vər dyōō′) *adj.* delayed past the time set for payment, arrival, etc. [an *overdue* bill; a bus long *overdue*].

o·ver·e·mo·tion·al (ō′vər ē mō′shə nəl) *adj.* too full of emotion or strong feeling [an *overemotional* speech].

o·ver·flow (ō vər flō′) *v.* 1 to flow across; flood [Water *overflowed* the streets.] 2 to have its contents flowing over [The sink is *overflowing*.] ◆*n.* (ō′vər flō) the act of overflowing.

o·ver·grown (ō′vər grōn′) *adj.* 1 covered with foliage or weeds [a lawn that is badly *overgrown*]. 2 having grown too large or too fast [an *overgrown* child].

o·ver·joyed (ō vər joid′) *adj.* filled with great joy.

o·ver·pro·tect (ō′vər prə tekt′) *v.* to protect more than is necessary or helpful, especially by trying to keep someone from the normal hurts and disappointments of life.

o·ver·sen·si·tive (ō′vər sn′sə tiv) *adj.* too quick to feel, notice, or respond to.

o·ver·weight (ō′vər wāt′) *n.* more weight than is needed or allowed; extra weight. ◆*adj.* (ō vər wāt′) weighing more than is normal or proper; too heavy.

oys·ter (ois′tər) *n.* a shellfish with a soft body enclosed in two rough shells hinged together. Some are used as food, and pearls are formed inside others.

oz. *abbreviation for* **ounce.** —*pl.* **oz.** or **ozs.**

Pp

parachute

pain·ful (pān′fəl) *adj.* causing pain; hurting; unpleasant [a *painful* wound]. —**pain′ful·ness** *n.*

pam·phlet (pam′flət) *n.* a thin booklet with a paper cover.

pap·ri·ka (pə prē′kə) *n.* a red seasoning made by grinding certain peppers.

par·a·chute (par′ə shōōt) *n.* a large cloth device that opens up like an umbrella and is used for slowing down a person or thing dropping from an airplane. ◆*v.* to jump with or drop by a parachute. —**par′a·chut·ed, par′a·chut·ing** —**par′a·chut·ist** *n.*

par·al·lel·o·gram (par′ə lel′ə gram) *n.* a figure having four sides, with the opposite sides parallel and of equal length.

par·ent (per′ənt) *n.* 1 a father or mother. 2 any animal or plant as it is related to its offspring. —**par′ent·hood** *n.*

pa·ren·the·sis (pə ren′thə sis) *n.* 1 a word, phrase, etc. put into a complete sentence as an added note or explanation and set off, as between curved lines, from the rest of the sentence. 2 either or both of the curved lines ( ) used to set off such a word, phrase, etc. —*pl.* **pa·ren·the·ses** (pə ren′thə sēz)

par·tial (pär′shəl) *adj.* 1 of or in only a part; not complete or total [a *partial* eclipse of the sun]. 2 favoring one person or side more than another; biased [A judge should not be *partial*.] —**par′tial·ly** *adv.*

par·tic·i·pate (pär tis′ə pāt) *v.* to take part with others; have a share [Sue *participated* in the school play.] —**par·tic′i·pat·ed, par·tic′i·pat·ing** —**par·tic′i·pa′tion** *n.* —**par·tic′i·pa′tor** *n.*

pas·sive (pas′iv) *adj.* 1 not active, but acted upon [Spectators have a *passive* interest in sports.] 2 not resisting; yielding; submissive [The *passive* child did as he was told.] —**pas′sive·ly** *adv.*

pa·tience (pā′shəns) *n.* the fact of being patient or the ability to be patient.

pa·tient (pā′shənt) *adj.* able to put up with pain, trouble, delay, boredom, etc. without complaining [The *patient* children waited in line for the theater to open.] ◆*n.* a person under the care of a doctor. —**pa′tient·ly** *adv.*

pa·ti·o (pat′ē ō *or* pät′ē ō) *n.* ☆1 in Spain and Spanish America, a courtyard around which a house is built. ☆2 a paved area near a house, with chairs, tables, etc. for outdoor lounging, dining, etc. —*pl.* **pa′ti·os**

pa·trol (pə trōl′) *v.* to make regular trips around a place in order to guard it [The watchman *patrolled* the area all night.] —**pa·trolled′, pa·trol′ling** u *n.* 1 the act of patrolling. 2 a person or group that patrols.

a	ask, fat
ā	ape, date
ä	car, lot
e	elf, ten
ē	even, meet
i	is, hit
ī	ice, fire
ō	open, go
ô	law, horn
oi	oil, point
ōō	look, pull
ōō	ooze, tool
ou	out, crowd
u	up, cut
u	fur, fern
ə	a in ago
	e in agent
	e in father
	i in unity
	o in collect
	u in focus
ch	chin, arch
ŋ	ring, singer
sh	she, dash
th	thin, truth
th	then, father
zh	s in pleasure

pause (pôz *or* päz) *n.* a short stop, as in speaking or working. ◆*v.* to make a pause; stop for a short time [He *paused* to catch his breath.] —**paused, paus′ing**

pave (pāv) *v.* to cover the surface of a road, walk, etc., as with concrete or asphalt. —**paved, pav′ing** —**pave the way,** to make the way ready for something; prepare.

pen·al·ty (pen′əl tē) *n.* **1** punishment for breaking a law. **2** a disadvantage, fine, etc. given to one side in a contest for breaking a rule. —*pl.* **pen′al·ties**

per·ceive (pər sēv′) *v.* **1** to become aware of through one of the senses, especially through seeing [to *perceive* the difference between two shades of red]. **2** to take in through the mind [I quickly *perceived* the joke.] —**per·ceived′, per·ceiv′ing**

per·cep·tion (pər sep′shən) *n.* **1** the act of perceiving or the ability to perceive [Jan's *perception* of color is poor.] **2** knowledge or understanding got by perceiving [She has a clear *perception* of her duty.]

per·pen·dic·u·lar (pur′pən dik′yoo lər) *adj.* **1** at right angles [The wall should be *perpendicular* to the floor.] **2** straight up and down; exactly upright [a *perpendicular* flagpole]. ◆*n.* a line that is at right angles to the horizon, or to another line or plane [The Leaning Tower of Pisa leans away from the *perpendicular*.]

per·son·al (pur′sə nəl) *adj.* of one's own; private; individual [a *personal* opinion; a *personal* secretary].

per·son·nel (pur sə nel′) *n.* persons employed in any work, service, etc. [office *personnel*].

per·spec·tive (pər spek′tiv) *n.* **1** the way things look from a given point according to their size, shape, distance, etc. [*Perspective* makes things far away look small.] **2** the art of picturing things so that they seem close or far away, big or small, etc., just as they look to the eye when viewed from a given point. **3** a certain point of view in understanding or judging things or happenings, especially one that shows them in their true relations to one another [Working in a factory will give you a new *perspective* on labor problems.]

pew·ter (pyōot′ər) *n.* **1** a grayish alloy of tin with lead, brass, or copper. **2** things made of pewter, especially dishes, tableware, etc. ◆*adj.* made of pewter.

phe·nom·e·non (fə näm′ə nän) *n.* **1** any fact, condition, or happening that can be seen, heard, and described in a scientific way, such as an eclipse. **2** an unusual or remarkable event or thing [Rain is a *phenomenon* in the desert.] —*pl.* **phe·nom·e·na** (fə näm′ə nə) or (for sense 2 usually) **phe·nom′e·nons**

pho·to·graph (fōt′ə graf) *n.* a picture made with a camera. ◆*v.* **1** to take a photograph of. **2** to look a certain way in photographs [She *photographs* taller than she is.]

piccolo

poncho

phrase (frāz) *n.* a group of words that is not a complete sentence, but that gives a single idea, usually as a separate part of a sentence ["Drinking fresh milk," "with meals," and "to be healthy" are *phrases*.] ◆*v.* to say or write in a certain way [He *phrased* his answer carefully.] —**phrased, phras′ing**

phy·si·cian (fi zish′ən) *n.* a doctor of medicine, especially one who is not mainly a surgeon.

pic·co·lo (pik′ə lō) *n.* a small flute that sounds notes an octave higher than an ordinary flute does.—*pl.* **pic′co·los**

pierce (pirs) *v.* **1** to pass into or through; penetrate [The needle *pierced* her finger. A light *pierced* the darkness.] **2** to make a hole through; perforate; bore [to *pierce* one's ears for earrings]. **3** to make a sharp sound through [A shriek *pierced* the air.] —**pierced, pierc′ing**

pig·ment (pig′mənt) *n.* **1** coloring matter, usually a powder, mixed with oil, water, etc. to make paints. **2** the matter in the cells and tissues that gives color to plants and animals.

pi·ta (pē′tə) *n.* a round, flat bread of the Middle East. It can be split open to form a pocket for a filling of meat, vegetables, etc.

☆**piz·za** (pēt′sə) *n.* an Italian dish made by baking a thin layer of dough covered with tomatoes, spices, cheese, etc.

pkg. *abbreviation for* **package** *or* **packages**.

plain·tiff (plān′tif) *n.* the person who starts a suit against another in a court of law.

plan·et (plan′ət) *n.* any of the large heavenly bodies that revolve around the sun and shine as they reflect the sun's light. The planets, in their order from the sun, are Mercury, Venus, Earth, Mars, Jupiter, Saturn, Uranus, Neptune, and Pluto. —**plan·e·tar·y** (plan′ə ter′ē) *adj.*

plaque (plak) *n.* **1** a thin, flat piece of metal, wood, etc. with decoration or lettering on it. **2** a thin film that forms on the teeth and hardens into tartar if not removed.

play·wright (plā′rīt) *n.* a person who writes plays; dramatist.

pledge (plej) *n.* **1** a promise or agreement [the *pledge* of allegiance to the flag]. **2** something promised, especially money to be given as to a charity. ◆*v.* **1** to promise to give [to *pledge* $100 to a building fund]. **2** to bind by a promise [He is *pledged* to marry her.] —**pledged, pledg′ing**

plumb·er (plum′ər) *n.* a person whose work is putting in and repairing the pipes and fixtures of water and gas systems in a building.

pol·y·gon (päl′i gän′) *n.* a flat, closed figure made up of straight lines, especially one having more than four angles and sides.

pon·cho (pän′chō) *n.* a cloak like a blanket with a hole in the middle for the head. It is worn as a raincoat, etc., originally in South America. —*pl.* **pon′chos**

por·trait (pôr′trit) *n.* a drawing, painting, or photograph of a person, especially of the face.

por·tray (pôr trā′) *v.* **1** to make a picture of, as in a painting. **2** to make a picture in words; describe [The writer *portrays* life in New York.] **3** to play the part of in a play, movie, etc. [The actress *portrayed* a scientist.]

po·si·tion (pə zish′ən) *n.* **1** the way in which a person or thing is placed or arranged [a sitting *position*]. **2** the place where a person or thing is; location [The ship radioed its *position*.] **3** a job or office; post [She has a *position* with the city government.] ◆*v.* to put in a certain position [They *positioned* themselves around the house.]

post·script (pōst′skript) *n.* a note added below the signature of a letter.

post·war (pōst′wôr′) *adj.* after the war.

po·ten·tial (pō ten′shəl) *adj.* that can be, but is not yet; possible [a *potential* leader; a *potential* source of trouble]. ◆*n.* power or skill that may be developed [a baseball team with *potential*]. —**po·ten′tial·ly** *adv.*

poul·try (pōl′trē) *n.* fowl raised for food; chickens, turkeys, ducks, geese, etc.

prac·ti·cal (prak′ti kəl) *adj.* **1** that can be put to use; useful and sensible [a *practical* idea; *practical* shoes]. **2** dealing with things in a sensible and realistic way [Wouldn't it be more *practical* to paint it yourself than pay to have it painted?]

praise (prāz) *v.* **1** to say good things about; give a good opinion of [to *praise* someone's work]. **2** to worship, as in song [to *praise* God]. —**praised, prais′ing** ◆*n.* a praising or being praised; words that show approval.

praise·wor·thy (prāz′wʉr′thē) *adj.* deserving praise; that should be admired.

pre·cau·tion (prē kô′shən *or* prē kä′shən) *n.* care taken ahead of time, as against danger, failure, etc. [She took the *precaution* of locking the door before she left.] —**pre·cau′tion·ar′y** *adj.*

pre·cede (prē sēd′) *v.* to go or come before in time, order, or rank [She *preceded* him into the room.]

pre·dict (prē dikt′) *v.* to tell what one thinks will happen in the future [I *predict* that you will win.] —**pre·dict′a·ble** *adj.*

pre·fer (prē fʉr′) *v.* to like better; choose first [He *prefers* baseball to football.] —**pre·ferred′, pre·fer′ring**

pre·lude (prel′yōōd *or* prā′lōōd) *n.* a part that comes before or leads up to what follows [The strong wind was a *prelude* to the thunderstorm.]

Pres. *abbreviation for* **President.**

pre·scrip·tion (prē skrip′shən) *n.* **1** an order or direction. **2** a doctor's written instructions telling how to prepare and use a medicine; also, a medicine made by following such instructions.

pre·sume (prē zōōm′ *or* prē zyōōm′) *v.* **1** to be so bold as to; dare [I wouldn't *presume* to tell you what to do.] **2** to take for granted; suppose [I *presume* you know what you are doing.] —**pre·sumed′, pre·sum′ing**

☆**pret·zel** (pret′s'l) *n.* a slender roll of dough, usually twisted in a knot, sprinkled with salt, and baked until hard.

pre·vent (prē vent′) *v.* **1** to stop or hinder [A storm *prevented* us from going.] **2** to keep from happening [Careful driving *prevents* accidents.] —**pre·vent′a·ble** or **pre·vent′i·ble** *adj.*

pre·vi·ous (prē′vē əs) *adj.* happening before in time or order; earlier [at a *previous* meeting; on the *previous* page]. —**pre′vi·ous·ly** *adv.*

prin·ci·pal (prin′sə pəl) *adj.* most important; chief; main [the *principal* crop of a State]. ◆*n.* the head of a school.

prin·ci·ple (prin′sə pəl) *n.* **1** a rule, truth, etc. upon which others are based [the basic *principles* of law]. **2** a rule used in deciding how to behave [It is against her *principles* to lie.]

pro·ceed (prō sēd′) *v.* **1** to go on, especially after stopping for a while [After eating, we *proceeded* to the next town.] **2** to begin and go on doing something [I *proceeded* to build a fire.] **3** to move along or go on [Things *proceeded* smoothly.]

proc·ess (prä′ses) *n.* **1** a series of changes by which something develops [the *process* of growth in a plant]. **2** a method of making or doing something, in which there are a number of steps [the refining *process* used in making gasoline from crude oil]. **3** the act of doing something, or the time during which something is done [I was in the *process* of writing a report when you called.] ◆*v.* to prepare by a special process [to *process* cheese].

pro·duce (prə dōōs′ *or* prə dyōōs′) *v.* **1** to bring forth; bear; yield [trees *producing* apples; a well that *produces* oil]. **2** to make or manufacture [a company that *produces* bicycles]. —**pro·duced′, pro·duc′ing** ◆*n.* (prō′dōōs) something that is produced, especially fruits and vegetables for marketing. —**pro·duc′er** *n.*

pro·found (prō found′) *adj.* **1** showing great knowledge, or thought [the *profound* remarks of the judge]. **2** deeply felt; intense [*profound* grief]. **3** thorough [*profound* changes].

prog·ress (präg′res) *n.* **1** a moving forward [the boat's slow *progress* down the river]. **2** a developing or improving [She shows *progress* in learning French.] ◆*v.* (prō gres′) **1** to move forward; go ahead. **2** to develop or improve; advance [Science has helped us to *progress*.]

pro·jec·tor (prə jek′tər) *n.* a machine for projecting pictures or movies on a screen.

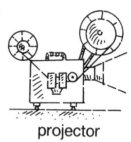

projector

a	ask, fat
ā	ape, date
ä	car, lot
e	elf, ten
ē	even, meet
i	is, hit
ī	ice, fire
ō	open, go
ô	law, horn
oi	oil, point
ʊ	look, pull
ōō	ooze, tool
ou	out, crowd
u	up, cut
ʉ	fur, fern
ə	a in ago
	e in agent
	e in father
	i in unity
	o in collect
	u in focus
ch	chin, arch
ŋ	ring, singer
sh	she, dash
th	thin, truth
th	then, father
zh	s in pleasure

prompt (prämpt) *adj.* **1** quick in doing what should be done; on time [He is *prompt* in paying his bills.] **2** done, spoken, etc. without waiting [We would like a *prompt* reply.] ◆*v.* **1** to urge or stir into action [Tyranny *prompted* them to revolt.] **2** to remind of something that has been forgotten [to *prompt* an actor when a line has been forgotten]. —**prompt'ly** *adv.* —**prompt'ness** *n.*

pro·noun (prō'noun) *n.* a word used in the place of a noun. *I, us, you, they, he, her, it* are some pronouns.

pro·nounce (prə nouns') *v.* **1** to say or make the sounds of [How do you *pronounce* "leisure"?] **2** to say or declare in an official or serious way [I now *pronounce* you husband and wife.] —**pro·nounced', pro·nounc'ing**

pro·pel (prə pel') *v.* to push or drive forward [Some rockets are *propelled* by liquid fuel.] —**pro·pelled', pro·pel'ling**

pros·e·cute (präs'ə kyōōt) *v.* to put on trial in a court of law on charges of crime or wrongdoing. —**pros'e·cut·ed, pros'e·cut·ing**

pros·e·cu·tor (präs'ə kyōōt'ər) *n.* a person who prosecutes; especially, a lawyer who works for the State in prosecuting persons charged with crime.

pro·te·in (prō'tēn) *n.* a substance containing nitrogen and other elements, found in all living things and in such foods as cheese, meat, eggs, beans, etc. It is a necessary part of an animal's diet.

pro·vi·sion (prō vizh'ən) *n.* **1** a providing or supplying. **2** something provided or arrangements made for the future [Her savings are a *provision* for her old age.] **3 provisions**, *pl.* a supply or stock of food.

pro·voke (prō vōk') *v.* **1** to excite to some action or feeling [to *provoke* a fight]. **2** to annoy or make angry [It *provoked* me to see litter on the lawn.] **3** to stir up [to *provoke* interest].

pt. *abbreviation for* **part, pint, point.** —*pl.* **pts.**

pur·pose (pur'pəs) *n.* **1** what one plans to get or do; aim; goal [I came for the *purpose* of speaking to you.] **2** the reason or use for something [a room with no *purpose*]. —**pur'pose·ful** *adj.* —**pur'pose·less** *adj.*

pur·sue (pər sōō' *or* pər syōō') *v.* **1** to follow in order to catch or catch up to [to *pursue* a runaway horse]. **2** to carry out or follow; go on with [She is *pursuing* a career in acting.] **3** to try to find; seek [to *pursue* knowledge]. —**pur·sued', pur·su'ing** —**pur·su'er** *n.*

quilt

qt. *abbreviation for* **quart or quarts.**

quad·ri·lat·er·al (kwäd'rə lat'ər əl) *adj.* having four sides. ◆*n.* a flat figure with four sides and four angles.

qual·i·fy (kwôl'ə fī *or* kwä'lə fī) *v.* to make or be fit or suitable, as for some work or activity [Your training *qualifies* you for the job. Does he *qualify* for the team?] —**qual'i·fied, qual'i·fy·ing**

qual·i·ty (kwôl'ə tē *or* kwä'lə tē) *n.* **1** any of the features that make a thing what it is; characteristic [Coldness is one *quality* of ice cream.] **2** degree of excellence [a poor *quality* of paper]. —*pl.* **qual'i·ties**

quan·ti·ty (kwänt'ə tē) *n.* **1** an amount or portion [large *quantities* of food]. **2** a large amount [The factory makes toys in *quantity*.] —*pl.* **quan'ti·ties**

ques·tion·naire (kwes chən ner') *n.* a written or printed list of questions used in gathering information from people.

quilt (kwilt) *n.* a covering for a bed, made of two layers of cloth filled with down, wool, etc. and stitched together in lines or patterns to keep the filling in place. ◆*v.* **1** to make in the form of a quilt [a *quilted* potholder]. ☆**2** to make quilts.

quiz (kwiz) *n.* a short test given to find out how much one has learned. —*pl.* **quiz'zes** ◆ *v.* **1** to ask questions of [The police *quizzed* the suspect.] **2** to test the knowledge of with a quiz [The teacher *quizzed* the class.] —**quizzed, quiz'zing**

quo·ta·tion (kwō tā'shən) *n.* **1** the act of quoting. **2** the words or section quoted [Sermons often have *quotations* from the Bible.]

quo·tient (kwō'shənt) *n.* the number got by dividing one number into another [In 32 ÷ 8 = 4, the number 4 is the *quotient*.]

ra·di·ance (ra'de əns) *n.* the quality or condition of being radiant; brightness.

re·al·ize (rē'ə līz) *v.* to understand fully [I *realize* that good marks depend upon careful work.] —**re'al·ized, re'al·iz·ing** —**re'al·i·za'tion** *n.*

rea·son·a·ble (rē'zən ə bəl) *adj.* **1** using or showing reason; sensible [a *reasonable* person; a *reasonable* decision]. **2** not too high or too low; fair [a *reasonable* price; a *reasonable* salary]. —**rea'son·a·bly** *adv.*

re · ceipt (rē sēt') *n.* **1** the act of receiving [We are in *receipt* of your letter.] **2** a written or printed statement that something has been received [My landlord gave me a *receipt* when I paid my rent.]

re · cent (rē'sənt) *adj.* of a time just before now; made or happening a short time ago [*recent* news]. —**re'cent · ly** *adv.*

rec·i·pe (res'ə pē) *n.* a list of ingredients and directions for making something to eat or drink [a *recipe* for cookies].

re · cruit (rē krōōt') *n.* a person who has recently joined an organization, group, or, especially, the armed forces. ✦ *v.* **1** to enlist new members in [to *recruit* an army]. **2** to get to join [Our nature club *recruited* six new members.]

re·fer (rē fʉr') *v.* **1** to speak of or call attention; mention [You seldom *refer* to your injury.] **2** to go for facts, help, etc. [Columbus had no accurate maps to *refer* to.] **3** to tell to go to a certain person or place for help, service, information, etc. [Our neighbor *referred* me to a good doctor.] —**re · ferred', re · fer'ring**

re · frig·er·a·tor (rē frij'ər āt'ər) *n.* a box or room in which the air is kept cool to keep food, etc. from spoiling.

reg · u · la · tion (reg yə lā'shən) *n.* **1** the act of regulating or the condition of being regulated [the *regulation* of the sale of alcohol]. **2** a rule or law that regulates or controls [safety *regulations*].

re·hearse (rē hʉrs') *v.* **1** to go through a play, speech, etc. for practice, before giving it in public. **2** to repeat in detail [They *rehearsed* all their troubles to me.] —**re·hearsed', re·hears'ing** —**re·hears'al** *n.*

reign (rān) *n.* the rule of a king, queen, emperor, etc.; also, the time of ruling [laws made during the *reign* of Victoria]. ✦ *v.* to rule as a king, queen, etc. [Henry VIII *reigned* for 38 years.]

rein·deer (rān'dir) *n.* a large deer found in northern regions, where it is tamed and used for work or as food. Both the male and female have antlers. —*pl.* **rein'deer**

re·joice (rē jois') *v.* to be or make glad or happy [We *rejoiced* at the news.] —**re·joiced', re·joic'ing** —**re·joic'ing** *n.*

re · late (rē lāt') *v.* **1** to tell about; give an account of [*Relate* to us what you did.] **2** to connect in thought or meaning; show a relation between [to *relate* one idea to another]. —**re · lat'ed, re · lat'ing**

re · lease (rē lēs') *v.* to set free or relieve [*Release* the bird from the cage.] ✦ *n.* the act of setting someone or something free [a *release* from prison].

re·li·a·ble (rē lī'ə bəl) *adj.* that can be trusted; dependable [This barometer gives a *reliable* weather forecast.] —**re·li·a·bil·i·ty** (ri lī'ə bil'ə tē) *n.* —**re·li'a·bly** *adv.*

re·lieve (rē lēv') *v.* **1** to free from pain, worry, etc. [We were *relieved* when the danger passed.] **2** to set free from duty or work by replacing [The guard is *relieved* every four hours.] —**re·lieved', re·liev'ing**

142

re·main·der (rē mān'dər) *n.* the part, number, etc. left over [I sold some of my books and gave the *remainder* to the library. When 3 is subtracted from 10, the *remainder* is 7.]

re·mark·a·ble (rē märk'ə bəl) *adj.* worth noticing because it is very unusual [the *remarkable* strength of Hercules]. —**re·mark'a·bly** *adv.*

rem·e·dy (rem'ə dē) *n.* **1** a medicine or treatment that cures, heals, or relieves [a *remedy* for sunburn]. **2** anything that corrects a wrong or helps make things better [a *remedy* for poor education]. —*pl.* **rem'e·dies** ✦ *v.* to cure, correct, make better, etc. [Some money would *remedy* her situation.] —**rem'e·died, rem'e·dy·ing**

re·peat·ed (ri pēt'əd) *adj.* said, made, or done again or often [*repeated* warnings]. —**re·peat'ed·ly** *adv.*

re · quire (rē kwīr') *v.* **1** to be in need of [Most plants *require* sunlight.] **2** to order, command, or insist upon [He *required* us to leave.] —**re·quired', re·quir'ing**

re·search (rē' sʉrch' *or* rē sʉrch') *n.* careful, patient study in order to find out facts and principles about some subject [to carry on *research* into the causes of cancer]. ✦ *v.* to do research.

re·sem·ble (rē zem'bəl) *v.* to be or look like [Rabbits *resemble* hares but are smaller.] —**re·sem'bled, re·sem'bling**

re · sign (rē zīn') *v.* to give up one's office, position, membership, etc. [We *resigned* from the club.]

re·sist·ance (rē zis'təns) *n.* **1** the act of resisting. **2** the power to resist or withstand [Her *resistance* to colds is low.] **3** the opposing of one force or thing to another [the fabric's *resistance* to wear].

re · solve (rē zälv' *or* rē zôlv') *v.* **1** to decide; make up one's own mind [I *resolved* to help them.] **2** to make clear; solve or explain [to *resolve* a problem]. ✦ *n.* firm purpose or determination [her *resolve* to be successful].

re·sound (rē zound') *v.* **1** to echo or be filled with sound [The hall *resounded* with music.] **2** to make a loud, echoing sound; to be echoed [His laughter *resounded* throughout the cave.]

re·trieve (rē trēv') *v.* **1** to get back; recover [to *retrieve* a kite from a tree]. **2** to find and bring back [The spaniel *retrieved* the wounded duck.] —**re·trieved', re·triev'ing**

re·veal (rē vēl') *v.* **1** to make known what was hidden or secret [The map *revealed* the spot where the treasure was buried.] **2** to show [She took off her hat, *revealing* her golden hair.]

rev·e·nue (rev'ə nōō *or* rev'ə nyōō) *n.* money got as rent, profit, etc.; income; especially, the money a government gets from taxes, duties, etc.

a	ask, fat
ā	ape, date
ä	car, lot
e	elf, ten
ē	even, meet
i	is, hit
ī	ice, fire
ō	open, go
ô	law, horn
oi	oil, point
ᴏᴏ	look, pull
ōō	ooze, tool
ou	out, crowd
u	up, cut
ʉ	fur, fern
ə	a in ago
	e in agent
	e in father
	i in unity
	o in collect
	u in focus
ch	chin, arch
ŋ	ring, singer
sh	she, dash
th	thin, truth
th	then, father
zh	s in pleasure

17

Franklin D.
Roosevelt

re·vers·i·ble (rē vur′sə bəl) *adj.* that can be reversed; made so that either side can be used as the outer side [a *reversible* coat].

☆**ro·de·o** (rō′dē ō) *n.* a contest or show in which cowboys match their skill in riding horses, roping and throwing cattle, etc. —*pl.* **ro′de·os**

Roo·se·velt, Franklin D. (rō′zə velt) 1882–1945; 32d president of the United States, from 1933 to 1945.

Roo·se·velt, Theodore 1858–1919; 26th president of the United States, from 1901 to 1909.

rough·en (ruf′ən) *v.* to make or become rough [to *roughen* a smooth surface with a coarse file].

row·boat (rō′bōt) *n.* a boat made to be rowed.

Ss

saxophone

sauce·pan (sôs′pan *or* säs′pan) *n.* a small metal pot with a long handle, used for cooking.

sau·té (sō tā′) *v.* to fry quickly in a pan with a little fat. **sau·téed** (sō tād′,) **sau·té·ing** (sō tā′iŋ) ◆*adj.* fried in this way [chicken livers *sauté*].

sax·o·phone (sak′sə fōn) *n.* a woodwind musical instrument with a curved metal body. Its mouthpiece has a single reed.

scald (skôld) *v.* **1** to burn with hot liquid or steam. **2** to use boiling liquid on, as to kill germs. **3** to heat until it almost boils [to *scald* milk for a custard]. ◆*n.* a burn caused by scalding.

scam·per (skam′pər) *v.* to move quickly or in a hurry [squirrels *scampering* through the trees]. ◆*n.* a quick run or dash.

scat·ter (skat′ər) *v.* **1** to throw here and there; sprinkle [to *scatter* seed over a lawn] . **2** to separate and send or go in many directions; disperse [The wind *scattered* the leaves. The crowd *scattered* after the game.]

sce·ner·y (sēn′ər ē) *n.* **1** the way a certain area looks; outdoor views [the *scenery* along the shore]. **2** painted screens, hangings, etc. used on a stage for a play.

sce·nic (sēn′ik) *adj.* **1** having to do with scenery or landscapes [the *scenic* wonders of the Rockies]. **2** having beautiful scenery [a *scenic* route along the river]. —**sce′ni·cal·ly** *adv.*

scent (sent) *n.* **1** a smell; odor [the *scent* of apple blossoms]. **2** the sense of smell [Lions hunt partly by *scent*.] **3** a smell left by an animal [The dogs lost the fox's *scent* at the river.] ◆*v.* to smell [Our dog *scented* a cat.]

sched·ule (skej′ool *or* ske′joo əl) *n.* ☆**1** a list of the times at which certain things are to happen; timetable [a *schedule* of the sailings of an ocean liner]. ☆**2** a timed plan for a project [The work is ahead of *schedule*.] ◆*v.* **1** to make a schedule of [to *schedule* one's hours of work]. ☆**2** to plan for a certain time [to *schedule* a game for 3:00 P.M.] —**sched′uled, sched′ul·ing**

scheme (skēm) *n.***1** a plan or system in which things are carefully put together [the color *scheme* of a painting]. **2** a plan or program, often a secret or dishonest one [a *scheme* for getting rich quick]. ◆ *v.* to make secret or dishonest plans; to plot [Lee is always *scheming* to get out of work.] —**schemed, schem′ing**

schol·ar·ship (skä′lər ship) *n.* a gift of money to help a student continue his or her education.

sci·en·tif·ic (sī′ən tif′ik) *adj.* **1** having to do with, or used in, science [a *scientific* study; *scientific* equipment]. **2** using the rules and methods of science [*scientific* procedure]. —**sci·en·tif′i·cal·ly** *adv.*

scis·sors (siz′ərz) *n.pl.* a tool for cutting, with two blades that are joined so that they slide over each other when their handles are moved: *also used with a singular verb. Also called* **pair of scissors.**

scour (skour) *v.* to clean by rubbing hard, especially with something rough or gritty [The cook *scoured* the greasy frying pan with soap and steel wool.]

scowl (skoul) *v.* to lower the eyebrows and the corners of the mouth in showing displeasure; look angry or irritated [She *scowled* upon hearing the bad news.] ◆ *n.* a scowling look; an angry frown.

scratch (skrach) *v.* **1** to mark or cut the surface of slightly with something sharp [Thorns *scratched* her legs. Our cat *scratched* the chair with its claws.] **2** to rub or scrape, as with the nails, to relieve itching [to *scratch* a mosquito bite]. **3** to cross out by drawing lines through [She *scratched* out what he had written.] ◆*n.* **1** a mark or cut made in a surface by something sharp. **2** a slight wound.

scream (skrēm) *v.* **1** to give a loud, shrill cry, as in fright or pain [They *screamed* as the roller coaster hurtled downward.] **2** to make a noise like this [The sirens *screamed*. We *screamed* with laughter.] ◆*n.* a loud, shrill cry or sound; shriek.

scrimp (skrimp) *v.* to spend or use as little as possible [to *scrimp* to save money].

sculp·ture (skulp′chər) *n.* **1** the art of carving wood, chiseling stone, casting or welding metal, modeling clay or wax, etc. into statues, figures, or the like. **2** a statue, figure, etc. made in this way. ◆*v.* to cut, chisel, form, etc. in making sculptures. —**sculp′tured, sculp′tur·ing** —**sculp′tur·al** *adj.*

seal (sēl) *n.* **1** a piece of paper, wax, etc. with a design pressed into it, fixed to an official document to show that it is genuine. Such wax designs were once also used to seal letters. **2** something that closes or fastens tightly. ◆*v.* to close or fasten tight [to *seal* cracks with putty; to *seal* a letter]. —**seal′er** *n.*

search (surch) *v.* **1** to look over or through in order to find something [We *searched* the house. The police *searched* the thief for a gun.] **2** to try to find [to *search* for an answer]. —**search′er** *n.*

sea·son·al (sē′zən əl) *adj.* of or depending on a season or the seasons [*seasonal* rains; *seasonal* work]. —**sea′son·al·ly** *adv.*

se·cu·ri·ty (si kyoor′ə tē) *n.* **1** the condition or feeling of being safe or sure; freedom from danger, fear, doubt, etc. **2** something that protects [Insurance is a *security* against loss.] **3** something given or pledged as a guarantee [A car may be used as *security* for a loan.] **4** **securities**, *pl.* stocks and bonds. —*pl.* **se·cu′ri·ties**

Seine (sān *or* sen) a river in northern France. It flows through Paris into the English Channel.

seize (sēz) *v.* to take hold of in a sudden, strong, or eager way; grasp [to *seize* a weapon and fight; to *seize* an opportunity]. —**seized, seiz′ing**

se·lec·tion (sə lek′shən) *n.* **1** a selecting or being selected; choice. **2** the thing or things chosen; also, things to choose from [a wide *selection* of colors].

sem·i·cir·cle (sem′i sur′kəl) *n.* a half circle. —**sem·i·cir·cu·lar** (sem′i sur′kyə lər) *adj.*

sem·i·co·lon (sem′i kō′lən) *n.* a punctuation mark (;) used to show a pause that is shorter than the pause at the end of a sentence, but longer than the pause marked by the comma [The *semicolon* is often used to separate closely related clauses, especially when they contain commas.]

sem·i·fi·nal (sem′i fī′nəl) *n.* a round, match, etc. that comes just before the final one in a contest or tournament. —**sem′i·fi′nal·ist** *n.*

sem·i·pre·cious (sem′i presh′əs) *adj.* describing gems that are of less value than the precious gems [The garnet is a *semiprecious* gem.]

ses·sion (sesh′ən) *n.* **1** the meeting of a court, legislature, class, etc. to do its work. **2** the time during which such a meeting or series goes on. **3** a school term or period of study, classes, etc.

sham·poo (sham poo′) *v.* to wash with foamy suds, as hair or a rug. —**sham·pooed′, sham·poo′ing** ◆*n.* **1** the act of shampooing. **2** a special soap, or soaplike product, that makes suds.

sharp (shärp) *adj.* **1** having a thin edge for cutting, or a fine point for piercing [a *sharp* knife; a *sharp* needle]. **2** easily seen; distinct; clear [a *sharp* contrast]. **3** very strong; intense; stinging [a *sharp* wind; *sharp* pain]. —**sharp′ly** *adv.* —**sharp′ness** *n.*

sheaf (shēf) *n.* **1** a bunch of cut stalks of wheat, rye, or straw tied up together in a bundle. **2** a bundle of things gathered together [a *sheaf* of papers]. —*pl.* **sheaves**

shoul·der (shōl′dər) *n.* **1** the part of the body to which an arm or foreleg is connected. **2** **shoulders,** the two shoulders and the part of the back between them.

shuf·fle·board (shuf′əl bôrd) *n.* a game in which the players use long sticks to slide disks along a smooth lane, trying to get them on numbered sections.

shut·ter (shut′ər) *n.* **1** a cover for a window, usually swinging on hinges. **2** a part on a camera that opens and closes in front of the lens to control the light going in.

shutter

siege (sēj) *n.* the act or an instance of surrounding a city, fort, etc. by an enemy army in an attempt to capture it.

sight·see·ing (sīt′sē′iŋ) *n.* the act of going about to see places and things of interest. —**sight′se′er** *n.*

sig·na·ture (sig′nə chər) *n.* **1** a person's name as he or she has written it. **2** a sign in music placed at the beginning of a staff to give the key or the time.

☆**sil·ver·ware** (sil′vər wer) *n.* things, especially tableware, made of or plated with silver.

sim·mer (sim′ər) *v.* to keep at or just below the boiling point, usually forming tiny bubbles with a murmuring sound [*Simmer* the stew about two hours.]

sim·ple (sim′pəl) *adj.* **1** easy to do or understand [a *simple* task; *simple* directions]. **2** without anything added; plain [the *simple* facts; a *simple* dress]. —**sim′pler, sim′plest**

sketch (skech) *n.* **1** a simple, rough drawing or design, usually done quickly and with little detail. **2** a short outline, giving the main points. ◆*v.* to make a sketch of; draw sketches.

☆**sleigh** (slā) *n.* a carriage with runners instead of wheels, for travel over snow or ice.

slop·py (släp′ē) *adj.* not neat or careful; messy [*sloppy* clothes; a *sloppy* piece of work]. —**slop′pi·er, slop′pi·est** —**slop′pi·ly** *adv.* —**slop′pi·ness** *n.*

smear (smir) *v.* **1** to cover with something greasy, or sticky [to *smear* the actor's face with cold cream]. **2** to rub or spread [*Smear* some grease on the axle.] **3** to make a mark or streak that is not wanted on something [He *smeared* the wet paint with his sleeve.] ◆*n.* **1** a mark or streak made by smearing. **2** the act of smearing or slandering someone.

a	ask, fat
ā	ape, date
ä	car, lot
e	elf, ten
ē	even, meet
i	is, hit
ī	ice, fire
ō	open, go
ô	law, horn
oi	oil, point
oo	look, pull
ōō	ooze, tool
ou	out, crowd
u	up, cut
u	fur, fern
ə	a in ago
	e in agent
	e in father
	i in unity
	o in collect
	u in focus
ch	chin, arch
ŋ	ring, singer
sh	she, dash
th	thin, truth
th	then, father
zh	s in pleasure

smooth (smōo̅th) *adj.* **1** having an even surface, with no bumps or rough spots [as *smooth* as marble; *smooth* water on the lake]. **2** even or gentle in movement; not jerky or rough [a *smooth* airplane flight; a *smooth* ride; *smooth* sailing]. **3** with no trouble or difficulty [*smooth* progress]. ◆*v.* **1** to make smooth or even [*Smooth* the board with sandpaper.] **2** to make easy by taking away troubles, difficulties, etc. [She *smoothed* our way by introducing us to the other guests.] ◆*adv.* in a smooth way [The engine is running *smooth* now.] —**smooth'ly** *adv.*

so·cial (sō'shəl) *adj.* **1** of or having to do with human beings as they live together in a group or groups [*social* problems; *social* forces]. **2** liking to be with others; sociable [A hermit is not a *social* person.] ◆*n.* a friendly gathering; party [a church *social*]. —**so'cial·ly** *adv.*

so·di·um (sō'dē əm) *n.* a soft, silver-white metal that is a chemical element. It is found in nature only in compounds. Salt, baking soda, lye, etc. contain sodium.

sof·ten (sôf'ən *or* säf'ən) *v.* to make or become soft or softer. —**sof'ten·er** *n.*

so·lar (sō'lər) *adj.* **1** of or having to do with the sun [a *solar* eclipse; *solar* energy]. **2** depending on light or energy from the sun [*solar* heating].

soldier

sol·dier (sōl'jər) *n.* a person in an army, especially one who is not a commissioned officer. ◆*v.* to serve as a soldier. —**sol'dier·ly** *adj.*

sol·emn (säl'əm) *adj.* serious; grave; very earnest [a *solemn* face; a *solemn* oath]. —**sol'emn·ly** *adv.*

so·lu·tion (sə lōo̅'shən) *n.* **1** the solving of a problem. **2** an answer or explanation [to find the *solution* to a mystery].

soothe (sōo̅th) *v.* **1** to make quiet or calm by being gentle or friendly [The clerk *soothed* the angry customer with helpful answers.] **2** to take away some of the pain or sorrow of; ease [I hope this lotion will *soothe* your sunburn.] —**soothed, sooth'ing** —**sooth'ing·ly** *adv.*

so·pra·no (sə pran'ō *or* sə prä'nō) *n.* **1** the highest kind of singing voice of women, girls, or young boys. **2** a singer with such a voice or an instrument with a range like this. —*pl.* **so·pra'nos**

spa·ghet·ti (spə get'ē) *n.* long, thin strings of dried flour paste, cooked by boiling or steaming and served with a sauce.

spear·mint (spir'mint) *n.* a common plant of the mint family, used for flavoring.

spearmint

spe·cies (spē'shēz *or* spē'sēz) *n.* a group of plants or animals that are alike in certain ways [The lion and tiger are two different *species* of cat.] —*pl.* **spe'cies**

spec·ta·tor (spek'tātər) *n.* a person who watches something without taking part; onlooker [We were *spectators* at the last game of the World Series.]

sports·man (spôrts'mən) *n.* **1** a man who takes part in or is interested in sports. **2** a person who plays fair and does not complain about losing or boast about winning. —*pl.* **sports'men** —**sports'man·like** *adj.* —**sports'man·ship** *n.*

square (skwer) *n.* **1** a flat figure with four equal sides and four right angles. **2** anything shaped like this [Arrange the chairs in a *square*.] ◆*adj.* **1** having the shape of a square. **2** forming a right angle [a *square* corner]. —**squar'er, squar'est** ◆*v.* to mark off in squares, as a checkerboard. —**squared, squar'ing**

squawk (skwôk *or* skäwk) *n.* a loud, harsh cry such as a chicken or parrot makes. ◆*v.* to let out a squawk. —**squawk'er** *n.*

squeeze (skwēz) *v.* **1** to press hard or force together [*Squeeze* the sponge to get rid of the water.] **2** to get by pressing or by force [to *squeeze* juice from an orange; to *squeeze* money from poor people]. —**squeezed, squeez'ing** ◆*n.* a squeezing or being squeezed; hard press. —**squeez'er** *n.*

stair·way (ster'wā) *or* **stair·case** (ster'kās) *n.* a flight of steps, usually with a handrail.

sta·tion·ar·y (stā'shə ner'ē) *adj.* **1** staying in the same place; not moving; fixed [A *stationary* bicycle is pedaled for exercise, but does not move from its base.] **2** not changing in condition or value; not increasing or decreasing [*stationary* prices].

stead·y (sted'ē) *adj.* not changing or letting up; regular [a *steady* gaze; a *steady* worker]. —**stead'i·er, stead'i·est** —**stead'ied, stead'y·ing** —**stead'i·ly** *adv.* —**stead'i·ness** *n.*

ster·e·o (ster'ē ō') *n.* a stereophonic record player, radio, sound system, etc. —*pl.* **ster'e·os'**

stew·ard (stōo̅'ərd *or* styōo̅'ərd) *n.* **1** a person, especially on a ship or airplane, whose work is to look after the passengers' comfort.

stiff (stif) *adj.* **1** that does not bend easily; firm [*stiff* cardboard]. **2** not able to move easily [*stiff* muscles]. —**stiff'ly** *adv.* —**stiff'ness** *n.*

stitch (stich) *n.* one complete movement of a needle and thread into and out of the material in sewing. —*pl.* **stitch'es** ◆ *v.* to sew or fasten with stitches [to *stitch* a seam].

stow·a·way (stō'ə wā) *n.* a person who hides aboard a ship, plane, etc. for a free or secret ride.

strain·er (strān'ər) *n.* a thing used for straining, as a sieve, filter, etc.

stretch (strech) **v.** **1** to draw out to full length, to a greater size, to a certain distance, etc.; extend [She *stretched* out on the sofa. Will this material *stretch*? *Stretch* the rope between two trees. The road *stretches* for miles through the hills.] **2** to pull or draw tight; strain [to *stretch* a muscle]. ◆**n.** **1** a stretching or being stretched [a *stretch* of the arms]. **2** an unbroken space, as of time or land; extent [a *stretch* of two years; a long *stretch* of beach].

strict (strikt) **adj.** **1** keeping to rules in a careful, exact way [a *strict* supervisor]. **2** never changing; rigid [a *strict* rule]. —**strict′ly** **adv.** —**strict′ness** **n.**

style (stīl) **n.** **1** the way in which anything is made, done, written, spoken, etc.; manner; method [pointed arches in the Gothic *style*]. **2** the way in which people generally dress, act, etc. at any particular period; fashion; mode [*Styles* in clothing keep changing.] **3** a fine, original way of writing, painting, etc. [This author lacks *style*.] —**styled, styl′ing**

sub · con · tract (sub′kän′trakt) **n.** a contract in which a company hires a second company to do part of a job that the first company has agreed to complete. ◆ **v.** to make a subcontract [to *subcontract* for plumbing and electrical work].

subj. *abbreviation for* **subject, subjunctive.**

sub · ma · rine (sub′mə rēn) **n.** a kind of warship that can travel under the surface of water. ◆**adj.** (sub mə rēn′) that lives, grows, happens, etc. under the surface of the sea [Sponges are *submarine* animals.]

sub · scrip · tion (səb skrip′shən) **n.** **1** the act of subscribing or something that is subscribed. **2** an agreement to take and pay for a magazine, theater tickets, etc. for a particular period of time.

sub · stan · tial (səb stan′shəl) **adj.** **1** of or having substance; material; real or true [Your fears turned out not to be *substantial*.] **2** strong; solid; firm [The bridge didn't look very *substantial*.] **3** more than average or usual; large [a *substantial* share; a *substantial* meal]. **4** wealthy or well-to-do [a *substantial* farmer]. —**sub · stan′tial · ly** **adv.**

sub · sti · tute (sub′stə tōōt *or* sub′stə tyōōt) **n.** a person or thing that takes the place of another [He is a *substitute* for the regular teacher.] ◆**v.** to use as or be a substitute [to *substitute* vinegar for lemon juice; to *substitute* for an injured player]. —**sub′sti · tut · ed, sub′sti · tut · ing** —**sub′sti · tu′tion** **n.**

suc · ceed (sək sēd′) **v.** **1** to manage to do or be what was planned; do or go well [I *succeeded* in convincing them to come with us.] **2** to come next after; follow [Carter *succeeded* Ford as president.]

suc · cess · ful (sək ses′fəl) **adj.** **1** having success; turning out well [a *successful* meeting]. **2** having become rich, famous, etc. [a *successful* architect]. —**suc · cess′ful · ly** **adv.**

su · crose (sōō′krōs) **n.** a sugar found in sugar cane, sugar beets, etc.

suf · fi · cient (sə fish′ənt) **adj.** as much as is needed; enough [Do you have *sufficient* supplies to last through the week?] —**suf · fi′cient · ly** **adv.**

suit · a · ble (sōōt′ə bəl) **adj.** right for the purpose; fitting; proper [a *suitable* gift]. —**suit′a · bil′i · ty** **n.** —**suit′a · bly** **adv.**

su · per · fi · cial (sōō′pər fish′əl) **adj.** of or on the surface; not deep [a *superficial* cut; a *superficial* likeness]. —**su · per · fi · ci · al · i · ty** (sōō′pər fish′ē al′ə tē) **n.** —**su′per · fi′cial · ly** **adv.**

su · per · son · ic (sōō′pər sän′ik) **adj.** **1** of or moving at a speed greater than the speed of sound. **2** *another word for* **ultrasonic.**

su · per · vise (sōō′pər vīz) **v.** to direct or manage, as a group of workers; be in charge of. —**su′per · vised, su′per · vis · ing**

sur · round (sər round′) **v.** to form or arrange around on all or nearly all sides; enclose [The police *surrounded* the criminals. The house is *surrounded* with trees.]

sur · vey (sər vā′) **v.** to measure the size, shape, boundaries, etc. of a piece of land by the use of special instruments [to *survey* a farm]. ◆**n.** (sur′vā) **1** a general study covering the main facts or points [The *survey* shows that we need more schools. This book is a *survey* of American poetry.] **2** the act of surveying a piece of land, or a record of this [He was hired to make a *survey* of the lake shore.] —*pl.* **sur′veys**

sur · vey · ing (sər vā′iŋ) **n.** the act, work, or science of one who surveys land.

Swede (swēd) **n.** a person born or living in Sweden.

Swiss (swis) **adj.** of Switzerland or its people. ◆**n.** a person born or living in Switzerland. —*pl.* **Swiss**

sym · me · try (sim′ə trē) **n.** **1** an arrangement in which the parts on opposite sides of a center line are alike in size, shape, and position [The human body has *symmetry*.] **2** balance or harmony that comes from such an arrangement.

syn · the · siz · er (sin′thə sī zər) **n.** ☆an electronic musical instrument that makes sounds that cannot be made by ordinary instruments.

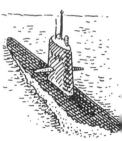

submarine

a	ask, fat
ā	ape, date
ä	car, lot
e	elf, ten
ē	even, meet
i	is, hit
ī	ice, fire
ō	open, go
ô	law, horn
oi	oil, point
oo	look, pull
ōō	ooze, tool
ou	out, crowd
u	up, cut
u	fur, fern
ə	a in ago
	e in agent
	e in father
	i in unity
	o in collect
	u in focus
ch	chin, arch
ŋ	ring, singer
sh	she, dash
th	thin, truth
th	then, father
zh	s in pleasure